The Official Rails-to-Trails
Conservancy Guidebook

# Rail-Trails
## Northern
## New England

The definitive guide to multiuse trails in Maine,
New Hampshire, and Vermont

 **WILDERNESS PRESS** . . . *on the trail since 1967*

**Rail-Trails: Northern New England**
1st Edition, 5th printing 2022
Copyright © 2018 by Rails-to-Trails Conservancy

Cover and interior photographs copyright © 2018 by Rails-to-Trails Conservancy
Maps: Lohnes+Wright; map data courtesy of Environmental Systems Research Institute
Cover design: Scott McGrew; Book design: Annie Long

### Library of Congress Cataloging-in-Publication Data

Names: Rails-to-Trails Conservancy.
Title: Rail-trails : Northern New England : the definitive guide to multiuse trails in Maine, New Hampshire, and Vermont.
Other titles: Great rail-trails series.
Description: First edition. | Birmingham, Alabama : Wilderness Press, an imprint of AdventureKEEN, [2018] | At head of title: The Official Rails-to-Trails Conservancy Guidebook. | "Distributed by Publishers Group West"—T.p. verso. | Includes index.
Identifiers: LCCN 2018006304| ISBN 9780899978970 (paperback) | ISBN 9780899978987 (ebook)
Subjects: LCSH: Rail-trails—New England—Guidebooks. | Rail-trails—Maine—Guidebooks. | Rail-trails—New Hampshire—Guidebooks. | Rail-trails—Vermont—Guidebooks. | Hiking—New England—Guidebooks. | Hiking—Maine—Guidebooks. | Hiking—New Hampshire—Guidebooks. | Hiking—Vermont—Guidebooks. | Bicycle trails—New England—Guidebooks. | Bicycle trails—Maine—Guidebooks. | Bicycle trails—New Hampshire—Guidebooks. | Bicycle trails—Vermont—Guidebooks. | Bicycle touring—New England—Guidebooks. | Bicycle touring—Maine—Guidebooks. | Bicycle touring—New Hampshire—Guidebooks. | Bicycle touring—Vermont—Guidebooks. | Outdoor recreation—New England—Guidebooks. | Outdoor recreation—Maine—Guidebooks. | Outdoor recreation—New Hampshire—Guidebooks. | Outdoor recreation—Vermont—Guidebooks. | Railroads—Right of way—Multiple use—United States. | New England—Guidebooks. | Maine—Guidebooks. | New Hampshire—Guidebooks. | Vermont—Guidebooks.
Classification: LCC GV191.42.N3 .R35 2018 | DDC 796.510974—dc23
LC record available at https://lccn.loc.gov/2018006304

Manufactured in China

Published by: **WILDERNESS PRESS**
An imprint of AdventureKEEN
2204 First Ave. S, Ste. 102
Birmingham, AL 35233
800-678-7008; fax 877-374-9016

Visit wildernesspress.com for a complete listing of our books and for ordering information. Contact us at our website, at facebook.com/wildernesspress1967, or at twitter.com/wilderness1967 with questions or comments. To find out more about who we are and what we're doing, visit blog.wildernesspress.com.

Distributed by Publishers Group West

*Front cover:* New Hampshire's Winnipesaukee River Trail (see page 158), photographed by Anthony Le; *back cover:* Vermont's Missisquoi Valley Rail-Trail (see page 187), photographed by Dennis Coello

# About Rails-to-Trails Conservancy

**H**eadquartered in Washington, D.C., Rails-to-Trails Conservancy (RTC) is a nonprofit organization dedicated to creating a nationwide network of trails from former rail lines and connecting corridors to build healthier places for healthier people.

Railways helped build America. Spanning from coast to coast, these ribbons of steel linked people, communities, and enterprises, spurring commerce and forging a single nation that bridges a continent. But in recent decades, many of these routes have fallen into disuse, severing communal ties that helped bind Americans together.

When RTC opened its doors in 1986, the rail-trail movement was in its infancy. Most projects focused on single, linear routes in rural areas, created for recreation and conservation. RTC sought broader protection for the unused corridors, incorporating rural, suburban, and urban routes.

Year after year, RTC's efforts to protect and align public funding with trail building created an environment that allowed trail advocates in communities across the country to initiate trail projects. These ever-growing ranks of trail professionals, volunteers, and RTC supporters have built momentum for the national rail-trails movement. As the number of supporters multiplied, so did the rail-trails.

Americans now enjoy more than 23,000 miles of open rail-trails, and as they flock to the trails to connect with family members and friends, enjoy nature, and get to places in their local neighborhoods and beyond, their economic prosperity, health, and overall well-being continue to flourish.

A signature endeavor of RTC is **TrailLink.com,** America's portal to these rail-trails, as well as other multiuse trails. When RTC launched TrailLink.com in 2000, our organization was one of the first to compile such detailed trail information on a national scale. Today, the website continues to play a critical role in both encouraging and satisfying the country's growing need for opportunities to ride, walk, skate, or run for recreation or transportation. This free trail-finder database—which includes detailed descriptions, interactive maps, photo galleries, and first-hand ratings and reviews—can be used as a companion resource to the trails in this guidebook.

The national voice for more than 160,000 members and supporters, RTC is committed to ensuring a better future for America made possible by trails and the connections they inspire. Learn more at **railstotrails.org.**

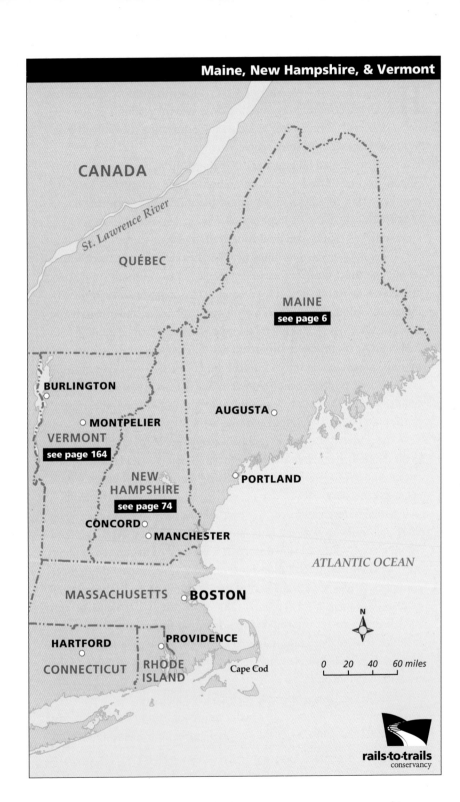

# Maine, New Hampshire, & Vermont

CANADA

St. Lawrence River

QUÉBEC

MAINE
see page 6

BURLINGTON

AUGUSTA

MONTPELIER

VERMONT
see page 164

NEW
HAMPSHIRE
see page 74

PORTLAND

CONCORD

MANCHESTER

ATLANTIC OCEAN

MASSACHUSETTS  BOSTON

HARTFORD  PROVIDENCE

CONNECTICUT  RHODE
ISLAND  Cape Cod

N

0   20   40   60 miles

rails·to·trails
conservancy

# Table of Contents

*Vermont's Missisquoi Valley Rail-Trail in Sheldon (see page 187)*

## VERMONT 164

# Foreword

For those of you who have already experienced the sheer enjoyment and freedom of riding on a rail-trail, welcome back! You'll find *Rail-Trails: Northern New England* to be a useful and fun guide to your favorite trails, as well as an introduction to pathways you have yet to travel.

For readers who are discovering for the first time the adventures possible on a rail-trail, thank you for joining the rail-trail movement. Since 1986, Rails-to-Trails Conservancy has been the leading supporter and defender of these priceless public corridors. We are excited to bring you *Rail-Trails: Northern New England,* so you too can enjoy some of the region's premier rail-trails and multiuse trails. These hiking and biking trails are ideal ways to connect with your community, with nature, and with your friends and family.

I've found that trails have a way of bringing people together, and as you'll see from this book, you have opportunities in every state you visit to get on a great trail. Whether you're looking for a place to exercise, explore, commute, or play, there is a trail in this book for you.

So I invite you to sit back, relax, pick a trail that piques your interest—and then get out, get active, and have some fun. I'll be out on the trails too, so be sure to wave as you go by.

Happy trails,

Keith Laughlin, President
Rails-to-Trails Conservancy

# Acknowledgments

Special thanks to editors Gene Bisbee and Amy Ahn for their work on this book. We are also appreciative of the following contributors and to all the trail managers we called on for assistance to ensure the maps, photographs, and trail descriptions are as accurate as possible.

Kevin Belanger

Ben Carter

Eli Griffen

Brandi Horton

Willie Karidis

Anthony Le

Kevin Mills

Liz Thorstensen

Torsha Bhattacharya

Andrew Dupuy

Katie Guerin

Amy Kapp

Joe LaCroix

Suzanne Matyas

Derek Strout

Patrick Wojahn

*Maine's Belfast Rail Trail on the Passagassawaukeag (see page 19)*

# Introduction

**R**ail-Trails: Northern New England highlights 60 of the top rail-trails and other multiuse pathways in Maine, New Hampshire, and Vermont. These trails offer a broad range of experiences to suit nearly every taste, from vibrant cities to remote forests, from sweeping coastal vistas to narrow wooded ravines, and from challenging mountain biking adventures to relaxing waterfront strolls.

Though short in length at 2.1 miles, the paved Eastern Promenade Trail in Portland, Maine, provides beauty in abundance as it skirts the shoreline of Casco Bay and Portland Harbor through a 73-acre park. On the opposite end of the spectrum is the Down East Sunrise Trail, an 87.9-mile crushed-stone, gravel, and sand trail that parallels the Gulf of Maine from Pembroke to Ellsworth. A major component of the 3,000-mile East Coast Greenway (ECG), the Down East Sunrise Trail features a variety of woodsy and marshy landscapes as it travels over 28 bridges and through a number of coastal villages—including Machias, site of the first naval battle of the American Revolution.

The Franconia Notch Recreation Path in New Hampshire provides a paved—but hilly—and scenic route that traverses the length of Franconia Notch State Park in the White Mountain National Forest. Here, you can see natural attractions such as Flume Gorge and the Old Man of the Mountain Historic Site.

And not to be outdone: Vermont's Island Line Rail Trail—a member of RTC's Rail-Trail Hall of Fame—is the highlight of the region, with Lake Champlain virtually at trail users' feet for long sections of its 13.4 miles. The path rolls through waterfront parks in Burlington and Colchester and crosses the lake on a 3-mile marble causeway to South Hero Island.

Several trails in this region are being stitched together in the developing ECG, which aims to link trails across 15 states, from Maine to Florida. You'll find many ECG-designated pathways in this book. You'll also learn about a number of trails that make up Maine's Interconnected Trail System, which comprises thousands of miles of all-terrain vehicle and snowmobile routes in the state.

No matter which routes in Rail-Trails: Northern New England you choose, you'll experience the unique history, culture, and geography of each, as well as the communities that have built and embraced them.

## What Is a Rail-Trail?

**R**ail-trails are multiuse public paths built along former railroad corridors. Most often flat or following a gentle grade, they are suited to walking, running, cycling, mountain biking, in-line skating, cross-country skiing, horseback

**OPPOSITE:** New Hampshire's Cotton Valley Rail Trail (see page 89)

riding, and wheelchair use. Since the 1960s, Americans have created more than 23,000 miles of rail-trails throughout the country.

These extremely popular recreation and transportation corridors traverse urban, suburban, and rural landscapes. Many preserve historical landmarks, while others serve as wildlife conservation corridors, linking isolated parks and establishing greenways in developed areas. Rail-trails also stimulate local economies by boosting tourism and promoting trailside businesses.

## What Is a Rail-with-Trail?

A rail-with-trail is a public path that parallels a still-active rail line. Some run adjacent to high-speed, scheduled trains, often linking public transportation stations, while others follow tourist routes and slow-moving excursion trains. Many share an easement, separated from the rails by extensive fencing. More than 300 rails-with-trails exist in the United States.

## What Is the Rail-Trail Hall of Fame?

In 2007 RTC began recognizing exemplary rail-trails around the country through its Rail-Trail Hall of Fame. Inductees are selected based on such merits as scenic value, high use, trail and trailside amenities, historical significance,  excellence in management and maintenance of facility, community connections, and geographic distribution. These iconic rail-trails, which have been singled out from more than 2,000 in the United States, have earned RTC's highest honor and represent tangible realizations of our vision to create a more walkable, bikeable, healthier America. Hall of Fame rail-trails are indicated in this book with a special blue icon; for the full list of Hall of Fame rail-trails, visit **railstotrails.org/halloffame.**

# How to Use This Book

**R**ail-Trails: Northern New England provides the information you'll need to plan a rewarding trek. With words to inspire you and maps to chart your path, it makes choosing the best route a breeze. Following are some of the highlights.

## Maps

**Y**ou'll find three levels of maps in this book: an **overall regional map, state locator maps,** and **detailed trail maps.**

The trails in this book are located in Maine, New Hampshire, and Vermont. Each chapter details a particular state's network of trails, marked on a locator map at the beginning of the chapter. Use these maps to find the trails nearest you, or select several neighboring trails and plan a weekend hiking or biking excursion. Once you find a trail on a state locator map, simply flip to the corresponding number for a full description. Accompanying trail maps mark each route's access roads, trailheads, parking areas, restrooms, and other defining features.

## Key to Map Icons

| Parking | Drinking Water | Restrooms | Featured Trail | Connecting Trail | Active Railroad |

## Trail Descriptions

**T**rails are listed in alphabetical order within each chapter. Each description leads with a set of summary information, including trail endpoints and mileage, a roughness index, the trail surface, and possible uses.

The map and summary information list the trail endpoints (either a city, street, or more specific location), with suggested points from which to start and finish. Additional access points are marked on the maps and mentioned in the trail descriptions. The maps and descriptions also highlight available amenities, including parking and restrooms, as well as such area attractions as shops, services, museums, parks, and stadiums. Trail length is listed in miles.

Each trail bears a **roughness index** rating from 1 to 3. A rating of 1 indicates a smooth, level surface that is accessible to users of all ages and abilities. A 2 rating means the surface may be loose and/or uneven and could pose a problem for road bikes and wheelchairs. A 3 rating suggests a rough surface that is only recommended for mountain bikers and hikers. Surfaces can range from asphalt or concrete to ballast, boardwalk, cinder, crushed stone, gravel, grass, dirt, sand, and/or wood chips. Where relevant, trail descriptions address alternating surface conditions.

All trails are open to pedestrians, and most allow bicycles, except where noted in the trail summary or description. The summary also indicates wheelchair access. Other possible uses include in-line skating, mountain biking, horseback riding, fishing, and cross-country skiing. While most trails are off-limits to motor vehicles, some local trail organizations do allow all-terrain vehicles (ATVs) and snowmobiles.

Trail descriptions suggest an ideal itinerary for each route, including the best parking areas and access points, where to begin, your direction of travel, and any highlights along the way. Following each description are directions to the recommended trailheads.

Each trail description also lists a local website for further information. Be sure to visit these websites in advance for updates and current conditions. **TrailLink.com** is another great resource for updated content on the trails in this guidebook.

## Trail Use

**R**ail-trails are popular destinations for a range of users, often making them busy places to enjoy the outdoors. Following basic trail etiquette and safety guidelines will make your experience more pleasant.

- ➤ **Keep to the right,** except when passing.
- ➤ **Pass on the left,** and give a clear audible warning: "Passing on your left."
- ➤ **Be aware** of other trail users, particularly around corners and blind spots, and be especially careful when entering a trail, changing direction, or passing, so that you don't collide with traffic.
- ➤ **Respect wildlife** and public and private property; leave no trace and take out litter.
- ➤ **Control your speed,** especially near pedestrians, playgrounds, and heavily congested areas.
- ➤ **Travel single file.** Cyclists and pedestrians should ride or walk single file in congested areas or areas with reduced visibility.
- ➤ **Cross carefully** at intersections; always look both ways and yield to through traffic. Pedestrians have the right-of-way.
- ➤ **Keep one ear open and volume low** on portable listening devices to increase your awareness of your surroundings.
- ➤ **Wear a helmet** and other safety gear if you're cycling or in-line skating.
- ➤ **Consider visibility.** Wear reflective clothing, use bicycle lights, or bring flashlights or helmet-mounted lights for tunnel passages or twilight excursions.

➤ **Keep moving,** and don't block the trail. When taking a rest, turn off the trail to the right. Groups should avoid congregating on or blocking the trails. If you have an accident on the trail, move to the right as soon as possible.

➤ **Bicyclists yield** to all other trail users. Pedestrians yield to horses. If in doubt, yield to all other trail users.

➤ **Dogs are permitted** on most trails, but **some trails through parks, wildlife refuges, or other sensitive areas may not allow pets;** it's best to check the trail website before your visit. If pets are permitted, keep your dog on a short leash and under your control at all times. Remove dog waste in a designated trash receptacle.

➤ **Teach your children** these trail essentials, and be especially diligent to keep them out of faster-moving trail traffic.

➤ **Be prepared,** especially on long-distance rural trails. Bring water, snacks, maps, a light source, matches, and other equipment you may need. Because some areas may not have good reception for cell phones, know where you're going, and tell someone else your plan.

## Key to Trail Use

| walking | cycling | wheelchair access | in-line skating | mountain biking |
| fishing | horseback riding | cross-country skiing | snowmobiling | ATV |

## Learn More

To learn about additional multiuse trails in your area or to plan a trip to an area beyond the scope of this book, visit Rails-to-Trails Conservancy's trail-finder website **TrailLink.com,** a free resource with more than 32,000 miles of mapped rail-trails and multiuse trails nationwide.

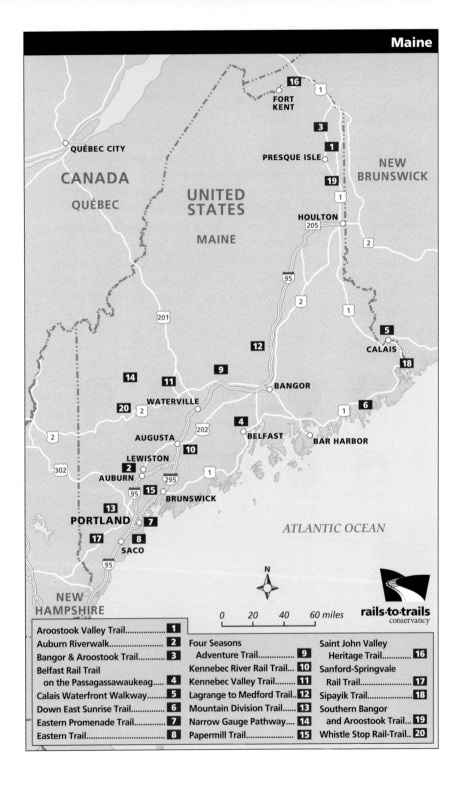

**Maine**

QUÉBEC CITY

CANADA

QUÉBEC

UNITED
STATES

MAINE

NEW
BRUNSWICK

**16** FORT
KENT
**3**
PRESQUE ISLE
**19**
HOULTON
205

95

12

9

14 11

20 2
WATERVILLE

202

4

201

BANGOR

5
CALAIS
18

1 6

AUGUSTA
10
LEWISTON
2
AUBURN
95 15
BRUNSWICK

302

13
PORTLAND 7

17
8
SACO

95

NEW
HAMPSHIRE

BAR HARBOR

BELFAST

ATLANTIC OCEAN

N

0   20   40   60 miles

rails·to·trails
conservancy

# Maine

*Kennebec River Rail Trail (see page 38) shares its corridor with active tracks, a configuration known as a rail-with-trail.*

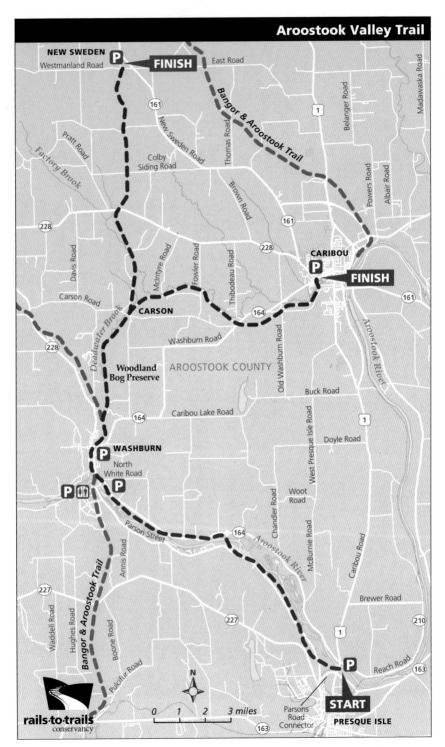

The Aroostook Valley Trail gets as much use from ATV riders and snowmobilers as it does from mountain bikers as it winds through the forests and potato farms of northeastern Maine. It's so far north that the United States and United Kingdom both laid claims to the area in the late 1830s in a dispute dubbed the Pork and Beans War, which ended without combat.

The rail-trail takes its name from the Aroostook Valley Railroad. (Local tribes translate Aroostook to "beautiful river.") A lumber baron built the railroad in 1910 to haul logs to his Presque Isle sawmill and used the river to generate electricity to power the railroad to Washburn. Over the years, it expanded to Caribou and New Sweden and provided full freight and passenger service, though it hauled more freshly picked potatoes than anything else. Switching to diesel in the 1940s, the line struggled until it ended operations in 1996.

Today the 28.8-mile trail connects with the Bangor & Aroostook Trail (see page 15) in Washburn and is part of

*In the far northeast reaches of Maine, this trail offers a rustic ride through quaint towns and remote areas.*

**County**
Aroostook

**Endpoints**
US 1/Main St. between ME 210/Reach Road and Parsons Road Connector/ME 163 (Presque Isle) to ME 164/Washburn St. between Willow Dr. and Roosevelt Ave. (Caribou) or Westmanland Road just east of Jepson Road (New Sweden)

**Mileage**
28.8

**Type**
Rail-Trail

**Roughness Index**
2–3

**Surfaces**
Crushed Stone, Dirt

the Interconnected Trail System, which comprises thousands of miles of ATV and snowmobile track in the state. Although it passes through four towns with food and lodging, most of the trail is remote, and travelers need to pack for backcountry emergencies. Note that in addition to snowmobiling and snowshoeing, dogsledding is permitted.

Starting at a riverside park on US 1 in Presque Isle, the largest town along the route, the trail follows the south bank of the Aroostook River. (A private ATV and snowmobile route heads east for 23 miles toward the Canadian border along the Canadian Pacific Railroad right-of-way.) You'll head through second-growth forests of spruce, fir, beech, poplar, and birch and, in the clearings, see the vast potato farms for which Aroostook County is known. The trail crosses the river in 5 miles, then rolls along the north riverbank for nearly 5 miles to its junction with the Bangor & Aroostook Trail in Washburn.

Leaving the banks of the Aroostook River and following the trail through town for a mile, you'll take the right fork to remain on the Aroostook Valley Trail heading north. After passing through the Woodland Bog Preserve and arriving in Carson at 3.8 miles, the trail splits: the right branch goes east toward Caribou, and the left continues north to New Sweden.

Caribou is 6.7 miles down the right branch, and, like other towns along the route, many businesses there cater to trail users. You'll find restaurants, bakeries, coffee shops, and even bed-and-breakfasts less than 0.5 mile east from the trailhead on Washburn Street. A branch of the Bangor & Aroostook Trail also ends in town.

Heading north from the trail junction in Carson, a separate 7-mile segment to New Sweden also passes through mostly woodland to Westmanland Road. New Sweden got its start after Maine invited immigrants to bolster its economy in the 1870s, and many Swedish events and traditions survive in the area. Light services are available in town, where you'll also find a museum, as well as historic homes and churches.

**CONTACT:** maine.gov/cgi-bin/online/doc/parksearch/details.pl?park_id=77 and caribourec.org

---

# DIRECTIONS

To reach the trailhead in Presque Isle from I-95, take Exit 302 north toward Presque Isle on US 1/North St. Go 26.4 miles north on US 1, and turn left to remain on US 1 in Mars Hill. Go another 15.8 miles, and turn right into the Star City ATV Club parking lot on the right, just before you cross the Aroostook River.

To reach the trailhead in Caribou from I-95, take Exit 302 north toward Presque Isle on US 1/North St. Go 26.4 miles north on US 1, and turn left to remain on US 1 in Mars Hill. Go another 26.8 miles, and turn left onto Lyndon St./Main St. in Caribou. Go 0.5 mile, and turn left onto Herschel St. Go 0.2 mile, turn left onto Prospect St., and then take your first right onto Sweden St. Go almost 0.1 mile, turn left onto Summer St. and then turn right onto ME 164/ Washburn St. Go 0.1 mile, bear left to stay on ME 164/Washburn St., go 0.1 mile farther, and look for trailhead parking on the left. (This lot is not recommended for ATVs and snowmobiles. Instead, continue 2.6 miles past this parking lot to the trail crossing on ME 164/Washburn Road, where you'll see parking on the right.)

A parking lot dedicated to snowmobiles and ATVs is located at the northern endpoint in New Sweden and is accessible by crossing Westmanland Road (look for the path immediately to your right, which heads northeast a few hundred feet). However, there is no dedicated parking lot for automobiles during the week. On weekends, parking is permitted at the New Sweden Consolidated School parking lot, which can be accessed by heading west from the trailhead on Westmanland Road about 0.3 mile, and turning right into the parking lot. To reach the endpoint from I-95, take Exit 302 toward Presque Isle on US 1/North St. Go 26.4 miles north on US 1, and turn left to remain on US 1 in Mars Hill. Go another 27.7 miles, and turn left again in Caribou to remain on US 1. In 0.8 mile turn left onto US 1. In 7.2 miles turn left onto Emond Road/Townline Road. Go 1.7 miles, and Emond Road becomes Station Road. Go another 3.8 miles. The trailhead is 0.1 mile past the New Sweden Covenant Church.

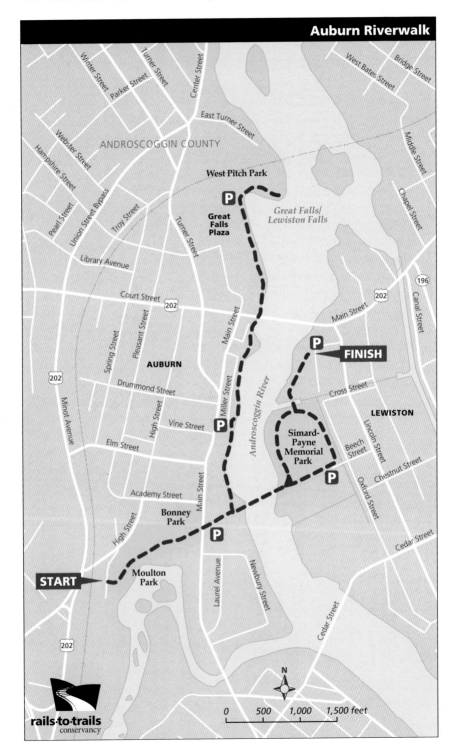

**Auburn Riverwalk**

West Bates Street

Bridge Street

Winter Street

Turner Street

Parker Street

Center Street

East Turner Street

Middle Street

ANDROSCOGGIN COUNTY

Webster Street

Hampshire Street

West Pitch Park

**P**

*Great Falls/
Lewiston Falls*

Chapel Street

Pearl Street

Union Street Bypass

Troy Street

**Great
Falls
Plaza**

Library Avenue

Turner Street

Court Street

202

Main Street

Main Street

196

202

Canal Street

Spring Street

Pleasant Street

**AUBURN**

Drummond Street

Miller Street

**P**

**FINISH**

Cross Street

**LEWISTON**

202

High Street

Vine Street

**P**

*Androscoggin River*

**Simard-
Payne
Memorial
Park**

Beech Street

Lincoln Street

Chestnut Street

Elm Street

**P**

Oxford Street

Academy Street

Main Street

**P**

Cedar Street

**START**

**Moulton
Park**

**Bonney
Park**

High Street

Laurel Avenue

Newbury Street

Cedar Street

202

N

0   500   1,000   1,500 feet

**rails·to·trails**
conservancy

Minot Avenue

The Auburn Riverwalk passes through the heart of the old mill district of the Twin Cities of Auburn and Lewiston. The 1.6-mile paved and gravel path offers many scenic views of the Androscoggin River, the powerhouse that fueled the historic mill industry. Lewiston is the second largest city in Maine and offers many dining opportunities. Keep an ear out for spoken French, as Lewiston is home to the largest French-speaking population in Maine (the language is spoken by nearly 15% of residents).

A section of trail crosses the Androscoggin River on a trestle built by the Grand Trunk Railroad in 1909. The railway started service in the 1850s, connecting Portland with Montreal. It later added a line to Auburn and Lewiston, serving the shoe and textile industries that boomed here in the second half of the 19th century. The Canadian National Railway later took over the railroad.

Starting in the west just past the skate park in Moulton Park, follow the gravel path for about 0.25 mile to a

*Moulton Park, in the heart of Auburn, offers a great starting point for your journey.*

**County**
Androscoggin

**Endpoints**
Moulton Park at Hutchins St. and High St. to Great Falls Plaza near Turner St. (Auburn) or Simard-Payne Memorial Park at Beech St. and Oxford St. (Lewiston)

**Mileage**
1.6

**Type**
Rail-Trail

**Roughness Index**
1

**Surfaces**
Gravel/Crushed Stone, Asphalt, Brick

fork in adjoining Bonney Park. The left fork heads north alongside the Andro-scoggin River for 0.7 mile to West Pitch Park and its overlook at Great Falls, also known as Lewiston Falls. One of only 15 urban waterfalls in the United States, it drops 37 feet over rocky outcrops and is still used for hydroelectric power. The segment is paved in bricks and offers benches for viewing wildlife or simply contemplating life.

Taking the right fork from Bonney Park carries you across the Androscog-gin River on a 425-foot converted railroad bridge. Viewing the river, you can appreciate the local efforts to clean up this waterway, once known as the most polluted in the state.

After crossing the bridge, you will run into Simard-Payne Memorial Park, which serves as a welcoming gateway to the trail and river. The park has several small walking paths that lead down to benches along the river and a paved loop encircling the park. At the top of the loop, a short trail leads to a gravel lot for parking and a picnic area. Depending on when you arrive, you could also experience the annual Great Falls Brewfest in June, the Great Falls Balloon Festival in August, or the Dempsey Challenge in September.

**CONTACT:** mainetrailfinder.com/trails/trail/Lewiston-auburn-greenway-trails

## DIRECTIONS

To reach the Auburn trailhead from I-95, take Exit 80 toward ME 196/Lewiston. Traveling north on I-95, turn right onto Alfred A. Plourde Pkwy.; traveling south on I-95, turn left onto Alfred A. Plourde Pkwy. Go about 0.5 mile, and turn right onto Goddard Road, and then go 0.9 mile, and turn right onto River Road, which becomes Lincoln St. Go 1.6 miles, and turn left onto Cedar St., and then go 0.4 mile, and turn right onto Mill St. in Auburn. Go 0.1 mile, and turn right onto S. Main St., and then go 0.3 mile, and look for parking on your right. The trail is at the bottom of the slope; go left 0.2 mile for the western endpoint.

To reach the Lewiston trailhead from I-95, take Exit 80 toward ME 196/Lewiston. Traveling north on I-95, turn right onto Alfred A. Plourde Pkwy.; traveling south on I-95 turn left onto Alfred A. Plourde Pkwy. Go about 0.5 mile, and turn right onto Goddard Road. Then go 0.9 mile, and turn right onto River Road, which becomes Lincoln St. Go 1.7 miles, and turn left onto Beech St. Cross the canal and park in Simard-Payne Memorial Park.

If you're looking for moose, the Bangor & Aroostook Trail (or BAT) is just the place. Moose watchers take to the 62.3-mile rail-trail on ATVs, snowmobiles, and mountain bikes to spot these large creatures that appear ungainly but can be unpredictably dangerous. The crushed-rock trail is part of the state's Interconnected Trail System that links more than a thousand miles of ATV and snowmobile trails around the state. (Snowshoeing and dogsledding are also permitted.)

The trail follows the former corridor of the Bangor and Aroostook Railroad (BAR) through northern Maine's bogs and forests. Founded in 1891 to combine two railroads, the rail line extended to Caribou in 1895 and Van Buren in 1899. The railroad stayed profitable by hauling the state's two big exports: potatoes and wood products. When farmers stopped shipping spuds by rail in the

*A branch of the trail connects to Caribou, located on the Aroostook River.*

**County**
Aroostook

**Endpoints**
Main St./US 1A and State St./US 1 (Van Buren) to Morrison St. between Station St. and Hughes Road (Mapleton) or Limestone St. and Broadway (Caribou)

**Mileage**
62.3

**Type**
Rail-Trail

**Roughness Index**
2–3

**Surface**
Gravel

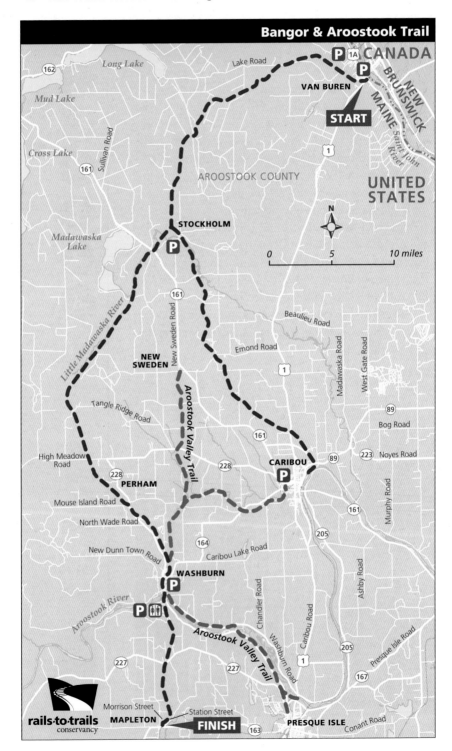

Bangor & Aroostook Trail

The trail offers views of the many scenic waterways that crisscross this part of northern Maine.

1970s, the company discontinued using some Aroostook County branch lines and eventually declared bankruptcy in 2002.

The trail runs south from Van Buren toward Stockholm, where it splits into branches to Caribou and Mapleton. It briefly joins the Aroostook Valley Trail (see page 8) in Washburn. Although the trail visits towns where lodging and restaurants are available, most of the trail is remote. Travelers should carry emergency gear along with extra food and water. Another leg of the old BAR from Phair to Houlton has been converted into the 38.8-mile Southern Bangor and Aroostook Trail (see page 66).

Starting at the north end of the trail in Van Buren, you're just across the Saint John River from the province of New Brunswick, Canada. If you hear French spoken here, don't be surprised. French settlers of Canadian Acadia who refused to swear allegiance to the British crown in the 1700s were deported or escaped—some to Maine. Many of those Acadians keep their culture alive in their language. Historic buildings from that era are collected at Acadian Village, 4.6 miles north of town on US 1/Main Street.

As you head out of Van Buren, you enter a forested wilderness where logging occurs. This is prime moose country, as the woods provide cover, but the open boggy areas provide food and allow the moose to move about with wide antlers. The trail splits in Stockholm, which was settled by Swedish immigrants in the 1870s.

The longest branch takes a sharp turn right, curves left, and then heads south for 30 miles to the small town of Mapleton. Along the way it passes through Washburn, where you can grab some food and perhaps hook up with the Aroostook Valley Trail. The country landscape transitions from forest to agriculture, primarily potato farming, which is still a major crop in Maine.

The left fork in Stockholm heads 16 miles to Caribou, located on the Aroostook River. Calling itself the most northeastern city in the United States, the town is a center for outdoor recreation in northern Maine. You'll find food and lodging here, as well as outfitters and guides for more outdoor adventures.

**CONTACT:** maine.gov/cgi-bin/online/doc/parksearch/details.pl?park_id=96

## DIRECTIONS

To reach the trailhead in Caribou from I-95, take Exit 302 toward Presque Isle on US 1. Go 26.4 miles north on US 1, and turn left to remain on US 1 in Mars Hill. Go another 27.7 miles, turn left to stay on US 1, and then bear right onto ME 89/Access Hwy. Go 0.4 mile, and turn left onto Otter St. Look for trailhead parking on the right in 0.3 mile at the street end. To reach the endpoint in Caribou, turn right from the north side of the parking lot, and use the underpass to reach the trail. Turn right, and go 1.5 miles to the endpoint.

To reach the trailhead in Van Buren from I-95, take Exit 302 toward Presque Isle on US 1. Go 26.3 miles north on US 1, and in Mars Hill take the right fork onto US 1A. Go 49.9 miles, and look for the trail and parking on the left just past the intersection with US 1/Main St.

To reach the trailhead in Washburn from I-95, take Exit 264 toward Patten on ME 158. Head northwest on ME 158, go 0.4 mile, and bear right onto ME 11/Station Road. Go 56.5 miles, and turn right onto ME 227/Station St. Go 14.6 miles, and turn left onto Castle Hill Road. Go 3.7 miles, and turn left onto ME 164/Washburn Road. Go 1.4 miles, turn left onto Station Road, and look for parking on the left.

Visitors to the Belfast Rail Trail on the Passagassawaukeag (pronounced pas-uh-gas-uh-WAH-keg and conveniently shortened to Passy Rail Trail by locals) can see vintage trains at one end of the trail or watch shipwrights at work at the other end. In between, the 2.3-mile rail-trail passes through woods alongside the Passagassawakeag River. The trail, named for the indigenous spelling of that tidal river instead of the common name, is relatively flat with a packed gravel and crushed stone surface.

The rail-trail, opened in 2016, follows the southern section of old railbed laid by the Belfast & Moosehead Lake Railroad, a historic short line railroad that operated over 33 miles from Belfast to Burnham beginning in 1871 until 2007. Most of the corridor, north of the trail, is an excursion and tourist train still named the Belfast & Moosehead Lake Railroad.

A good place to start is the northern trailhead on Oak Hill Road, adjacent to the City Point Central Railroad Museum. Located in a vintage late-19th-century railroad

*The Belfast Armistice Bridge is a highlight on the southern end of the trail.*

**County**
Waldo

**Endpoints**
Oak Hill Road and Kaler Road/Hills to Sea Trail to Pierce St. at Water St. and Harbor Walk (Belfast)

**Mileage**
2.3

**Type**
Rail-Trail

**Roughness Index**
2

**Surfaces**
Crushed Stone, Gravel

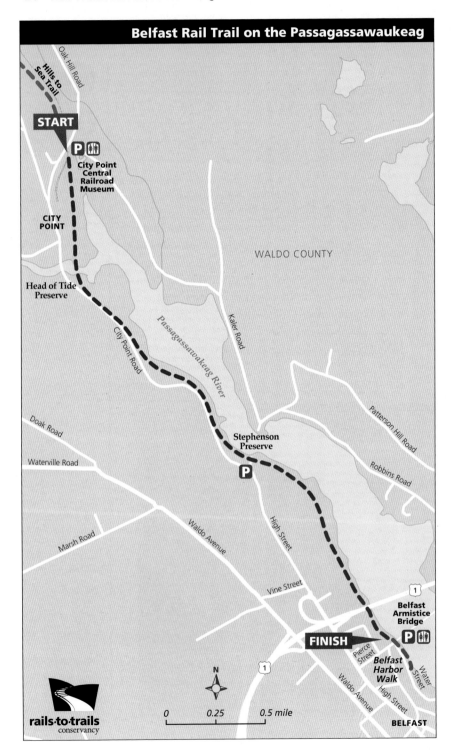

# Belfast Rail Trail on the Passagassawaukeag

Oak Hill Road

**Hills to Sea Trail**

**START**

P

City Point Central Railroad Museum

**CITY POINT**

Head of Tide Preserve

City Point Road

*Passagassawaukeag River*

Kaler Road

WALDO COUNTY

Doak Road

Waterville Road

Stephenson Preserve

P

Patterson Hill Road

Robbins Road

Marsh Road

Waldo Avenue

High Street

Vine Street

1

Belfast Armistice Bridge

**FINISH**

P

*Belfast Harbor Walk*

Pierce Street

Waldo Avenue

High Street

Water Street

1

N

0    0.25    0.5 mile

**rails·to·trails**
conservancy

**BELFAST**

station, the museum serves as the depot for the excursion train. Some of the rolling stock in use include electric locomotives, an observation car, a Pullman car, a coach/café car, and a caboose. The trailhead also is the terminus of the 47-mile Hills to Sea Trail, a walking path that heads west to the town of Unity.

Heading south on the Passy Rail Trail, you'll come to a bridge across a narrow section of the Passagassawakeag River in 0.4 mile. The 92-acre Head of Tide Preserve just west of the trail after crossing the bridge marks the end of the river's tidal zone. A couple of loop trails pass through the woods and along the river.

The trail runs alongside City Point Road for the next mile with some clear views of the river. Keep your eyes open for seals running the tide in the river and nesting eagles and ospreys in the woods along the shoreline. About 1.3 miles from the trailhead, you'll come to a parking lot. The 8-acre Stephenson Preserve, with a loop trail heading uphill, is located just north of here on City Point Road.

The trail continues along the river another mile, passing beneath the US 1 bridge and next to a potato processing plant, to the southern trailhead on Pierce Street. Here it connects to Belfast Harbor Walk at the Belfast Armistice Bridge (also known as Footbridge). The Harbor Walk connects to the Footbridge and continues south along the west side of the river, where the surface is a combination of asphalt and boardwalks. The southern end of the Harbor Walk has restaurants, docks, and shops, and hosts events and festivals.

**CONTACT:** belfastandmooseheadlakerail.org/portal/index.php/menu-rail-trail

## DIRECTIONS

To reach the northern trailhead, take US 1 N to Belfast, and take the exit for ME 7/ME 137 to Waldo Ave. Go straight onto Field St., and then go 0.1 mile and turn left onto High St. Go 2.1 miles on High St./City Point Road, and look for parking on the right at the City Point Central Railroad Museum.

To reach the northern trailhead from US 1 S/ME 3/Searsport Road in Belfast, turn right onto Swan Lake Ave./ME 141. Go 0.1 mile, and turn left onto Robbins Road, and then go 1 mile, and turn right onto Kaler Road. Go 1.3 miles, and turn left onto Oak Hill Road. Trailhead parking is on the left at the City Point Central Railroad Museum.

To reach the southern trailhead, take US 1 N to Belfast, and take the exit for ME 7/ME 137 to Waldo Ave. Go straight onto Field St., then go 0.1 mile and turn right onto High St. Go 0.1 mile, and turn left onto Pierce St., then go 0.2 mile for parking at the intersection with Water St.

To reach the southern trailhead from US 1 S/ME 3/Searsport Ave. in Belfast, take the ME 7/ME 137 exit toward downtown Belfast after crossing the bridge over the Passagassawakeag River. Turn right onto High St., then go 0.3 mile and turn left onto Pierce St. Go 0.2 mile for parking at the intersection with Water St.

## Calais Waterfront Walkway

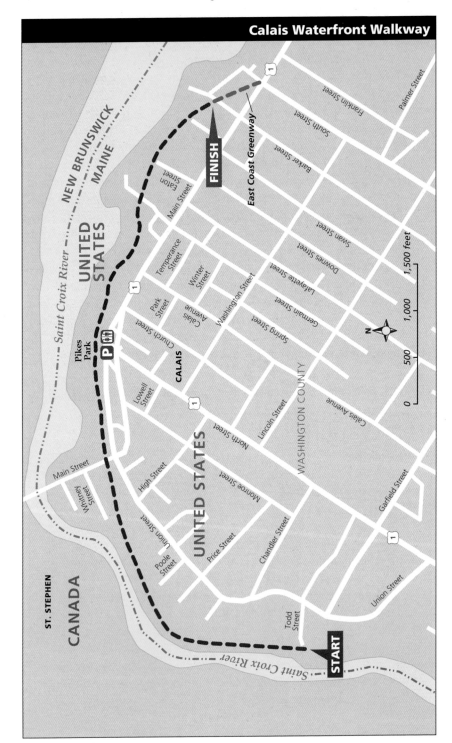

The Calais Waterfront Walkway provides a path for a short stroll along the Saint Croix River on the border between Calais and Canada, but it's also the start of something much longer. The 1.5-mile rail-trail marks the first mile of the East Coast Greenway, a project envisioned as a 3,000-mile off-road trail for non-motorized transportation, stretching from the border in Calais to Key West, Florida.

The gravel path got its start as a railroad, the first to be granted a charter by the state in 1832. When the 2-mile railroad between Milltown and Calais opened a few years later, horses provided the power to haul lumber from a nearby mill. The rail route then extended south to Baring and became the Calais & Baring Railroad. More extensions and ownership changes followed until 1904, when the Maine Central Railroad took over. The line eventually became the Calais Branch, with service to Bangor more

*The tree-lined trail is nestled between the Saint Croix River and downtown Calais.*

**County**
Washington

**Endpoints**
Todd St. between the St. Croix River and Union St. to Barker St. and South St. (Calais)

**Mileage**
1.5

**Type**
Rail-Trail

**Roughness Index**
2

**Surface**
Gravel

than 130 miles away. Although the railroad eventually discontinued use on most of the line (including the section that's now a trail), a segment from the western end of the trail carries pulp wood products between Calais and Milltown and then into Canada.

Calais is an international town with three entrances into New Brunswick, Canada. The northernmost crossing at the midpoint of the trail marks the beginning of the East Coast Greenway. It travels east along the Calais Waterfront Walkway for 0.8 mile until the trail ends. From there, East Coast Greenway travelers use road shoulders until they encounter the next off-road section.

The Calais Waterfront Walkway trailhead is located about midpoint at the riverfront Pikes Park, although it's easily accessible anywhere along the river. Heading east, the trail immediately passes the brick Calais Free Library, built in 1892. It's just one of the 19th-century brick buildings standing in downtown, much of which was destroyed in a calamitous fire in the 1870s. In front of the library you'll find the sculpture *Nexus,* one of more than 30 erected as part of a 200-mile-long sculpture trail in coastal Down East Maine. About 0.2 mile east of the trailhead, a narrow side path heads right to Main Street and the Dr. Job Holmes Cottage, which dates to at least 1805. A museum displays photos and artifacts from early Calais. The trail ends at Barker Street, where the East Coast Greenway continues onto South Street.

Returning to the trailhead and heading west, you'll pass beneath Main Street spanning the river to St. Stephen in New Brunswick. The Canadian town's scenic skyline is easy to see from Calais. If you have proper identification for crossing borders, you can ride on St. Stephen's mile-long Riverfront Walking Trail and visit the town's Chocolate Museum.

Emerging from the underpass, the trail continues west and then south as it follows the river's forested banks for another 0.6 mile. Keep your eyes open for bald eagles that feed along the river in this area.

**CONTACT:** calaismaine.org/directories/30-211/calais-waterfront-walkway

---

# DIRECTIONS

To reach the trailhead in Calais from I-395 in Bangor, take Exit 6A onto US 1A E toward Bar Harbor. Go 5.4 miles east, and turn left onto ME 46. Go 4.9 miles, and turn right onto ME 9. Go 76.5 miles, and turn right onto US 1 S/ME 9 toward Calais. Go 4.7 miles, go through a traffic circle, and continue on Baring St. 0.5 mile. Continue on North St. 1.7 miles, and then stay straight on North St. to reach the trailhead and parking (about 400 feet after passing Main St.).

The 87.9-mile Down East Sunrise Trail passes through the woods, marshlands, and coastal villages of southern Maine. It takes its name from its location in Down East Maine, dubbed by early mariners for being "downwind" from more western ports such as Boston. Also, it's one of the first trails to experience sunrise in the United States. ATV riders are the most frequent trail users and maintain the crushed stone and gravel trail surface. It's also a major off-road component on the East Coast Greenway, a future Calais, Maine–to–Key West, Florida, route for bicyclists, hikers, and equestrians.

The rail-trail follows a section of a 19th-century railroad that ran between Calais and Bangor, later becoming the Calais Branch of the Maine Central Railroad in 1911. The branch closed after Maine Central was sold in the 1980s, and the Maine Department of Transportation

*A bridge over the Narraguagus River in Cherryfield shows off the trail's railroad roots.*

**Counties**
Hancock, Washington

**Endpoints**
ME 214/Ayers Junction Road 0.5 mile south of Mt. Tom Road (Pembroke) to US 1/ME 3/High St. and Beals Ave. (Ellsworth)

**Mileage**
87.9

**Type**
Rail-Trail

**Roughness Index**
2–3

**Surfaces**
Crushed Stone, Gravel, Sand

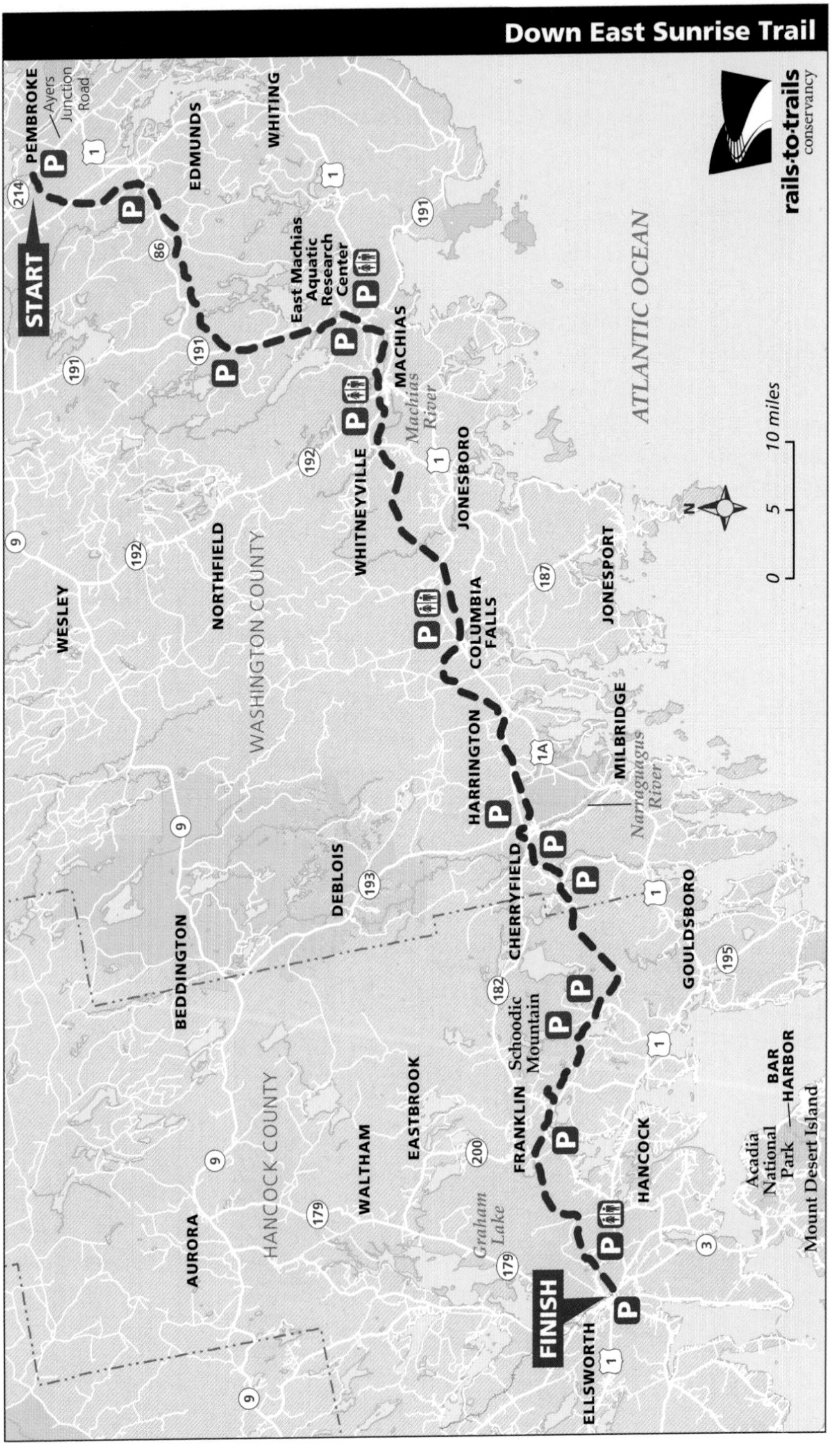

**Down East Sunrise Trail**

rails-to-trails
conservancy

START

FINISH

Ayers
Junction
Road

PEMBROKE

EDMUNDS

WHITING

East Machias
Aquatic
Research
Center

MACHIAS

Machias
River

WHITNEYVILLE

JONESBORO

COLUMBIA
FALLS

JONESPORT

HARRINGTON

MILBRIDGE

Narraguagus
River

CHERRYFIELD

WASHINGTON COUNTY

WESLEY

NORTHFIELD

DEBLOIS

BEDDINGTON

GOULDSBORO

Schoodic
Mountain

FRANKLIN

HANCOCK

BAR
HARBOR

Acadia
National
Park

Mount Desert Island

AURORA

HANCOCK COUNTY

WALTHAM

EASTBROOK

Graham
Lake

ELLSWORTH

ATLANTIC OCEAN

N

0   5   10 miles

214

86

191

191

192

1

1

187

1A

1

195

1

182

200

193

179

9

9

9

9

179

3

1

acquired the railbed in 1987. The first section of trail opened in 2009, and crews completed the 2-mile-long final section in Ellsworth in 2016.

The trail begins on Ayers Junction Road near Pembroke, site of a future extension eastward to the Sipayik Trail (see page 63). Your first leg heads mostly southwest through forestland for 29 miles toward the coastal village of Machias, site of the first naval battle of the American Revolution. Along the way, you can visit the East Machias Aquatic Research Center at 13 Willow Street, where you'll find native fish from local rivers and hatchery tanks filled with Atlantic salmon. Food and lodging are available in the village on the Machias River.

Leaving Machias, you'll cross many bridges over coastal rivers as you head west. In 3.5 miles, you'll cross the Machias River on a trestle, one of 28 bridges on the trail. The next 12 miles cross a remote landscape from Whitneyville to Columbia Falls, where you'll find drive-ins and cafés. After Harrington, the trail runs alongside US 1 on the way into Cherryfield, which calls itself the Wild Blueberry Capital of the World. Sandy soil and fog contribute to bountiful blueberry crops.

Crossing the Narraguagus River on the way out of Cherryfield, you'll begin another lonely section for 15 miles to the 150-acre Schoodic Bog at the foot of scenic Schoodic Mountain. You'll find insect-eating plants and turtles here, as well as beavers. Nearby, North End Road leads to a public beach and camping at the Donnell Pond Public Reserved Land. Refreshments are available about 5 miles past Schoodic Bog in Franklin. Watch for deer and other wildlife on the final 12 miles to Ellsworth, where you'll find restaurants and groceries. The rail yard for the Downeast Scenic Railroad excursion train is about 0.3 mile north of the trailhead. Plans call for a connection with the Ellsworth Rail Trail less than a mile north.

**CONTACT:** sunrisetrail.org and **maine.gov/downeastsunrisetrail**

---

## DIRECTIONS

To reach the eastern trailhead from I-395 in Bangor, take Exit 6A onto US 1A E toward Bar Harbor. Go 5.4 miles east, then turn left onto ME 46. Go 4.9 miles, then turn right onto ME 9. Go 67.9 miles, and turn right onto Davis Road. Go 0.8 mile, and turn right onto Arm Road. After another 1.2 miles, turn right onto Cooper Road/N. Union Road, and go 5.8 miles. Turn left onto ME 191, go 4.7 miles, and stay straight onto ME 214/Conant Hill Road, which will become ME 214/Ayers Junction Road. Go 6.2 miles, and look for parking on the right.

To reach the western trailhead in Ellsworth from I-395 in Bangor, take Exit 6A onto US 1A E toward Bar Harbor. Go 23.1 miles, and stay straight onto US 1/ME 3. Go 0.4 mile, turn left onto Beals Ave., and look for trailhead parking on the right.

# Eastern Promenade Trail

Back Cove Trail

Back Cove

Bayside Trail

Casco Bay

START

295

Sewage Plant Road

Loring Memorial Trail

Loring Memorial Park

Eastern Promenade

Eastern Promenade Midslope Trail

North Street

Walnut Street

Montreal Street

Melbourne Street

Quebec Street

Turner Street

Eastern Promenade

Cutter Street

East End Beach

26

Washington Avenue

Anderson Street

Fort Sumner Park

Lafayette Street

Merrill Street

Vesper Street

Morning Street

Fish Point

Fox Street

Greenleaf Street

Anderson Street

Cumberland Avenue

Congress Street

Monument Street

Munjoy Street

Atlantic Street

St Lawrence Street

Fore Street

Fort Allen Park

26

CUMBERLAND COUNTY

Mayo Street

Smith Street

Boyd Street

Mountfort Street

Kellogg Street

Maine Narrow Gauge Railroad Museum

1A

PORTLAND

Federal Street

Newbury Street

Hancock Street

Fore River

Wilmot Street

Franklin Street

Hampshire Street

India Street

Pearl Street

Congress Street

Lincoln Park

Middle Street

Fore Street

Portland Harbor

Federal Street

Market Street

FINISH

N

Commercial Street

Harborwalk Trail

rails-to-trails
conservancy

0    0.125    0.25 mile

Old salts should love the Eastern Promenade Trail, as it skirts the shoreline of Portland's Casco Bay and Portland Harbor. The 2.1-mile paved trail is always within sight of the water and is one of more than 30 trails and greenways in the state's largest city.

The trail runs through the city's Eastern Promenade, a 73-acre park that has been hosting visitors on the seaward flank of Munjoy Hill (once known as Mount Joy) since the 1830s. The Olmsted Brothers firm, noted architects of New York City's Central Park, created a park design in the early 20th century that has been followed over the years.

The trail, however, wasn't part of that plan. The Grand Trunk Railway (later the Canadian National Railroad) made Portland its terminus, and trains rolled right between the green space and the beaches. A fire in the 1980s destroyed the bridge that carried trains across Back Cove into Portland, and the city acquired the right-of-way

*Alongside the path, you'll see the tracks for the Maine Narrow Gauge Railroad Co. & Museum.*

**County**
Cumberland

**Endpoints**
Sewage Plant Road near I-295/Bayside Trail to Maine State Pier at Franklin St./US 1A and Commercial St. (Portland)

**Mileage**
2.1

**Type**
Rail-with-Trail

**Roughness Index**
1

**Surface**
Asphalt

and built the trail in the late 1990s. The paved trail is about 18 feet wide and can be used by pedestrians, bicyclists, and skaters. (While cross-country skiing is permitted, snow is usually plowed from the trail a day or two after falling.) A narrow stone dust trail runs parallel and midway up the slope in places.

In the northern end of the park, the Eastern Promenade Trail starts at the 1-mile Bayside Trail, which connects with the Back Cove Trail that encircles Back Cove. The Eastern Promenade Trail also is the path through Portland for the East Coast Greenway, an off-road trail project that stretches from Calais, Maine, to Key West, Florida. The Loring Memorial Trail (comprising a series of stairs) climbs the hill at the beginning of the trail to Loring Memorial Park, where you'll get an even better view of the islands in Casco Bay.

Back to the waterfront, you'll pass a wastewater treatment plant and see the remains of the trestle across Back Cove. Just past the sewage facility, the dirt Eastern Promenade Mid-Slope Trail heads partway up the hillside for those seeking a more scenic option. Alongside the main trail in this area, you'll see the tracks for the Maine Narrow Gauge Railroad Co. & Museum. The tourist railroad preserves equipment used historically for logging in remote parts of the state.

Crossing the parking lot and kayak launch at Cutter Street, you'll pass East End Beach and then turn southwest along the Fore River at Fish Point. Just uphill is Fort Allen Park, an earthen fort built to protect the harbor during the Revolutionary War and War of 1812. Vintage cannons are still posted here, and visitors get a good view of the harbor.

Heading upriver, you'll pass the narrow gauge train museum on the right and marinas on the left before the trail ends at ferry terminals to the outer islands. The Harborwalk Trail continues south on sidewalks through the Old Port and across Casco Bay Bridge to the Eastern Trail (see page 31).

**CONTACT: easternpromenade.org**

## DIRECTIONS

To reach the Cutter St. trailhead from I-295, take Exit 7 toward US 1A/Franklin St. Go 0.7 mile south on Franklin St./US 1A, and turn left onto Fore St./Eastern Promenade. Go 0.8 mile, and turn right onto Cutter St. The parking lot is straight ahead in 0.3 mile. The trail is downhill from the parking lot; left (northwest) goes 0.8 mile to the junction with the Bayside Trail, and right (southeast) goes 1.1 miles south toward the Maine State Pier.

The 28.9-mile Eastern Trail connects the historic towns along Maine's southern coast from the woods near Kennebunk to South Portland's harbor lighthouse. Nearly 22 miles of the route follows off-road rail-trail and greenway interrupted by two major on-road gaps in Saco/Biddeford and Scarborough. Plans are underway to close at least one of these gaps and extend the trail another 19 miles southwest to Kittery. The East Coast Greenway incorporates the Eastern Trail on its 3,000-mile-long trail project between Maine and Key West, Florida.

A significant distance uses the old Eastern Railroad route, chartered in the 1830s to run passenger and freight trains between Boston and Portland. Its rival, the Boston & Maine Railroad, leased the Eastern in 1884 and then bought it outright in 1900. Guilford Transportation,

*The Eastern Trail provides a pleasant ride through natural areas along Maine's southern coast.*

**Counties**
Cumberland, York

**Endpoints**
Warrens Way and ME 35/Alewive Road (Kennebunk) to W. Cole Road near ME 111/Alfred St. (Biddeford); Clark St. near Nott St. (Saco) to Eastern Road near ME 207/Black Point Road (Scarborough); Gary L. Maietta Way near Highland Ave. to Bug Light Park at Madison St. 0.5 mile north of Breakwater Dr. (South Portland)

**Mileage**
28.9

**Type**
Rail-Trail

**Roughness Index**
1

**Surfaces**
Asphalt, Crushed Stone, Sand

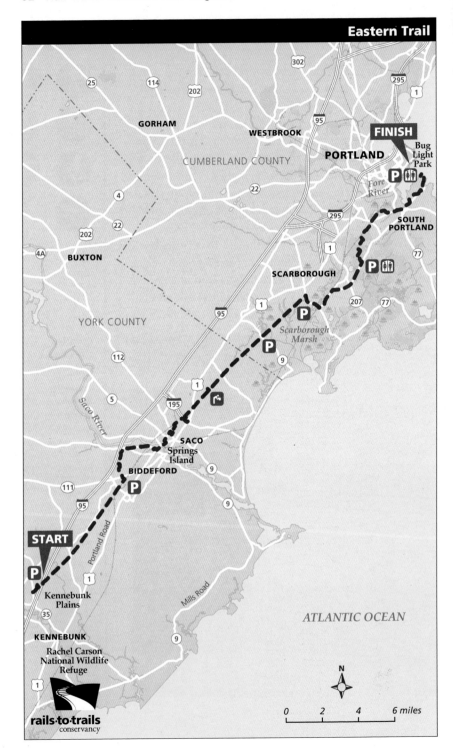

Eastern Trail

302

295

1

GORHAM

WESTBROOK

FINISH

Bug Light Park

25

114

202

95

PORTLAND

CUMBERLAND COUNTY

P

4

22

Fore River

295

SOUTH PORTLAND

22

202

1

77

4A

BUXTON

SCARBOROUGH

P

207

77

YORK COUNTY

95

1

P

Scarborough Marsh

112

P

9

5

1

195

SACO
Springs Island

9

BIDDEFORD

P

111

95

9

START

Portland Road

P

Kennebunk Plains

1

Mills Road

ATLANTIC OCEAN

35

KENNEBUNK

9

Rachel Carson National Wildlife Refuge

1

N

rails·to·trails
conservancy

0    2    4    6 miles

*A highlight of the route is Scarborough Marsh, a breathtaking expanse of saltwater wetlands that is Maine's largest at 3,100 acres.*

which became Pan Am Railways, purchased the Boston & Maine in the 1980s, and later discontinued use on many underperforming routes.

In the southwest, the trail starts just north of the town center of Kennebunk, where quaint, old New England architecture draws tourists in the summer. The Kennebunk Plains blueberry barrens, where you can pick the berries after August 1, and the Rachel Carson National Wildlife Refuge are nearby. The trail surface switches between packed dirt, gravel, and sand as it crosses small roads and streams for 6.2 miles to the first gap in Biddeford. Follow directional signs for 4.5 miles through Biddeford on streets and sidewalks and across the Saco River at Springs Island to regain the trail on Clark Street at Thornton Academy in Saco.

After about 2 miles of paved and crushed stone surface, you'll cross US 1 on an overpass about 0.5 mile south of Funtown Splashtown USA, a Saco tourism destination. About 4 miles later, you'll arrive at Scarborough Marsh, a breathtaking expanse of saltwater wetlands that is Maine's largest at 3,100 acres. Keep an eye out for marine birds and enjoy the ride along nearly 2 miles of beautiful coastal trail. The trail ends after the marsh, and a 4-mile on-road section begins. It's well marked, but traffic is heavy and fast, so be cautious riding on the shoulder. The Eastern Trail Alliance has been raising funds to close this gap to the Wainwright Recreation Complex, where the trail starts again.

The final 5-mile leg soon becomes urbanized. As you approach the Fore River, which separates South Portland from Portland, the corridor meanders between off-road trail and on-street routes. Follow signs for the South Portland Greenbelt. The trail ends at Bug Light Park, named for the smallish lighthouse that has stood here since 1875. Enjoy the views of tankers and sailboats in the harbor and the Portland skyline.

**CONTACT:** easterntrail.org

## DIRECTIONS

To reach the Kennebunk trailhead from I-95 N, take Exit 25 toward ME 35/Kennebunk/Kennebunkport. Go 0.4 mile, and turn right onto ME 35, and then go 0.2 mile, and turn right to stay on ME 35/Alewive Road. Go 0.8 mile, and turn right into the Kennebunk Elementary School parking lot. A short path to the trail is at the south end of the parking lot. From I-95 S, take Exit 25, and turn right onto ME 35/Alewive Road. In less than 0.5 mile, the Kennebunk Elementary School will be on your right.

To reach the South Portland trailhead from I-295 N, take Exit 4 toward Casco Bay Bridge/Portland Waterfront. Go 0.7 mile, and merge onto the Veterans Memorial Bridge, and then go 0.4 mile, and merge onto US 1A/Fore River Pkwy./W. Commercial St. Go 1 mile, turn left at the traffic light near Goodyear, and merge onto ME 77/Casco Bay Bridge. Go 1 mile, and continue onto Broadway; then go 1.6 miles, and turn left onto Breakwater Dr./Benjamin W. Pickett St. Go 0.1 mile, and turn right onto Madison St. Go 0.4 mile, and look for parking straight ahead.

To reach the South Portland trailhead from I-295 S, take Exit 4 toward US 1/Main St. Merge onto US 1, go 0.4 mile, and merge onto US 1 S/Main St., and then immediately turn left onto Alton St./Huntress Ave. Go 0.3 mile, and turn left onto Broadway, and then go 1.8 miles, and turn right to stay on Broadway. Go 1.6 miles, and turn left onto Breakwater Dr./Benjamin W. Pickett St. Go 0.1 mile, and turn right onto Madison St. Go 0.4 mile, and look for parking straight ahead.

The Four Seasons Adventure Trail skirts several scenic lakes as it passes through forests and farmland, linking Newport, Corinna, Dexter, and Dover-Foxcroft in central Maine. The trail experiences frequent ATV use on summer weekends, mountain bikers and horseback riders share the trail in warmer months, and snowmobilers and cross-country skiers appear when the snow flies. Snowshoeing and dogsledding are also permitted. Both ends of the trail tie into the 1,000-mile-plus-long Maine Interconnected Trail System.

The trail follows the old railbed of the Dexter and Newport Railroad, which blazed north in 1868. The Maine Central Railroad leased the line and then extended it northward to Foxcroft in 1889. A transporter of wood products, the railway became known as the Foxcroft Branch. Maine Central ceased operations on the branch in 1993, setting the stage for the state's purchase of the corridor for recreational use. It has been known variously as the Moosehead Trail and the Newport/Dover-Foxcroft Trail before adoption of the Four Seasons Adventure Trail name.

Starting in Newport, the trail passes through a business district and then some woods before it crosses ME 7 for the

*Much of the trail runs through the dense forests of central Maine.*

**Counties**
Penobscot, Piscataquis

**Endpoints**
Spring St. between South St. and W. Spring St. (Newport) to Fairview Ave. and Depot St. (Dover-Foxcroft)

**Mileage**
29.8

**Type**
Rail-Trail

**Roughness Index**
2–3

**Surfaces**
Crushed Stone, Dirt, Sand

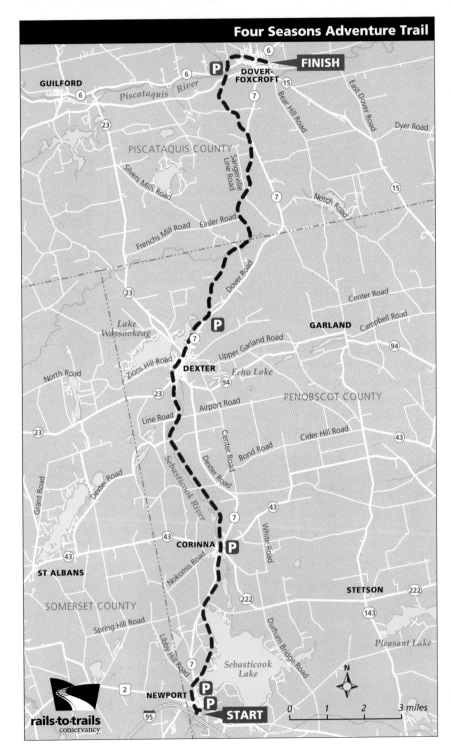

## Four Seasons Adventure Trail

FINISH

GUILFORD

Piscataquis River

DOVER-FOXCROFT

PISCATAQUIS COUNTY

Silvers Mills Road

Sangerville Line Road

Bear Hill Road

East Dover Road

Dyer Road

Frenchs Mill Road

Easler Road

Notch Road

Dover Road

Lake Wassookeag

Upper Garland Road

GARLAND

Center Road

Campbell Road

DEXTER

Echo Lake

Zions Hill Road

North Road

Airport Road

PENOBSCOT COUNTY

Line Road

Center Road

Bond Road

Cider Hill Road

Grant Road

Dexter Road

Sebasticook River

Dexter Road

CORINNA

White Road

ST ALBANS

Nokomis Road

STETSON

SOMERSET COUNTY

Spring Hill Road

Durham Bridge Road

Pleasant Lake

Libby Hill Road

Sebasticook Lake

NEWPORT

START

N

rails·to·trails
conservancy

0    1    2    3 miles

second time and plays peekaboo with the 4,000-acre Sebasticook Lake. Although this area may seem remote, wooden stakes used in prehistoric fish traps discovered at the north end of the lake in the 1990s show that people lived here some 3,000 years ago. Today the lake is stocked with largemouth bass and crappie.

Leaving the lake, the trail wends north another 2.5 miles to the old mill town of Corinna, where an antiques shop, general store, and café offer distractions. The imposing brick building with a clock tower and belfry, a couple of blocks away, is the Free Library, built in 1898 and easily the most eye-catching landmark.

The trail offers a glimpse of a reservoir on the Sebasticook River as it leaves town, and then plunges into woods for about 7 miles to Dexter. (When you cross Line Road at 5.6 miles past Corinna, you're crossing the 45th Parallel, halfway between the Equator and North Pole.) This old mill town, former home of the shoe manufacturer of the same name, offers cafés, groceries, and shady parks for resting. It's easy to wander a couple of blocks east of the trail on Center Street to Water Street, where you'll find the historical society museum housed in an old gristmill with a period home and schoolhouse nearby.

The trail rolls out of town behind some businesses and Lake Wassookeag (which means "shining water"), where you'll see boaters and swimmers in the summer and people fishing through the ice in the winter. Leaving the lakeside, the trail meanders north for 11 miles through woods interrupted infrequently by farm lots on its way to Dover-Foxcroft.

After crossing the old railroad bridge spanning the Piscataquis River, which powered the mills that once thrived here, you'll find food and services on the commercial outskirts of town where the trail crosses ME 6. You'll encounter more interesting fare as you proceed across the north side of town. If you're lucky, you'll arrive during the annual Maine Whoopie Pie Festival in June. The town goes all out to celebrate this sandwich-sized cookie, a nice reward for a day of exercise.

CONTACT: maine.gov/cgi-bin/online/doc/parksearch/details.pl?park_id=95

## DIRECTIONS

To reach the southern trailhead in Newport from I-95, take Exit 157 toward Newport/Dexter on ME 11/ME 100. Go 0.5 mile northeast on ME 11/ME 100, and stay straight through the US 2 intersection to stay on ME 7/ME 11/Moosehead Trail. Go 0.8 mile, and turn right into the small parking lot adjacent to the trailhead, or go another 0.1 mile, and look for parking on your left. The trail's endpoint is about 1.2 miles south along the trail in Newport.

To reach the northern trailhead in Dover-Foxcroft from I-95, take Exit 185 onto ME 15 N/Broadway. Go 35.2 miles northwest on ME 15 to Dover-Foxcroft, and turn left onto ME 6/ME 15/ME 16/W. Main St. Go 1.2 miles to the trail crossing, where trail parking can be found at the Irving service station on the right. The trail continues north of Main St. for 2 miles.

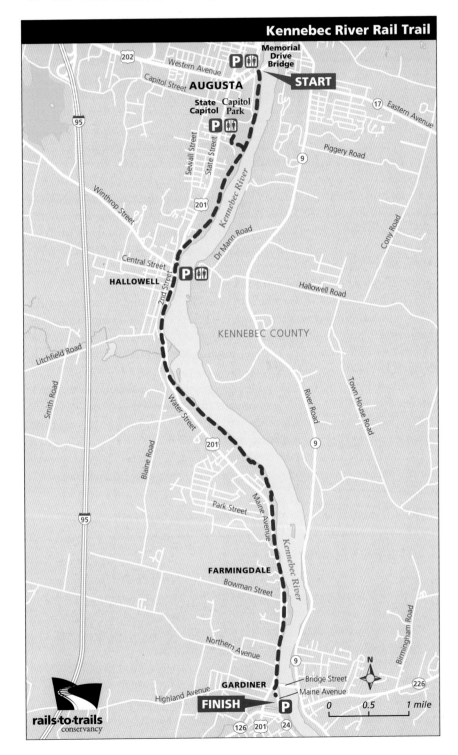

**Kennebec River Rail Trail**

Visitors to the 6.5-mile-long Kennebec River Rail Trail mostly stay within sight of the wide river as the paved trail links the state capital of Augusta with the river towns of Hallowell, Farmingdale, and Gardiner. The trail is part of the off-road East Coast Greenway, which will connect Calais, Maine, with Key West, Florida, when it is complete. No motorized use is allowed on the trail, which is plowed of snow in the winter.

The trail shares the corridor with railroad tracks that the Maine Department of Transportation preserved in hopes that trains will one day return. It follows the route of the Kennebec and Portland Railroad, which the state chartered in 1836 and reached Augusta by 1851. The Maine Central Railroad subsequently bought the 63-mile line and provided rail service to communities along the river until 1983. The new owners, Guilford Transportation

*True to its name, the trail stays within sight of the beautiful Kennebec River for almost its entire distance.*

**County**
Kennebec

**Endpoints**
Water St. and Gage St.
(Augusta) to Maine Ave.
and Bridge St. (Gardiner)

**Mileage**
6.5

**Type**
Rail-with-Trail

**Roughness Index**
1

**Surface**
Asphalt

(later Pan Am Railways), eventually closed the Augusta-Brunswick segment, which the state acquired.

Beginning at a riverside parking lot in Augusta, the trail heads south beneath the US 201/Memorial Drive bridge. The first mile of trail is often crowded with office workers stretching their legs during lunchtime and after work. About 0.7 mile from the trailhead, a side trail heads right to more parking and Capitol Park at the foot of the State Capitol building. The Maine State Museum and State Library are nearby.

At mile 2, measured by 0.25-mile trailside markers, you'll arrive at the waterfront in Hallowell, once a logging, mill, and shipbuilding center. Parking and restrooms are at a riverfront park that's home to the farmers market in season. You might be drawn to the colorful Adirondack chairs that overlook the river here, or you can visit antiques stores, art studios, or restaurants along Water Street.

Leaving Hallowell, the trail veers away from the rail corridor for a short distance, then hugs the shoreline of Kennebec River to Farmingdale. At one time polluted by industrial discharges, the river Kennebec—named so by the area's original inhabitants for its "large body of still water"—has benefited from clean water laws. Removal of the Edwards Dam in Augusta in 1999 has helped bring back migratory fish. You may see osprey or bald eagles that feed on the river life.

The trail ends at a shopping center on the north end of Gardiner, a former mill town. About a block south is a vintage Maine Central Railroad depot built in 1911 and used by the railroad into the 1950s. Just a few blocks farther south, you'll find Gardiner Waterfront Park, a popular event space and put-in for boats, kayaks, and canoes. The future Merrymeeting Trail project is proposed to follow the rail corridor south of here for 32 miles to Brunswick on the coast.

**CONTACT: kennebecriverrailtrail.org**

## DIRECTIONS

To reach the trailhead in Augusta from I-95, take Exit 109A toward Augusta on US 202/ME 11/ Western Ave. Go 1.4 miles east on US 202 to the Memorial Circle roundabout, and take the third exit onto Water St. Go 0.3 mile, and turn right into Downtown Parking. The trail begins at the south end of the parking lot.

To reach the trail in Gardiner from I-295, take Exit 51 onto ME 9/ME 126/Cobbossee Ave./ Lewiston Road. Go 1.8 miles east, and cross the bridge onto ME 9/ME 126/Water St. Go another 1.1 miles, and stay straight on Water St. Go 0.2 mile, and turn left onto Maine Ave. Go 0.2 mile, and turn left into the parking lot. The trailhead is at the north end of the lot.

**K**eep your ears open for the haunting call of loons along the scenic Kennebec Valley Trail. They're just one example of the wildlife—another is the moose—that inhabits the river, woods, and fields surrounding this nearly 14.5-mile rail-trail from Bingham to North Anson. The trail traces part of the grueling river route that Benedict Arnold's troops took in their ill-fated Revolutionary War attack on British forces in Quebec in December 1775.

American Indians—and later settlers and railroad builders—considered the Kennebec Valley a natural corridor for traveling in the wilderness. In the 1870s, the Somerset Railroad eyed the route as it began pushing toward Quebec from southern Maine. Running out of money when it reached North Anson in 1877, the company reorganized as the Somerset Railway and laid track to Solon by 1889 and Bingham by 1890. The Maine Central Railroad

*The Kennebec is so wide and calm in places that you have to remind yourself that it's a river and not one of Maine's lakes.*

**County**
Somerset

**Endpoints**
Goodrich Road between Somerset Lane and River Road (Bingham) to Fahi Pond Road just north of US 201A/N. Main St. (North Anson)

**Mileage**
14.5

**Type**
Rail-Trail

**Roughness Index**
3

**Surfaces**
Crushed Stone, Dirt, Sand

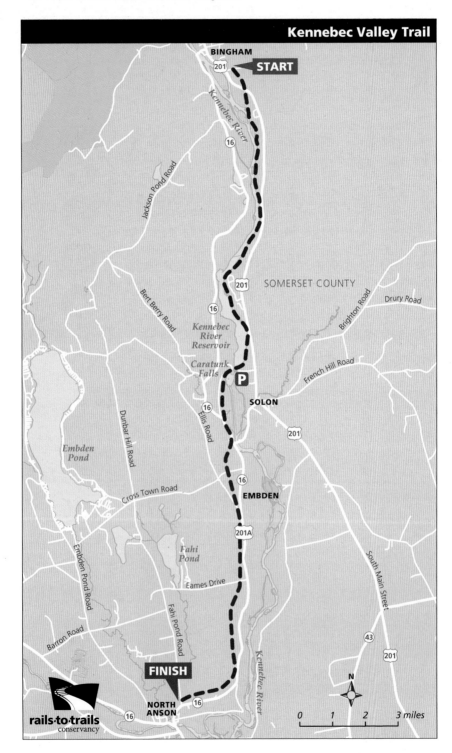

**Kennebec Valley Trail**

took over in 1911, hauling timber and agricultural products. Traffic declined with road improvements in the area, and the Maine Central discontinued using this section in 1976 after the last sawmill closed in Bingham.

Folks on ATVs and mountain bikes travel this remote rail-trail until the first snowfall, which brings out snowmobilers and cross-country skiers. Snowshoeing and dogsledding are also permitted. Mountain bikes are recommended for cycling, as parts of the trail suffer rough conditions. In Bingham, the trail links to more than a thousand miles of trail in Maine's Interconnected Trail System.

The Kennebec Valley Trail starts in Bingham, where sawmills used to process timber floated downriver from the north. Consider stopping in town for provisions, as there are few towns with services ahead. The trailhead is south of town on Goodrich Road.

Gazing at the river as you head south, you'll soon realize why it's named Kennebec: it translates to "large body of still water or large bay" in local tribal language. The Kennebec is so wide and calm in places that you have to remind yourself that it's a river and not one of Maine's lakes.

The riverbank is forested for most of the next 6.5 miles to just north of Solon, where the trail veers right and crosses the river on an old railroad bridge across rocky Caratunk Falls and a modern hydroelectric facility. On October 7, 1775, Arnold's force arrived at a point below the falls that's now called Arnolds Landing. His boats were leaking, and his men were wet, cold, and sick. After a good night's sleep, they carried the boats around the falls and continued their journey through the wilderness to Quebec. You can take a footpath to Arnolds Landing before crossing the river. Falls Road heads into Solon before you cross the bridges.

After a 1.1-mile jaunt on Levee Road along a tamed section of river, you'll pick up the Kennebec Valley Trail again as it enters a more agricultural district. Traveling along the high ground, you'll catch only occasional glimpses of the river in the valley below. After passing through Embden in 2.1 miles, the trail gets rougher in places over the next 4.5 miles until you arrive in North Anson.

**CONTACT:** maine.gov/cgi-bin/online/doc/parksearch/details.pl?park_id=74

## DIRECTIONS

To reach official trail parking in Solon from I-95, take Exit 133 toward Skowhegan on US 201. Go 30.1 miles north on US 201 through Solon, and turn left onto Falls Road. Go 0.4 mile to a parking lot. From here, the Bingham trailhead is 6.7 miles north; the North Anson trailhead is 7.8 miles south.

There are no official trail parking areas near the endpoints in Bingham or North Anson.

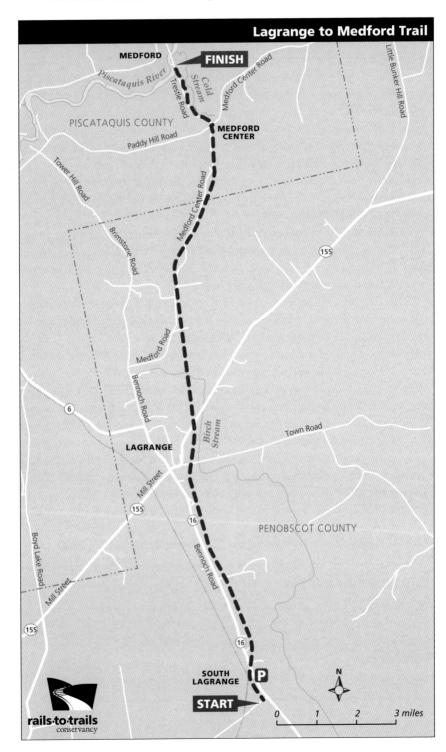

**Lagrange to Medford Trail**

MEDFORD

FINISH

Piscataquis River

Cold Stream

Trestle Road

Medford Center Road

Little Bunker Hill Road

PISCATAQUIS COUNTY

Paddy Hill Road

MEDFORD CENTER

Tower Hill Road

Brimstone Road

Medford Center Road

155

Medford Road

Bennoch Road

6

LAGRANGE

Birch Stream

Town Road

Mill Street

155

16

PENOBSCOT COUNTY

Boyd Lake Road

Mill Street

Bennoch Road

155

16

SOUTH LAGRANGE

P

START

N

0    1    2    3 miles

rails·to·trails
conservancy

The Lagrange to Medford Trail fills the bill if you're looking for a remote trail experience. The gravel rail-trail runs for 11.4 miles from Lagrange to Medford Center, where it crosses a 100-year-old railroad trestle across the Piscataquis River. An ATV and snowmobile route continues north on the old railroad bed to remote Schoodic Lake at Lake View Plantation. You're as likely to see evidence of beavers and moose as people along the out-of-the-way route.

The Bangor and Aroostook Railroad built the 600-foot-long trestle some 60 feet over the river as part of its Medford Cutoff in 1907. After a local ferry closed in the 1940s, the bridge was the only connection between the towns of Medford and Medford Center, located on opposite sides of the river. Some daring locals took to crossing the bridge in cars and on foot after the railroad discontinued using the line in

*Keep your eyes open for wildlife in the ponds, marshes, and bogs as you travel along Birch and Cold Streams.*

**Counties**
Penobscot, Piscataquis

**Endpoints**
S. Lagrange Road just west of Bennoch Road/ ME 16 (Lagrange) to Trestle Road and River Road at the Piscataquis River (Medford Center)

**Mileage**
11.4

**Type**
Rail-Trail

**Roughness Index**
2–3

**Surfaces**
Crushed Stone, Dirt

1978. The town later bought and refurbished the bridge just as crews were about to dismantle it.

The area's remoteness means that you should carry provisions to get through the day, including insect repellent in the spring and early summer. The trail is shared by folks on ATVs, horses, and mountain bikes in warm months, and snowmobiles, cross-country skis, snowshoes, and dogsleds in the winter. It's best to avoid the trail during muddy seasons.

Starting at the trailhead in South Lagrange, the trail rolls north through a heavily wooded area where you'll catch occasional glimpses of houses or small farms through the trees. In about 4 miles, you'll pass about 0.5 mile east of the old lumber mill town of Lagrange, home to a service station/general store via the Town Road crossing.

Keep your eyes open for waterfowl and signs of beavers in the ponds, marshes, and bogs as you head north along Birch Stream and later Cold Stream. Fishermen are attracted here as well. Moose have been sighted in these woods and bogs, so use extreme caution around these unpredictable creatures.

About 6 miles north of Lagrange you'll arrive in Medford Center, where a few buildings cluster around a restored barn that serves as the town hall. The state park's trail ownership ends at Paddy Hill Road, and local ATV and snowmobile clubs maintain a section of trail for Medford that parallels Trestle Road for 1.3 miles to the south bank of the Piscataquis River.

Across the bridge, the old railroad corridor is controlled by private landowners and state easements. ATV clubs use Railroad Bed Road to reach the eastern shore of Schoodic Lake, while snowmobilers find connections to continue their journeys on the Maine Interconnected Trail.

CONTACT: maine.gov/cgi-bin/online/doc/parksearch/details.pl?park_id=79

## DIRECTIONS

To reach the trailhead in South Lagrange from I-95 N, take Exit 199 toward Lagrange on ME 16/Bennoch Road. Turn left onto ME 16/Bennoch Road, go 10.4 miles, and turn left onto Railroad Road. Trailhead parking is about 500 feet ahead. The southern end of the trail is about 0.4 mile south. From I-95 S, take Exit 217, and turn right (west) onto ME 155 S/ME 6 W/Lagrange Road, and go 10.6 miles. Turn left onto ME 16 E, and go 3.8 miles. Turn right onto Railroad Road.

To reach parking in Medford Center from I-95, take Exit 217 onto ME 6/ME 155 toward Lagrange. Head west on ME 6/ME 155, go 0.4 mile, and turn right toward Maxfield onto River Road/Maxfield Road. Go 9.7 miles (River Road becomes Medford Center Road), and turn right onto Trestle Road in Medford Center. Go 0.1 mile, and look for parking at the trail crossing.

The Mountain Division Trail exists as two separate segments of what will eventually be a more than 50-mile-long trail from Fryeburg to Portland. The southern section rolls for about 6 miles between Windham and Standish; the northern section runs for nearly 4 miles through Fryeburg on the New Hampshire border. The paved trail segments run alongside currently dormant train tracks owned by the Maine Department of Transportation. Long-range plans call for a trail alongside the roughly 45 miles of existing rail corridor that the state owns between Fryeburg and Westbrook. The state wants to acquire and install trail on the final 5-mile rail link to Portland.

**Counties**
Cumberland, Oxford

**Endpoints**
US 202/ME 4 between Depot St. and Elderberry Lane (Windham) to ME 35/Chadbourne Road 0.25 mile east of School St. (Standish) and ME 113/Portland St. at Lyman Dr. to US 302/E. Main St. at Haley Town Road (Fryeburg)

**Mileage**
9.7

**Type**
Rail-with-Trail

**Roughness Index**
1–2

**Surfaces**
Asphalt, Gravel

*The paved path runs alongside train tracks owned by the Maine Department of Transportation.*

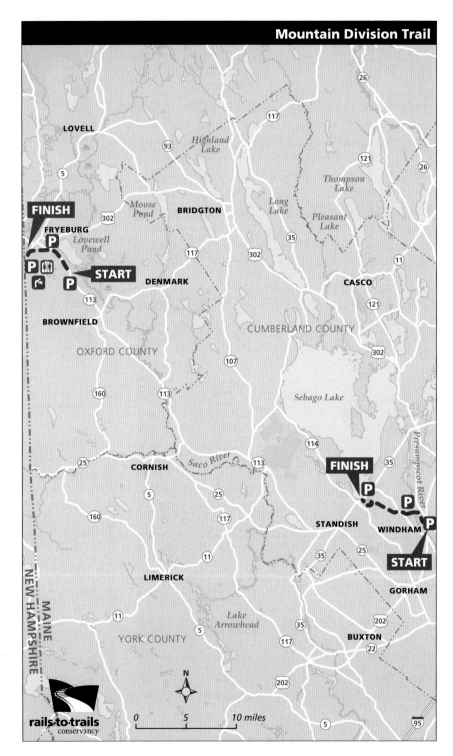

## Mountain Division Trail

The Mountain Division Trail takes its name from the Maine Central Railroad's Mountain Division that ran from Portland through New Hampshire's White Mountains to Vermont. Chartered in 1867 as the Portland and Ogdensburg Railroad, Maine Central took over in the early 20th century. Passenger service on the scenic run ended in 1958, and freight trains stopped rolling after Guilford Transportation (later Pan Am Railways) acquired it in the 1980s. The Maine DOT owns and maintains the tracks today in hopes of reestablishing rail service.

## Windham to Standish Segment: 5.6 miles

The southern section of the Mountain Division Trail comprises a segment of the 28-mile Sebago to the Sea Trail that runs between the southern tip of Sebago Lake to Casco Bay in Portland. You can start at the parking lot for the post office in Windham, about 0.25 mile north of the trailhead. The 10-foot-wide paved trail follows the unused tracks for 1.6 miles to a crossing over the Presumpscot River. Just past the bridge, a side trail heads downhill for 0.7 mile past Shaw Park, where you can swim and rent kayaks or canoes. The trail ends at a bridge just above Gambo Dam. A footpath heads into the woods where you can explore the ruins of a canal and the Oriental Powder Mill, which supplied the Union Army with one-quarter of its gunpowder.

Returning to the main trail, you'll continue west across the rural landscape for 3 miles to a gate and stop sign blocking access to the railroad corridor across some ponds. The Mountain Division Trail continues up a hill as a gravel path for 1.2 miles to the trailhead at the south shore of Sebago Lake.

## Fryeburg Segment: 4.0 miles

The northern section starts about 30 miles away at a trailhead on Portland Street in Fryeburg. Heading west, the paved trail is wooded and lined with wildflowers. You'll have occasional mountain views through breaks in the vegetation. The trail parallels the road for 2.5 miles before it passes south of the historic town center. It travels another 1.5 miles to a trailhead near the New Hampshire state line.

**CONTACT:** maine.gov/mdot/bikeped

**SOUTHERN SECTION:** windhammaine.us/documentcenter/view/219 and sebagotothesea.org

**NORTHERN SECTION:** facebook.com/pages/Fryeburg-Rail-Trail-Mountain-Division -Trail/191670854301192

## DIRECTIONS

To reach the western trailhead for the south segment from the intersection of ME 25 and ME 35 in Standish, head north on ME 35 N/Northeast Road (it becomes Chadbourne Road), and go 2.5 miles. Turn right into the parking lot by Standish Skate Park.

To reach the eastern trailhead for the south segment from the intersection of ME 25 and US 202 in Gorham, head northeast on US 202 E/ME 4/Gray Road, and go 4 miles. The trailhead is on the left, but no parking is available.

To reach the eastern trailhead for the north segment from the intersection of US 302 and ME 113 in Fryeburg, head south on ME 5/ME 113 toward Brownfield and Old Orchard Beach. Go 3.4 miles, and look for parking on the right.

To reach the western trailhead for the north segment from the intersection of US 302 and ME 113 in Fryeburg, head southwest on US 302, and go 1.1 miles. Find the Maine Tourism Association parking lot near the New Hampshire border just north of Haley Town Road.

There's plenty of room for backcountry experiences on the Narrow Gauge Pathway (also known as Carrabassett River Trail) nestled between Sugarloaf Mountain and the 36,000-acre Bigelow Preserve. The firm, crushed-stone surface hugs the north shore of the Carrabassett River for 5 miles as it rolls through a rocky channel in a forest. The trail surface, which is groomed in the winter for cross-country skiing, calls for the wider tires of hybrid or mountain bikes. Unlike most other remote rail-trails in the state, motorized vehicles such as ATVs and snowmobiles are prohibited.

The trail follows the bed of the Kingfield and Dead River Railroad that served loggers and sawmills in the area. The railroaders chose a 2-foot-wide narrow gauge for track separation instead of the 4-foot-8-inch standard gauge because it was easier and cheaper to build and operate through rough, mountainous terrain. The narrow

*Groomed in winter, the pathway provides backcountry experiences for cross-country skiing and snowshoeing.*

**County**
Franklin

**Endpoints**
Huston Brook Road at the Carrabassett River Pedestrian Bridge, 1 mile north of Carriage Road, to Carrabassett Dr./ ME 16/ME 27 just northwest of Access Road (Carrabassett Valley)

**Mileage**
5.4

**Type**
Rail-Trail

**Roughness Index**
2

**Surfaces**
Crushed Stone, Dirt

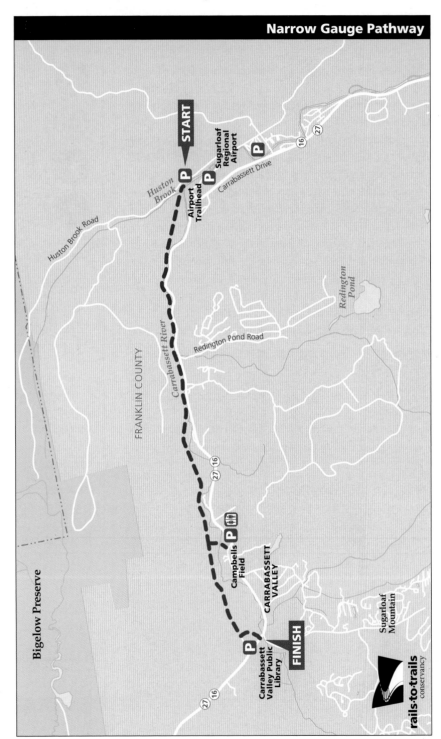

**Narrow Gauge Pathway**

START

Sugarloaf Regional Airport

Huston Brook

Airport Trailhead

Carrabassett Drive

16

27

Huston Brook Road

Redington Pond

Carrabassett River

Redington Pond Road

FRANKLIN COUNTY

Bigelow Preserve

27  16

Campbells Field

CARRABASSETT VALLEY

Sugarloaf Mountain

FINISH

Carrabassett Valley Public Library

27  16

rails-to-trails
conservancy

gauge railroad reached Carrabassett Valley from the south in 1894, extending in 1900 to Bigelow, where the old railroad station still stands. The Bigelow branch fell out of use in the late 1920s, and the town of Carrabassett Valley constructed the recreational path in 2001.

Starting at the Airport Trailhead, follow a trail that heads north into the woods and cross the Carrabassett River on a footbridge. Signs at a kiosk point to the Narrow Gauge Pathway on the left fork, where you'll immediately cross a short footbridge over Huston Brook. The trail offers a slight uphill grade all the way to the endpoint near the entrance to the Sugarloaf ski resort.

The trail rolls through forests uphill from the river for about 0.8 mile until the trail meets the river. You'll have river views most of the rest of the way to the western endpoint, about 4 miles away. There are several picnic tables at scenic overlooks along this section. If you have your fishing license with you, there are many good places to throw in a line. A path on the Maine Huts and Trails System veers off to the right in this area.

Trailside wildflowers bloom in profusion from early spring through fall, while birch, aspen, and maple trees offer splashes of spectacular color during the fall foliage season. You'll cross a boardwalk over a beaver flowage just shy of 4 miles from the trailhead. A left fork here crosses the river on a 0.2-mile trail to restrooms and parking at Campbell Field on ME 16/ME 27.

In another mile, another fork sends travelers left toward the trailhead and parking at the Carrabassett Valley Public Library. The right fork goes a short distance down Bigelow Station Road to the old railroad station set amid a collection of ski huts. The 2,200-mile Appalachian Trail is about 2 miles north on ME 16/27.

**CONTACT:** carrabassettvalley.org/narrow-gauge-pathway

## DIRECTIONS

To reach the airport trailhead in Carrabassett Valley from I-95, take Exit 112 or 112B toward Belgrade, heading north on ME 8/ME 11/ME 27. Go 24.6 miles north, and turn left onto ME 27/US 2. Go 9.6 miles and turn right to stay on ME 27. Go 3.1 miles, and bear right to stay on ME 27. Go 19.6 miles, and join ME 16/ME 27. Go 10.2 miles, turn right into the Carrabassett Valley Airport, and go straight to the parking lot. Follow a trail 0.2 mile north into the woods and across a footbridge over the Carrabassett trailhead to find the trail.

To reach the western trailhead at the Carrabassett Valley Public Library from I-95, take Exit 112 or 112B toward Belgrade on ME 8/ME 11/ME 27. Go 24.6 miles north, and turn left onto ME 27/US 2. Go 9.6 miles, and turn right to stay on ME 27. Go 3.1 miles, and bear right to stay on ME 27. Go 19.6 miles, and join ME 16/ME 27; then go 15.2 miles, and turn left into the parking lot for the Carrabassett Valley Public Library. The trailhead is 0.1 mile to the left (northwest) on the right side of ME 16/ME 27.

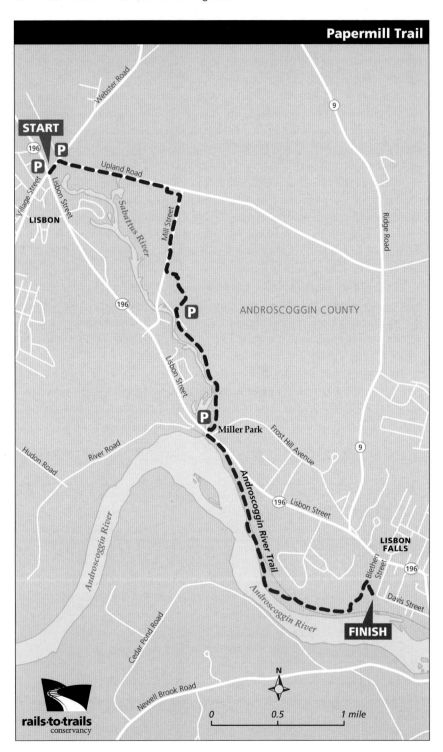

**Papermill Trail**

The Papermill Trail celebrates the heritage of mills in the development of the town of Lisbon and the surrounding area while providing an easy, pleasant trail experience for users of all abilities. The trail also serves as a transportation link between the town center and the community of Lisbon Falls, passing two schools and several access points and parking areas.

Inadequate signage can make finding the start of the trail next to the Sabattus River at Village Street near Lisbon Street a challenge. The trail crosses the Sabattus River on the sidewalk of a bridge with a striking view of a three-story, 160-year-old woolen mill that's been transformed into apartments. The off-road portion begins after the bridge and follows Upland Road and Mill Street while passing through open fields and farmland on a section also known as the Ricker Farm Trail.

*The sections along the Sabattus and Androscoggin Rivers are popular with birders; watch for herons, bald eagles, osprey, and other types of birds.*

**County**
Androscoggin

**Endpoints**
Village St. and Lisbon St./ME 196 to Davis St. and Blethen St. (Lisbon)

**Mileage**
4.0

**Type**
Rail-with-Trail

**Roughness Index**
1

**Surface**
Asphalt

About 1.2 miles from the start, the trail veers toward the Lisbon Community School and passes through a more wooded and scenic area for the rest of the way. The trail follows the Sabattus River across slightly undulating—but rarely steep—terrain. Remnants of a bridge built as part of mill-related development are visible shortly after the trail comes within view of the river.

About 0.6 mile past the bridge ruins you'll come to Miller Park, where the Sabattus River meets the much wider Androscoggin River. There's parking, a boat launch, and a trail information panel here. The trail goes left, running along inactive tracks that historically carried trains on the Maine Central Railroad's Rumford Branch. This newest section of the trail to Lisbon Falls, also known as the Androscoggin River Trail, is less densely wooded and reveals open sections of wildflowers with unobstructed views of the river.

These river sections are popular with birders, who find warblers, indigo buntings, and vireos in the woods and fields, as well as herons and waterfowl in the river. Bald eagles and osprey are often spotted here.

The 1.8-mile section along the Androscoggin River ends shortly after you pass the Lisbon High School football stadium in the community of Lisbon Falls, childhood home of horror writer Stephen King. There's no parking lot at the trailhead. Food is available at nearby restaurants, including a pub in the old railroad depot on Lisbon Street.

If you arrive during the second weekend in July, be prepared for crowds in town for the annual Moxie Festival. The event celebrates a regional soft drink that got its start as a patent medicine in the 19th century and whose advertising added the word *moxie* (meaning "force of character or determination") to the English language.

**CONTACT:** lisbontrails.wordpress.com/about

## DIRECTIONS

To reach the trailhead in Lisbon from I-95, take Exit 80 to ME 196 toward Lewiston. Head north on Alfred A. Plourde Pkwy., go 0.3 mile, and turn right onto ME 196 E/Lisbon St. Go 5 miles, and turn left onto Village St./Webster Road. Look for municipal parking on the left. The trail starts across Village St./Webster Road on the shoulder and bridge sidewalk. Parking also is available 300 feet farther on the left at St. Ann St.

To reach the trailhead at Miller Park from I-295, take Exit 31 or 31B onto ME 196/Lisbon St. toward Lisbon. Head northwest on ME 196/Lewiston Road, go 7.6 miles, and turn right onto Frost Hill Ave. Parking for Miller Park is immediately on the left.

History seems to appear around every corner in Fort Kent and Saint Francis for travelers getting underway on the Saint John Valley Heritage Trail. The gravel trail rolls along the south bank of the Saint John River for nearly 17 miles between the two towns and offers clear views of forests and farmland across the river in New Brunswick. It's used primarily by mountain bikers, ATV riders, and snowmobilers who can connect to more than a thousand miles of off-roading on Maine's Interconnected Trail System. (In the winter, snowshoeing and dogsledding are also permitted.)

The trail traces the former Fish River Railroad, which opened in 1902 and was sold a year later to the Bangor and Aroostook Railroad (BAR). The old Fish River Railroad Station, taken over by BAR, remained in operation until 1979 on Market Street about 0.8 mile north of the trailhead. It's now a museum open during the summer and run by the Fort Kent Historical Society.

Beginning on Market Street in Fort Kent, the trail immediately crosses the Fish River, a tributary of the Saint

*The pathway follows the Saint John River through a mixed forest that is quiet and serene.*

**County**
Aroostook

**Endpoints**
Market St./ME 161 between W. Market St. and N. Perley Brook Road (Fort Kent) to Sunset Dr. south of Main St./ME 161 (Saint Francis)

**Mileage**
16.9

**Type**
Rail-Trail

**Roughness Index**
2

**Surface**
Crushed Stone

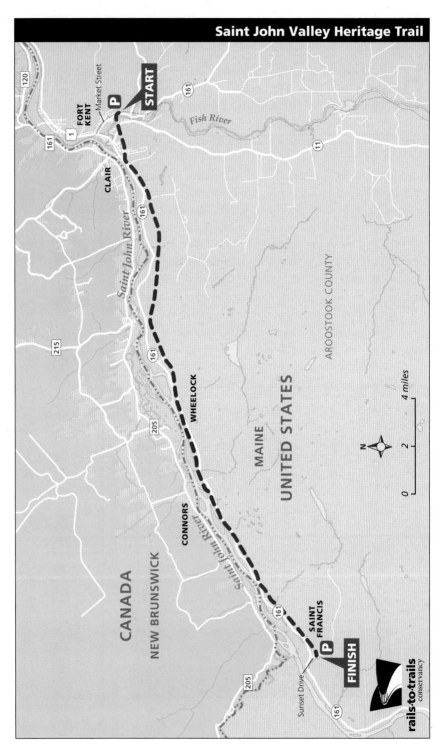

John River. Leaving the trail at the first cross street (Aroostook Road) with a wide shoulder and sidewalk, you can visit the Fort Kent State Historic Site 0.6 mile north. The wooden blockhouse is the only remaining fortification of the Aroostook War, also known as the Pork and Beans War, which took place in 1838–39. Diplomats settled the border dispute between Canada and the United States before battles broke out, although militias were mustered throughout the region.

Back on the trail, watch for road crossings and spurs that lead to restaurants, service stations, and other businesses. When you stop, you may overhear a local dialect of French spoken in stores and cafés. Descendants of French colonists settled all along the Saint John River Valley in the 1700s after the British government deported them from Acadia for refusing to support the crown. The families and Acadian culture survive to this day.

Beyond town, the trail follows the Saint John River through forests and wetlands. Although the trail parallels ME 161 for several miles, the mixed forest remains quiet and serene. The trail crosses to the north side of ME 161 at mile 8.2 in Wheelock and rolls along the riverbank, offering the best views of villages and farms in New Brunswick. About 4 miles later, the trail again crosses ME 161, passing behind homes and shops.

About 0.25 mile from the trail's end on Sunset Drive in Saint Francis, you'll pass a 1904 vintage railroad turntable that local high school students restored for the Saint Francis Historical Society Museum. A path leads from the turntable to the museum on ME 161/Main Street (across the street from the Saint Francis Town Office), which is open Sunday, Wednesday, and Friday afternoons from May through September. There's also a Bangor and Aroostook Railroad caboose, covered picnic tables, and a memorial display at the museum.

**CONTACT: maine.gov/cgi-bin/online/doc/parksearch/details.pl?park_id=78**

## DIRECTIONS

To reach the trailhead in Fort Kent from I-95, take Exit 302 onto US 1 heading north. Go 26.4 miles north on US 1, and turn left to remain on US 1 in Mars Hill. Go another 27.7 miles, and in Caribou, bear right onto ME 161. Go 3.6 miles, turn right to stay on ME 161, and then go 39.4 miles to Fort Kent. Look for parking on the left side of ME 161/Market St. just after passing a convenience store with gasoline pumps on the right.

To reach the trailhead in Saint Francis from I-95, take Exit 302 onto US 1 heading north. Go 26.4 miles north on US 1, and turn left to remain on US 1 in Mars Hill. Go another 27.7 miles, and in Caribou, bear right onto ME 161. Go 3.6 miles, and turn right to stay on ME 161. Go 40.2 miles to Fort Kent, and turn left to stay on ME 161. Go 16.9 miles, and turn left onto Sunset Dr.; look for parking on the left in 0.2 mile.

# Sanford-Springvale Rail Trail

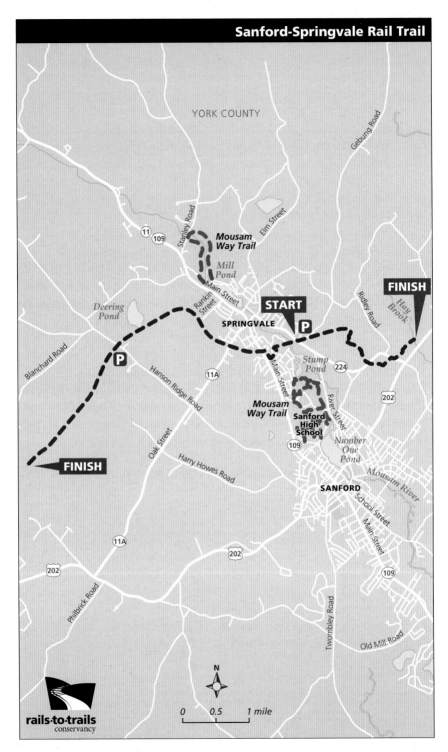

The Sanford-Springvale Rail Trail (also known as Railroad Trail) traverses the woods on either side of Sanford's scenic Springvale community in southern Maine. Founded by a mill owner in the 17th century, it later became home for textile mills powered by the Mousam River. When the mills relocated in the 1950s, the town diversified its industrial base, with woolen mills and aircraft and their parts now making up the area's commerce.

The gravel trail runs for nearly 6 miles as it links a shady brook in the east to a woodsy property line in the west. A couple of segments meander off the historic rail corridor onto private easements. Its gravel surface ranges from firm to loose and is best suited to bicycles with wide tires; ATVs, snowmobiles, and horses also use the trail.

The trail tracks the corridor of the Sanford and Eastern Railroad, the last survivor of railroads that began serving the area in the 1840s. The Worcester, Nashua and Rochester Railroad combined those original rail lines in

*Carpenter's Crossing is named for Hazen Carpenter, a Springvale resident who was one of the driving forces behind the rail-trail.*

**County**
York

**Endpoints**
Alfred/Sanford town line, about 0.3 mile north of the intersection of Shaws Ridge Road/ ME 224 and US 202, to Lebanon/Sanford town line 0.4 mile southeast of Blanchard Road and 1.7 miles south of Hanson Ridge Road (Sanford)

**Mileage**
5.9

**Type**
Rail-Trail

**Roughness Index**
3

**Surface**
Gravel

1883 and later was acquired by the Boston and Maine Railroad (B&M). The B&M began to discontinue use on rail segments in Maine in the 1940s, however, and sold off its line from Rochester to Portland in 1949. That became the Sanford and Eastern Railroad that existed in the Sanford area until 1961.

Starting at the trailhead on Pleasant Street/ME 224 in Springvale, trail users can go east toward US 202 or west toward Deering Pond. Those traveling east will find a rougher trail. First you'll pass an old freight depot that's currently a private business. Then, in about 0.6 mile, the trail leaves the rail corridor and turns right onto a power line right-of-way. Look for the trail heading left into the woods in about 0.1 mile. From there the trail travels through the woods and crosses ME 224/Shaws Ridge Road, then a field, and then crosses ME 224/Shaws Ridge Road again. The trail goes to the right of a clump of trees and ends at Hay Brook in less than 0.5 mile.

You'll find a firmer trail surface heading west from the Pleasant Street trailhead. In a few feet you'll cross the Mousam River that powered mills in the 1800s. Just past the river, the Mousam Way Trail splits to the left and passes Stump Pond on its way to Sanford High School, the YMCA, and several parks in Sanford. The Sanford-Springvale Rail Trail briefly leaves the corridor at Mousam Street. Turn left here and then right onto Witham Street. The trail reappears on the right in 0.1 mile and runs behind some businesses to Main Street. Back on the rail corridor, the trail gently climbs past Deering Pond to Hanson Ridge Road in 2 miles. From there, the trail passes through more forest to its endpoint in 0.8 mile at the town line.

**CONTACT:** sanfordmaine.org/trailmaps

## DIRECTIONS

To reach the eastern trailhead on Pleasant St./ME 224 from I-95, take Exit 19 onto ME 109/Sanford Road. Turn right (northwest) onto ME 109/Sanford Road, and go 9.5 miles. At the traffic circle, take the first exit right onto ME 4 N/Alfred Road. Go 2.1 miles north on ME 4/Alfred Road, turn left onto Grammar Road, and go another 2.1 miles. Continue straight onto ME 224 W, and go 1.4 miles. Turn right onto Railroad Ave., and almost immediately turn right into the trailhead parking lot. The endpoint is located 1.7 miles farther east along the trail.

To reach the western trailhead on Hanson Ridge Road from I-95, take Exit 19 onto ME 109/Sanford Road. Turn right (northwest) onto ME 109/Sanford Road, go 9.5 miles, and take the second exit off the traffic circle to continue on ME 109/ME 4A/Main St. Go 2.7 miles, and turn left onto US 202/ME 11/Lebanon St. Go 0.4 mile, and turn right onto Hanson Ridge Road. Go 2.7 miles, and look for trailhead parking on the right. The endpoint is located 1.6 miles farther west along the trail.

**S**ipayik translates to "along the edge" in the Passamaquoddy tribal language, which is a good description for the Sipayik Trail as it rolls through the Pleasant Point Reservation. The 1.9-mile paved rail-trail hugs the edge of the water along Little River, Gleason Cove, and the Western Passage. It's also on the edge of the continent, located so far east that dawn strikes the Sipayik Trail before any other rail-trail in the United States.

The Passamaquoddy tribe built the trail in 2004 as an alternative for pedestrians and bicyclists using busy ME 190, which connects Pleasant Point with Perry on US 1. They installed the trail on the railbed left behind in 1977 when the Maine Central Railroad discontinued using a spur route that ran through the reservation between Ayers Junction and Eastport to serve that city's sardine-canning industry.

The trail starts in the small community on Pleasant Point on Passamaquoddy Bay. This is just one of the locations where tribal members lived throughout the bay

*The waterfront trail hugs the edge of Little River, Gleason Cove, and the Western Passage.*

**County**
Washington

**Endpoints**
Treatment Plant Road north of Side Road and Bayview Dr. intersection (Pleasant Point) to US 1/S. River Road between S. Meadow Road and Shore Road (Perry)

**Mileage**
1.9

**Type**
Rail-Trail

**Roughness Index**
1

**Surface**
Asphalt

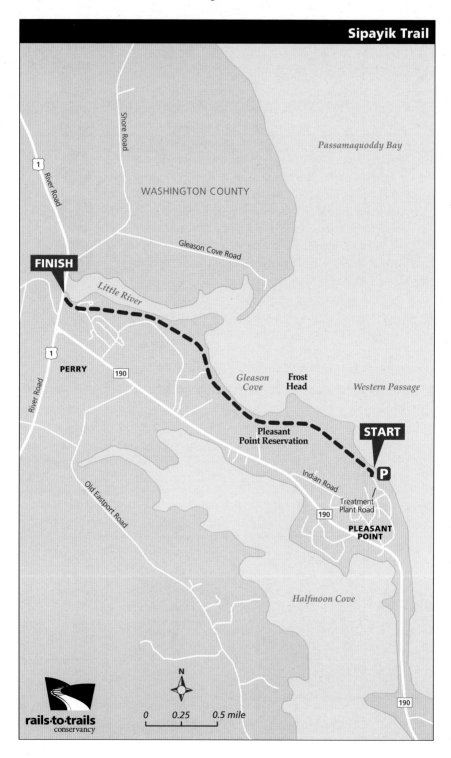

**Sipayik Trail**

Passamaquoddy Bay

Shore Road

1

River Road

WASHINGTON COUNTY

Gleason Cove Road

**FINISH**

Little River

1

**PERRY**

190

River Road

Gleason Cove

Frost Head

Western Passage

Pleasant Point Reservation

**START**

P

Indian Road

190

Treatment Plant Road

**PLEASANT POINT**

Old Eastport Road

Halfmoon Cove

N

190

0    0.25    0.5 mile

**rails·to·trails**
conservancy

region for thousands of years before the arrival of Europeans. They spent the warmer months on the bay fishing, clamming, and hunting marine mammals. Today the tribe is split between those living in several locations in Maine and Saint Andrews in Canada.

If you're lucky enough to be here for the second weekend in August, you'll get to participate in the annual Sipayik Indian Days Festival. The event features the arrival of warrior canoes from Calais, a morning service at the sacred Split Rock site, concerts, and a traditional meal. For those interested in learning more about the local culture, the Waponahki Museum presents demonstrations by local artisans, dancers, chefs, and storytellers on the second Saturday of each month April–September.

As you stand at the trailhead, Canada's Deer Island dominates the view across the bay; to the north, Saint Andrews is visible. Gazing across the bay, keep an eye open for seals, porpoises, and the occasional whales that still patrol these waters.

The trail dips out of sight of the bay for a short distance at Frost Head and then emerges in Gleason Cove. You can get down to the beach from the trail at low tide and look for critters in the tidal pools. You'll also see seagulls and many shorebirds here; songbirds and deer populate the woods elsewhere along the trail.

The trail crosses behind another forested point of land and then comes out on the southern bank of the tidal Little River. The trail passes through a residential neighborhood before it ends on US 1, across from the post office in Perry.

A dirt track that drills into the woods across the road is a future extension of the Down East Sunrise Trail (see page 25) that heads to Ayers Junction on the former Maine Central Railroad right-of-way. Currently, it's Route 82 on snowmobile maps.

**CONTACT: wabanaki.com**

## DIRECTIONS

To reach the eastern trailhead in Pleasant Point from the intersection of ME 9 and US 1 in Baileyville, take US 1 S 27.3 miles through Perry, and turn left (east) onto County Road 190. Go 1.4 miles. Turn left onto Indian Road, and go 0.4 mile. Turn left onto Side Road, go 0.1 mile, and turn left onto Treatment Plant Road. The trailhead and parking are straight ahead.

There is no official parking for the trail in Perry.

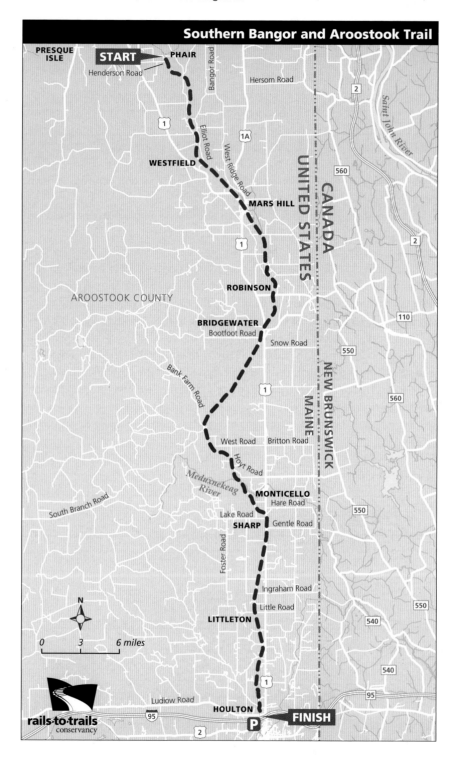

# Southern Bangor and Aroostook Trail

PRESQUE ISLE

**START** — PHAIR

Henderson Road

Bangor Road

Hersom Road

2

Saint John River

1

Elliot Road

1A

**WESTFIELD**

West Ridge Road

560

CANADA

UNITED STATES

**MARS HILL**

1

2

**ROBINSON**

AROOSTOOK COUNTY

**BRIDGEWATER**
Bootfoot Road

Snow Road

110

550

Bank Farm Road

1

560

MAINE

NEW BRUNSWICK

West Road   Britton Road

Hoyt Road

Meduxnekeag River

South Branch Road

**MONTICELLO**
Hare Road

550

Lake Road   Gentle Road
**SHARP**

Foster Road

Ingraham Road

550

Little Road

**LITTLETON**

540

N

0    3    6 miles

540

1

95

Ludlow Road

**HOULTON**   P   **FINISH**

95

**rails·to·trails**
conservancy

2

Northern Maine's pine trees and potatoes inspired the railroad that survives today as the 38.8-mile Southern Bangor and Aroostook Trail. Located in eastern Aroostook County near the Canadian border, the trail extends from near Presque Isle south to Houlton, mostly through farmland with occasional excursions into forests and wetlands. The county is a cultural center for Acadian French heritage and a destination for vacationers interested in viewing wildlife and exploring the outdoors.

The trail is part of a 1,200-mile network of private and public thoroughfares for ATVs in the county, the largest east of the Mississippi River. Trail users can expect infrequent brushes with logging trucks using the hard-packed

*The trail provides an excursion through forests, farmlands, and wetlands.*

**County**
Aroostook

**Endpoints**
Henderson Road and Williams Cross Road (Presque Isle) to Ludlow Road and Stewart Road (Houlton)

**Mileage**
38.8

**Type**
Rail-Trail

**Roughness Index**
2

**Surfaces**
Crushed Stone, Gravel

*The trail offers a forested adventure with many opportunities to view local wildlife, such as white-tailed deer, beavers, red foxes, coyotes, moose, and even black bears.*

crushed rock and gravel trail. In addition to walking, biking, and ATV use, permitted activities also include cross-country skiing, snowmobiling, snowshoeing, and dogsledding.

The trail traces the railbed of the Bangor and Aroostook Railroad, incorporated in 1891 to take over two previous rail lines. The company extended its tracks north from the existing terminus in Houlton, reaching Presque Isle in 1895. Although it carried passengers until 1961, the railroad mainly served the forest products and potato industries. At one time the county was the nation's largest spud producer. That potato traffic disappeared in the 1970s after mishandling by another railroad, and many of the Aroostook County lines ceased use.

Starting in the community of Phair, about 5 miles south of downtown Presque Isle, the northern part of the trail passes through pine forests along Williams Brook and Prestile Stream for nearly 9 miles until it opens up along a utility corridor south of Westfield. The trail continues south flanked by vast stretches of farmland.

About 5 miles past Westfield, the trail enters Mars Hill, named for the Mars Hill Mountain that rises 1,200 feet above the countryside to the east. You'll find grocery stores and diners in the town, which is a destination for snow sports enthusiasts in the winter.

Heading south from Mars Hill, vast stretches of farmland flank the trail as it follows Prestile Stream to Robinson. The trail follows US 1 most of the way and crosses the highway in Bridgewater. It enters another forest south of town and climbs a gentle slope for about 7 miles before descending to cross a bridge between Hoyt Road and Station Road over the North Branch of the Meduxnekeag River. There are many opportunities here to view local wildlife, such as white-tailed deer, beavers, and red squirrels. More cautious animals, such as black bears, coyotes, and red foxes live here as well, and moose might be seen in wetlands.

About 2 miles after the river crossing, the trail runs alongside US 1 through the community of Sharp, which has a café. The trail continues south through more farmland for about 12 miles to Houlton. A gas station mini-mart on US 1 about 2.5 miles south of Sharp offers the only services along this stretch. It's 0.4 mile east of the trail via Station Road.

CONTACT: visitaroostook.com/story/southern-bangor-and-aroostook-trail /vtm5AE51A5679903CE9B and maine.gov/cgi-bin/online/doc/parksearch/details .pl?park_id=75

## DIRECTIONS

To reach the northern trailhead in Presque Isle from I-95, take Exit 302, and head north on US 1. Go 26.4 miles, and turn left to remain on US 1 in Mars Hill. Go 9.6 miles, and turn right onto Centerline Road. Go 0.2 mile, and turn right onto Henderson Road. Go 1.5 miles, and look for the trailhead on the right.

To reach the southern trailhead from I-95, take Exit 302, and head north on US 1. Go 0.2 mile, and turn left onto Ludlow Road. Go 0.2 mile, and turn left into the Maine Visitor Information Center. To get to the trailhead, leave the parking lot, and turn left onto Ludlow Road. Go 0.2 mile, and turn right into an access road for a grocery store. The trail starts behind the building.

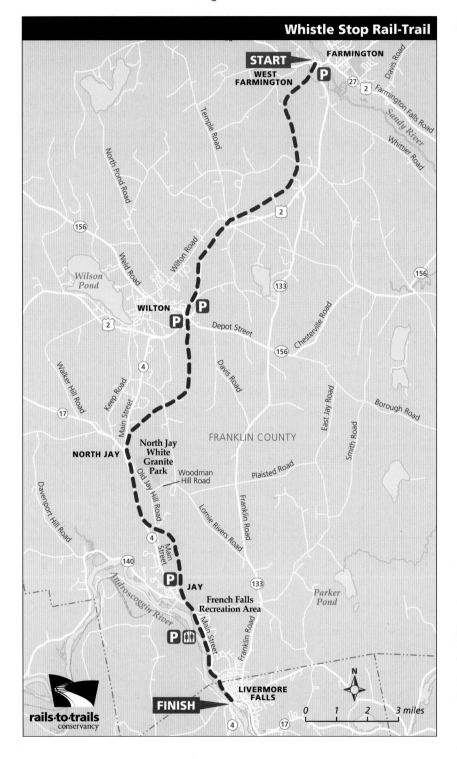

# Whistle Stop Rail-Trail

**A**former Maine Central Railroad line provides a year-round playground for motorized and nonmotorized trail users to explore the western hills of Maine. The long, flat, mostly straight stretches of the Whistle Stop Rail-Trail, running from Farmington to Livermore Falls, primarily serve ATVs and off-road vehicles in warmer months and snowmobiles in winter, but the trail is also accessible to mountain bikers, hikers, dog walkers, horseback riders, cross-country skiers, and snowshoers. Hybrid cyclists will find sandy sections passable but difficult.

Trees shade the trail as it passes through wetlands and rural farmland. Several small towns with services stand along the trail, but most interactions with civilization are limited to the occasional road crossing or the backyards of scattered houses or industrial buildings, including some remnants of rock quarrying from years gone by.

The trail follows the historic corridor of the Androscoggin Railroad, which served mill industry and agricultural centers on the Sandy and Androscoggin Rivers. The

*The scenic pathway provides a peaceful alternative to busy US 2 and ME 4.*

**County**
Franklin

**Endpoints**
Oak St. between Bridge St. and Thomas McClellan Road (Farmington) to Bridge St. and Water St. (Livermore Falls)

**Mileage**
15.8

**Type**
Rail-with-Trail

**Roughness Index**
2–3

**Surfaces**
Dirt, Sand, Gravel

railroad reached Livermore Falls in 1852 and Farmington in 1859, becoming part of the Maine Central Railroad in 1871. Guilford Transportation, which has become Pan Am Railways, acquired the railroad in the 1980s. While much of the original line is not in use, the trail follows still-active tracks for a very short distance in Livermore Falls.

From the community of West Farmington on the Sandy River, the packed dirt and gravel trail surface is easier for bicyclists to traverse than sections farther south. In 6.5 miles the trail arrives in Wilton, formerly a booming manufacturing center where Bass shoes and boots were made for 122 years until the factory closed in 1998. A mile or two south of town, the trail surface turns to deeper sand that poses more of a challenge to bicyclists.

You'll pass marshy lowlands to the east along the middle section of the trail from Wilton to North Jay. At 3.7 miles past Wilton, you can take a 1-mile side trip on Old Jay Hill Road to Woodman Hill Road to visit the North Jay White Granite Park. A hiking trail goes to the edge of a lookout over the quarry, where desirable white granite was mined for many uses, such as monuments in Washington, D.C.

The sandier surface continues south to the town of Jay, where the trail comes into view of the Androscoggin River. On the final 2.5 miles to Livermore Falls, you'll see signs for the French Falls Recreation Area, which can serve as another trailhead with bathrooms and parking closer to the southern end. At this point, sand yields to a harder-packed—albeit somewhat rutted and potholed—surface.

You'll have scenic views of the Androscoggin River and a railroad trestle that carries tracks across the river for the final mile to Livermore Falls. The trail ends in the heart of the town of Livermore Falls near various retail establishments.

**CONTACT: mainetrailfinder.com/trails/trail/whistle-stop-trail** and **maine.gov/cgi -bin/online/doc/parksearch/details.pl?park_id=76**

## DIRECTIONS

To reach the trailhead in West Farmington from I-95, take Exit 113 toward Belgrade on ME 3. Head north on ME 3, go 1.4 miles, and turn right onto ME 8/ME 27/New Belgrade Road. Go 22.4 miles, and turn left to join US 2/ME 27. Go 9.6 miles, turn left onto Intervale Road/US 2, and almost immediately after crossing the Sandy River, turn right onto Bridge St. Go 0.2 mile, turn left onto Oak St., and look for parking in 300 feet.

To reach the trailhead at the French Falls Recreation Area in Jay from US 202 and ME 41/ ME 133 in Winthrop, turn onto northbound ME 133/ME 41 in Winthrop. Go 1.5 miles, and bear left to stay on ME 133/Wayne Road. Go 15.8 miles, and turn left onto ME 133/ME 17/Depot St. Go 0.2 mile, and turn right onto ME 4/ME 17/Main St. Go 1.7 miles, and turn left onto French Falls Lane. Go 0.2 mile, and look for parking straight ahead. The southern endpoint is 1.7 miles south along the trail.

*Down East Sunrise Trail (see page 25)*

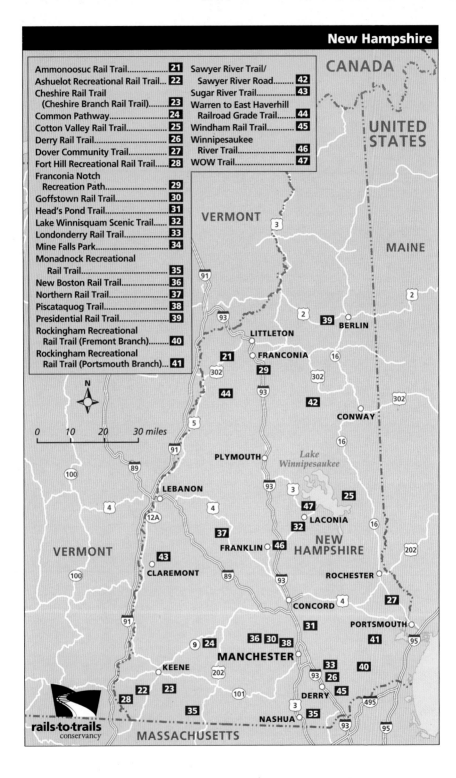

# New Hampshire

# New Hampshire

*Franconia Notch Recreation Path (see page 102)*

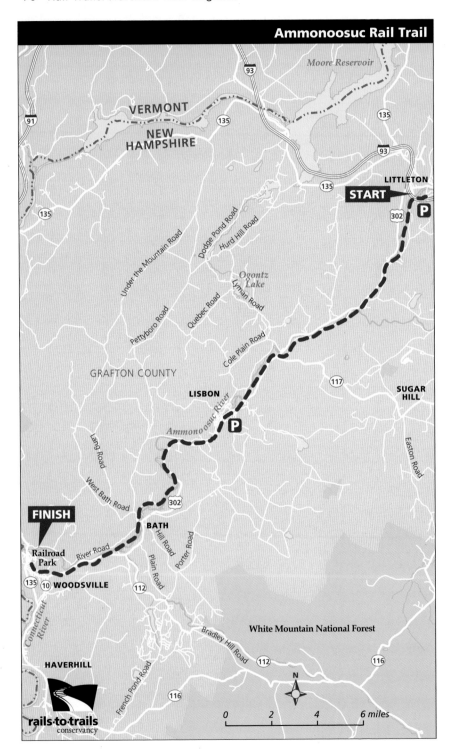

# Ammonoosuc Rail Trail

Moore Reservoir

VERMONT

NEW
HAMPSHIRE

LITTLETON

START

Dodge Pond Road

Hurd Hill Road

Under the Mountain Road

Ogontz
Lake

Lyman Road

Pettyboro Road

Quebec Road

Cole Plain Road

GRAFTON COUNTY

LISBON

SUGAR
HILL

Ammonoosuc River

Lang Road

Easton Road

West Bath Road

FINISH

BATH

Railroad
Park

River Road

Hill Road

Porter Road

WOODSVILLE

Plain Road

White Mountain National Forest

HAVERHILL

Bradley Hill Road

French Pond Road

rails·to·trails
conservancy

N

0    2    4    6 miles

The Ammonoosuc Rail Trail carries its users for 19.2 miles along the scenic river that shares its name and is itself a destination for fishing, kayaking, and canoeing. The trail passes through a variety of landscapes and several small historic mill towns that are ideal for sightseeing, shopping, or relaxing. The trail draws ATV riders, hikers, snowmobilers, snowshoers, and cross-country skiers—and also permits dogsledding—but cyclists should note that parts are very rough and challenging, and would be best handled on fat tires.

The northern end of the trail is in the town of Littleton, which is the birthplace of author Eleanor H. Porter, who introduced the world to the inspiringly optimistic *Pollyanna*. A statue in front of the library at 92 Main Street, only a mile from the trailhead's parking area, and an umbrella-draped gateway arch across the street honor the character.

*Nearly 4 miles southwest of Lisbon, you'll cross the Ammonoosuc River on a former railroad bridge.*

**County**
Grafton

**Endpoints**
Industrial Park Road near Riverside Dr. (Littleton) to US 302/Central St. and Highland St. (Woodsville)

**Mileage**
19.2

**Type**
Rail-Trail

**Roughness Index**
2–3

**Surfaces**
Ballast, Gravel, Dirt, Sand

After leaving Littleton on the former railbed of the Boston and Maine Railroad, you'll alternate between shady deciduous forest, wetlands, fields, and farmland before reaching Lisbon in 9.5 miles. A refurbished 1868 railroad station serves as the town's Historical Society Museum and rest area. Rich in history, Lisbon was chartered in the mid-1700s (at the time, wigwams were visible from the town's center) and has been home to the world's largest piano sounding board manufacturer, peg mills, and the state's first ski rope tow. Refreshments are available near the trail.

Nearly 4 miles past Lisbon you will cross the Ammonoosuc River over a former railroad trestle bridge. Just 2 miles later you'll arrive in Bath, which is known for its three covered bridges. The longest, built in 1832 and 375 feet long, spans the trail and an adjacent waterfall in the river. You may see people fishing and tubing here.

The trail crosses the river again and offers views of forest and farmland on its final 4-mile leg to the Woodsville community in the town of Haverhill. There's no parking at the trail's endpoint, but on-street parking is available nearby or at Railroad Park on the Connecticut River via US 302. A segment of the Cross Vermont Trail (Montpelier & Wells River Trail), see page 169, starts about 2 miles away in Vermont across the Connecticut River.

CONTACT: nhstateparks.org/visit/recreational-rail-trails/ammonoosuc-rec reational-trail.aspx

## DIRECTIONS

To reach the Littleton trailhead from I-93, take Exit 42 onto US 302/Meadow St. toward Littleton. Head east 0.5 mile, turn right onto Industrial Park Road, and then go 0.3 mile to the dirt parking lot on the left. The trailhead is across the street.

To reach the Woodsville trailhead from I-91, take Exit 17 onto US 302 toward Woodsville. Head east 2.6 miles, and bear right onto US 302/Main St. N. Then go 0.1 mile, and turn left onto US 302/Railroad St. Go 0.3 mile, cross the bridge, and stay straight onto US 302/Central St. Go 0.5 mile, and look for the trail on the left at Highland St. Although there is no parking lot at the trail endpoint, street parking is available on Central St.

The Ashuelot Recreational Rail Trail passes such scenic and historical landmarks as covered bridges, abandoned mills, and postcard-perfect towns. Starting on asphalt in Keene, the rail-trail can be marked by deep puddles and potholes as it follows the Ashuelot River south to Hinsdale in southern New Hampshire. Mountain bikes are recommended in warmer months, and in winter, cross-country skiing, snowmobiling, snowshoeing, and dogsledding are all permitted.

The 21.5-mile trail traces the corridor of the Ashuelot Railroad, which began serving the area in 1851. The Connecticut River Railroad acquired the route in 1877, and the Boston and Maine Railroad took over in 1893. It ran until 1983, helping to spark the late-19th-century manufacturing boom for mills along the river by supplying raw materials and getting products to market.

Starting in Keene, the trail begins as an asphalt path that passes through the campus of Keene State College. It crosses a secluded trestle on the Ashuelot River and then

*Several nods to its railroad history dot the rail-trail, including trestle bridges over the Ashuelot River.*

**County**
Cheshire

**Endpoints**
Emerald St. at Ralston St./Cheshire Rail Trail (Keene) to Northfield Road/NH 63 1.75 miles south of Tower Hill Road and 1.3 miles north of S. Parish Road (Hinsdale)

**Mileage**
21.5

**Type**
Rail-Trail

**Roughness Index**
2–3

**Surfaces**
Asphalt, Crushed Stone, Ballast, Sand, Dirt

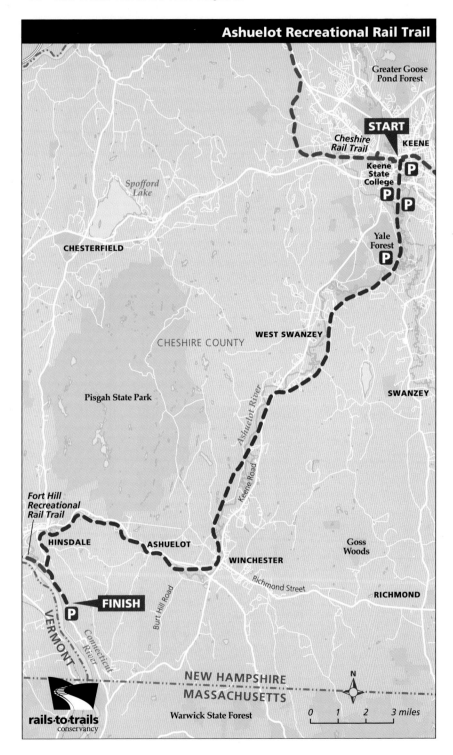

# Ashuelot Recreational Rail Trail

Greater Goose Pond Forest

Cheshire Rail Trail

**START**

KEENE

Keene State College

Spofford Lake

CHESTERFIELD

Yale Forest

WEST SWANZEY

CHESHIRE COUNTY

SWANZEY

Pisgah State Park

Ashuelot River

Keene Road

Fort Hill Recreational Rail Trail

HINSDALE

ASHUELOT

WINCHESTER

Goss Woods

Richmond Street

RICHMOND

**FINISH**

Burt Hill Road

VERMONT

Connecticut River

NEW HAMPSHIRE

MASSACHUSETTS

Warwick State Forest

N

0    1    2    3 miles

**rails·to·trails** conservancy

takes a pedestrian bridge over busy NH 12/101. The packed gravel here becomes ballast, dirt, and sand a mile south of the bridge.

About 2.5 miles past the pedestrian bridge, you'll cross Sawyers Crossing Road, where the circa 1859 Cresson Covered Bridge sits about 500 feet to the left. The trail crosses the river in 0.3 mile near West Swanzey in an area considered moose territory. Passing on the east side of West Swanzey, a 0.3-mile detour right onto Railroad Street, and then another right onto Main Street, leads to the 1832 Thompson Covered Bridge.

Between West Swanzey and Winchester, the rail-trail passes east of Pisgah State Park. At Holbrook Avenue, you can detour off the trail to the right for 0.7 mile to find the 1862 Slate Covered Bridge (from Holbrook Avenue, turn right onto Westport Village Road). The trail crosses the Ashuelot River on a trestle about halfway to Winchester, where you'll find the old railroad depot on Elm Street put to use in a lumberyard.

About 2.2 miles past the old depot in Winchester, you arrive in the town of Ashuelot, where there's another restored railroad depot at the Gunn Mountain Road intersection. Next to the trail is the Ashuelot Covered Bridge, built in 1864 to bring wood across the Ashuelot River to fuel the burners of the railroad's steam engines. Considered one of New England's most sophisticated covered bridges, the span is 169 feet long and decorated with intricate latticework.

The slope drops over the next 3 miles to Hinsdale, where you'll pass abandoned mills and rusting boxcars on a siding that marks another railroad depot—this one restored and converted into a residence. The trail sticks to a ridge above the town, which is festooned with a clock tower and church steeples. The Ashuelot River empties into the Connecticut River shortly past Hinsdale, and the trail ends 2.6 miles south of town at a trailhead on NH 63. You can pick up the Fort Hill Recreational Rail Trail (see page 98) near here to continue to Brattleboro, Vermont.

**CONTACT:** nhstateparks.org/visit/recreational-rail-trails/ashuelot-recreational -rail-trail.aspx

## DIRECTIONS

To reach the trailhead in Keene from I-91, take Exit 3 onto NH 9/Franklin Pierce Hwy. east toward Keene. Go 14.7 miles, and stay straight onto NH 10/NH 12. Go 0.4 mile, and at the roundabout take the third exit (left) onto Winchester St. Go 0.6 mile, and turn left onto Ralston St. Go 0.2 mile, and turn left onto Emerald St. Parking is available in the shopping center lot across from the trailhead.

To reach the trailhead near Hinsdale from I-91, take Exit 28 (from I-91 S) or Exit 28A (from I-91 N) onto MA 10 heading east toward Northfield. Go 4.4 miles east, and turn left onto MA 10/ MA 63/Main St. Go 2.5 miles, and turn left to stay on MA 63/NH 63. Go 3.2 miles, and turn left into the parking lot. To reach the trailhead, backtrack 0.2 mile on NH 63/Northfield Road.

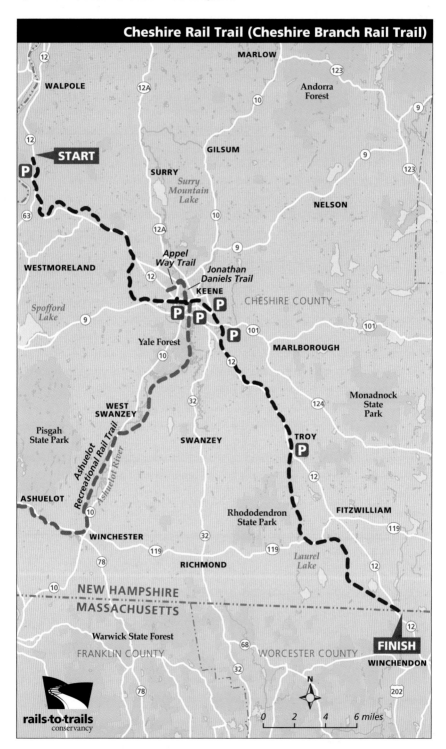

**Cheshire Rail Trail (Cheshire Branch Rail Trail)**

Formerly comprising two separate segments—one running northward from Keene to Walpole, and the other running southward from Keene to Fitzwilliam—the Cheshire Rail Trail now runs a continuous 32.9 miles through connections made in 2017 between the two sections and the former 1-mile Industrial Heritage Trail in Keene.

Initially settled in the 1730s, Keene developed a reputation as a manufacturing center in the mid-1800s when it served as a meeting point for three railroads: the Manchester & Keene Railroad, the Ashuelot Railroad, and the Cheshire Railroad. After the decline of the railroads in the 20th century, both the Ashuelot Railroad and Cheshire Railroad were transformed into rail-trails. Today, Keene is sustained by the tourism, insurance, and education industries.

*In Keene you'll cross a stone arch bridge with a river overlook.*

**County**
Cheshire

**Endpoints**
Bellows Road/NH 12 at Bookseller Road (Walpole) to the NH–MA state line just east of McAllister Road and State Line Cir. (Fitzwilliam)

**Mileage**
32.9

**Type**
Rail-Trail

**Roughness Index**
1–3

**Surfaces**
Asphalt, Ballast, Cinder, Dirt, Gravel, Sand

*In Troy you'll find an old train depot that has been refurbished into a museum.*

The Cheshire Rail Trail now plays host to a variety of uses, including mountain biking and horseback riding, and in winter, cross-country skiing and snowshoeing are permitted. Note that the entire route may also be used by snowmobilers, who help maintain the trail.

The trail begins in the north at NH 12 between Alyson's Lane and Blackjack Crossing in Walpole. Most of the northern segment between Walpole and Keene is surfaced with hard-packed gravel. Cyclists should use a mountain bike; however, a small stretch between NH 9 and the center of Keene is paved and can accommodate wheelchairs.

Those who persevere along this part of the trail will be rewarded with abundant scenery, including wooded landscapes and natural rock walls; however, trail use is sparse until you reach Keene, and there is little to draw users off the trail. Note also the challenging terrain prior to Keene, including large rocks, flooding, and erosion; turns in the trail that can be challenging to spot; and several steep inclines. After crossing NH 9, a short paved segment takes you into Keene, host to Keene State College and Antioch University.

The town is also the meeting point for three other trails, including the 0.9-mile Jonathan Daniels Trail, located one block north along Island Street; the 1.3-mile Appel Way Trail, which meets up with the Jonathan Daniels Trail and begins just east of Keene High School; and the Ashuelot Recreational Rail Trail (see page 79), which connects to the Cheshire Rail Trail at Emerald and Ralston Streets and stretches 21.5 miles southwest to Hinsdale.

Heading south, the Cheshire Trail's second segment offers a much smoother and less-challenging experience for trail users than the northern segment as it travels just under 19 miles to Fitzwilliam. This segment feels more removed from town, and the mostly gravel surface is suitable for hybrid bikes.

Passing the Marlboro Street trailhead in Keene (there is a small parking area there), you'll head up a short, steep dirt hill and cross a quaint stone arch bridge before crossing the Ashuelot River. In about 9 miles you'll reach Troy, where you'll find a few restaurants, some railroad relics, and an old train depot that has been refurbished into a museum.

Continuing southeast, you'll pass through the town of Fitzwilliam, where an old railroad depot is undergoing renovation. The route then becomes relatively remote, officially ending in the outskirts of Fitzwilliam at the New Hampshire–Massachusetts border. Note that the most convenient southern terminus for bikers and hikers is at the trailhead at State Line Circle and NH 12, as the section of trail east of NH 12 is prone to flooding in the rainy season.

CONTACT: keenepaths.com/trails/cheshire-rail-trail and nhstateparks.org/visit /recreational-rail-trails/cheshire-recreational-rail-trail.aspx

## DIRECTIONS

To reach the northern endpoint in Walpole from I-91, take Exit 5 toward US 5/Walpole NH/ Westminster. Head east on Westminster St., and go 0.8 mile. Turn right onto US 5 heading south, go 0.7 mile, and then turn left onto VT 123 E (entering New Hampshire). Go 0.3 mile, and then continue onto NH 123 E. After 0.1 mile, turn right onto NH 12 S, go 4.2 miles, and turn left onto Blackjack Crossing. The parking area will be directly ahead in 0.1 mile. The trail endpoint is 0.3 mile north along the trail.

To reach the Troy trailhead from the intersection of NH 101 and US 202 in Peterborough, follow Grove St./US 202 W/Jaffrey Road, and go 6 miles. Turn right onto Main St./NH 124, and go 6.4 miles. Turn left onto Troy Road, which becomes Monadnock St. Go 2.6 miles, and turn right onto NH 12 N. Immediately turn left onto Water St. The parking lot will be to your left after about 450 feet. The southern endpoint is located about 10.9 miles south along the trail; note that there is no dedicated parking available for trail users.

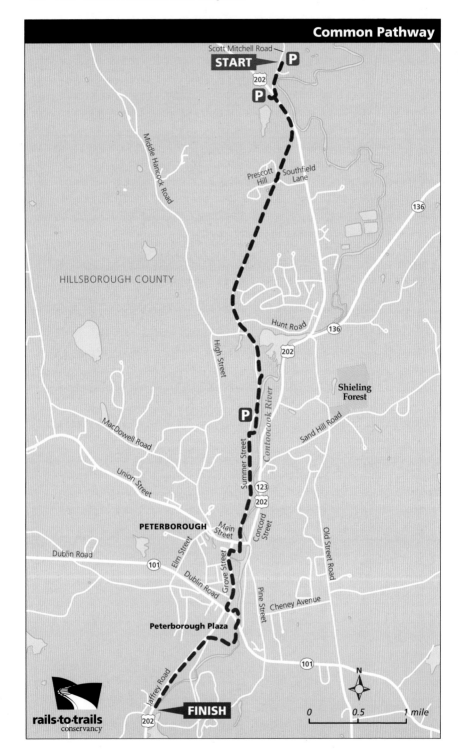

**Common Pathway**

Scott Mitchell Road

START

P

202

P

Middle Hancock Road

Prescott Hill

Southfield Lane

136

HILLSBOROUGH COUNTY

Hunt Road

136

202

High Street

Contoocook River

Shieling Forest

Sand Hill Road

P

Summer Street

MacDowell Road

Union Street

123

202

Old Street Road

PETERBOROUGH

Main Street

Concord Street

Dublin Road

101

Elm Street

Grove Street

Dublin Road

Pine Street

Cheney Avenue

Peterborough Plaza

101

Jaffrey Road

N

FINISH

202

0        0.5        1 mile

rails·to·trails
conservancy

The Common Pathway travels 5.5 miles from the outskirts of Peterborough south to downtown's Noone Falls area, paralleling US 202 and the Contoocook River for most of its journey. The small town of Peterborough boasts the Peterborough Town Library, the oldest tax-supported public library in the United States. Founded in 1833 by Reverend Abiel Abbot, the library collection has grown from 100 to more than 43,000 books, and the space supports research and hosts a variety of educational programs and events.

The pathway offers easy, mostly level terrain, with crushed stone making up the very northern portion of trail and a paved portion spanning from Southfield Lane to the trail's southern endpoint. Note that there are a few small, narrow, or poorly maintained sections, so hybrid bikes are recommended.

Beginning at the northern trailhead on Scott Mitchell Road, you'll find a small parking lot adjacent to the

*North of Peterborough, travelers will enjoy one of the trail's wooded off-road sections.*

**County**
Hillsborough

**Endpoints**
Old Railroad Trail just south of the W. Ridge Dr. and Scott Mitchell Road intersection to US 202 and Cabana Dr. (Peterborough)

**Mileage**
5.5

**Type**
Rail-Trail

**Roughness Index**
1–2

**Surfaces**
Asphalt, Crushed Stone

trailhead, and additional parking just south where US 202 intersects Scott Mitchell Road. This trailhead also serves the Old Railroad Trail, which seamlessly connects to the northern endpoint of the Common Pathway and heads 2.7 miles into Hancock.

Heading south, the trail alternates between quiet on-road and wooded off-road segments. Bike route signs help with wayfinding, although they are not prevalent, so proceed carefully. About 2.5 miles along the trail from Scott Mitchell Road, you'll pass another parking area accessible from Summer Street.

The trail runs south to and beyond the small town of Peterborough, which is a hot spot for home-based entrepreneurs and telecommuters, and a popular tourist spot for those seeking outdoor pursuits such as fishing. Access to downtown Peterborough is provided through mostly residential, low-traffic streets; here, you'll find a quaint main street with restaurants, shops, preserved historical buildings (to reach the Peterborough Town Library on Concord Street head east on Main Street for one block), and a restored train depot that now hosts shops and a café.

South of downtown Peterborough, the route is not well signed and may be difficult to navigate for those not familiar with the trail. You'll continue south on US 202 to the intersection with NH 101, turn left, and loop around a gas station to the NH 101 underpass by the Contoocook River. You'll then head around the east side of the Peterborough Shopping Plaza and then west to a side-path portion of the trail (composed of asphalt that is not regularly maintained), which travels on the left side of busy US 202 S (across the highway is another strip mall) to the trail's end just before Cabana Drive.

**CONTACT:** peterboroughopenspace.org/success-stories/common-pathway.html

## DIRECTIONS

To reach the northern trailhead near the Peterborough Recycling Center from the intersection of NH 101/Wilton Road and NH 123, head north on Granite St./US 202, and go 4.1 miles (the road becomes Pine St., then US 202 E/Concord St., then Hancock Road). Turn right onto Scott Mitchell Road, go 0.2 mile, and turn right into the trailhead parking lot (immediately after Sanitation Lane).

To reach the alternate northern trailhead and the Old Railroad Trail, follow the directions above, but turn left instead of right at Scott Mitchell Road. Look for the parking lot immediately on your left. The northern endpoint is located about 0.2 mile north along the trail.

To reach the trailhead on Summer St., from the intersection of NH 101/Wilton Road and NH 123, head north on Granite St./US 202, and go 0.6 mile (the road becomes Pine St.). Turn left onto Main St., and then immediately turn right onto Summer St. Go 0.9 mile, and turn right into the small trailhead parking lot.

There is no parking at the southern endpoint.

The Cotton Valley Rail Trail connects the small town of Wakefield, near the Maine border, and the quintessentially quaint New England vacation town of Wolfeboro. In 2017 the towns held a ribbon-cutting ceremony to celebrate the completion of a short segment between Cotton Valley Road in East Wolfeboro and Clark Road in Wakefield—resulting in a continuous 12-mile route.

The trail is bookended by wonderful glimpses of its railroad history, making it a must-see for any railcar enthusiast. From the easternmost point in Wakefield, the trail begins at a small park surrounding the old-fashioned Old Boston and Maine Railroad Turntable, which was refurbished in the 1990s for the benefit of riders and park patrons. The trail makes no bones about its past as a railroad corridor, delightfully switchbacking along either side of the rails and even providing some well-paved opportunities for users to ride between the irons through the canopied northeastern woods. The eastern section includes some small hills that might prove difficult for some.

Continuing west, the Cotton Valley Rail Trail travels on a heavily wooded path leading toward Lake Wentworth.

**County**
Carroll

**Endpoints**
Meadow St. between Forest St. and High St. (Wakefield) to Railroad Ave. just north of Depot St. (Wolfeboro)

**Mileage**
12.0

**Type**
Rail-Trail/Rail-with-Trail

**Roughness Index**
1

**Surface**
Gravel

*The rail-trail embraces its railroad past—in some sections you'll be riding between the old iron rails.*

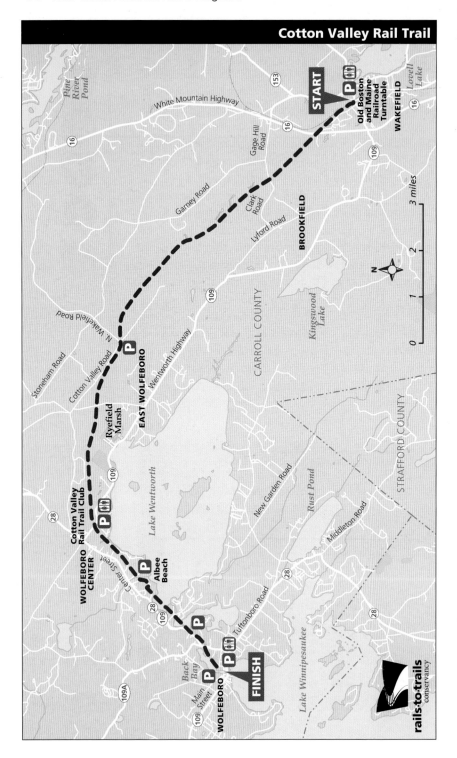

**Cotton Valley Rail Trail**

The western portion of the trail is very flat, making it ideal for horseback riding and cross-country skiing. In 3.1 miles, you will find a resting point where the trail intersects NH 109, complete with a restroom, picnic benches, shelter, and the headquarters of the Cotton Valley Rail Trail Club. In 1.3 miles, you'll come across the Albee Beach access point and a short, winding trail portion before finding gorgeous straightaways, including some narrow causeways over beautiful lake basins. The trail passes through the Linda Baldwin Preserve before finding the edge of the Back Bay, which is surrounded by parks, eateries, and charming shops that help make Wolfeboro a vacation destination.

**CONTACT:** **cottonvalley.org**

# DIRECTIONS

To reach the easternmost trailhead at the Old Boston & Maine Railroad Turntable in Wakefield from the intersection of US 202 and NH 16 in Rochester, head north on NH 16 toward Ossipee/Conway. Go 18.6 miles. Turn right onto NH 109 S, and go 0.5 mile. A small parking lot and the trailhead will be on your left, just after you cross Forest St.

To reach the Cotton Valley Road/N. Wakefield Road endpoint, follow the directions above to NH 109, but turn left instead of right. Head west toward Wolfeboro on NH 109, and go 6.4 miles. Turn right onto Bryant Road, and go 1.2 miles. Turn right onto Cotton Valley Road, and go 1.3 miles. Turn left onto N. Wakefield Road, where two to three cars can park on a small gravel patch on the corner immediately to your right.

To reach the Cotton Valley Rail Trail Club trailhead, follow the directions above to NH 109. Turn left (west) onto NH 109, and go 8.7 miles. Parking at the Cotton Valley Rail Trail Club is situated on the right of NH 109/Governor John Wentworth Hwy., across from Fernald Crossing.

To reach the Albee Beach parking lot, follow the directions above to NH 109, and turn left. Go 9 miles, and turn left onto NH 109/NH 28/Center St. Go 1.1 miles, then turn left onto Albee Beach Road. Follow it 0.3 mile, at which point the parking lot entrance branches off from Albee Beach Road.

To reach the northwesternmost endpoint in Wolfeboro from the intersection of US 202 and NH 16 in Rochester, head north on US 202/NH 16, and in less than a mile, take Exit 15. Turn left (northwest) onto NH 11, and go 14.6 miles. At the traffic circle, take the second exit (straight) onto NH 28 N/S. Main St. In 2.5 miles turn right onto Glendon St. then make an immediate left onto Depot St. Public parking can be found immediately surrounding the Wolfeboro Chamber of Commerce, which resides in a retrofitted train depot.

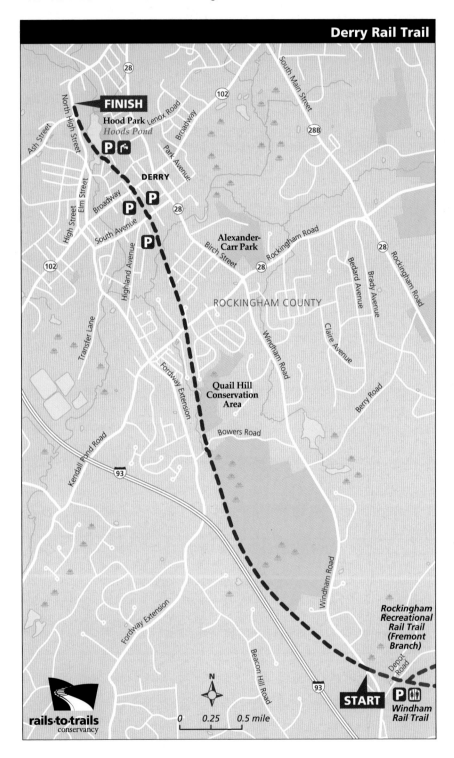

**Derry Rail Trail**

FINISH

Hood Park
*Hoods Pond*

North High Street

Ash Street

High Street

Elm Street

Broadway

South Avenue

**DERRY**

Lenox Road

Broadway

Park Avenue

Highland Avenue

Transfer Lane

Kendall Pond Road

93

Fordway Extension

Fordway Extension

102

102

28

28

28

28

28B

South Main Street

**Alexander-
Carr Park**

Birch Street

Rockingham Road

Rockingham Road

Rockingham Road

Bedard Avenue

Brady Avenue

Claire Avenue

Berry Road

Windham Road

Windham Road

**ROCKINGHAM COUNTY**

**Quail Hill
Conservation
Area**

Bowers Road

Beacon Hill Road

93

**START**

*Windham
Rail Trail*

**Rockingham
Recreational
Rail Trail
(Fremont
Branch)**

Depot Road

N

0    0.25    0.5 mile

**rails·to·trails**
conservancy

This exquisitely maintained trail slices through forested areas and wetlands for a wonderful experience in southern New Hampshire. The trail will eventually be part of the Granite State Rail Trail, which is realizing the grand vision of creating a 125-mile trail from the Massachusetts to Vermont border. The Derry Rail Trail already makes a seamless connection with the 4.3-mile Windham Rail Trail (see page 155) at its southern endpoint and will eventually connect in the north with the Londonderry Rail Trail (see page 114), which stretches 3.3 miles to Manchester. You can also access the 18.3-mile Rockingham Recreational Rail Trail (Fremont Branch), see page 139, by heading southwest for 0.2 mile on the Windham Rail Trail and turning left onto the new trail just after Depot Road.

Starting at the southern end, just north of the Windham Depot, the asphalt trail immediately enters a wooded area that invokes a very remote feel for such a populated area. You may see the occasional heron or turtle venturing out of the neighboring wetlands.

*The paved, well-maintained trail slices through forested areas and wetlands for a fun and easy experience even for novice riders.*

**County**
Rockingham

**Endpoints**
Windham Rail Trail at N. Lowell Road/Windham Road at Brown Road to N. High St. between Madden Road and Ash St. Ext. (Derry)

**Mileage**
3.6

**Type**
Rail-Trail

**Roughness Index**
1–3

**Surface**
Asphalt

The trail crosses Beaver Brook over a beautiful stone arch bridge; the middle of the bridge is known locally as Lover's Leap, and while the origin of this name is not confirmed, it is rumored to have American Indian roots. The trail then enters the quaint downtown area of Derry and crosses East Broadway, where there are bike shops, restaurants, and ice cream shops.

The paved section of trail ends in Hood Park, which has a variety of outdoor and recreational amenities, including picnic tables, a playground, basketball courts, and a large pond with a waterfront area. The pond contains multiple species of fish and is stocked annually with brook trout and rainbow trout.

If you are feeling adventurous, you can continue on the trail along the west side of Hoods Pond on a dirt path for another 0.3 mile until the path ends. Because this section is not paved, it is only suited for mountain biking and hiking. The plan is to eventually pave this section and create a seamless connection with the Londonderry Rail Trail (see page 114), which currently begins approximately 1 mile to the north.

**CONTACT:** derryrailtrail.org

## DIRECTIONS

To reach the trailhead at Windham Depot from I-93 N, take Exit 3 onto NH 111 W toward Windham. Head west 1.6 miles, and turn right onto N. Lowell Road. Go 2.6 miles, and turn right onto Depot Road. Go 0.1 mile, and turn right into the depot parking lot. The Derry Rail Trail is located 0.2 mile northwest along the Windham Rail Trail. Parking is prohibited at Windham Depot from 30 minutes after sunset to 30 minutes before sunrise.

To reach the trailhead at Windham Depot from I-93 S, take Exit 4 onto NH 102 toward Derry/Londonderry. Turn left (east) onto NH 102/Nashua Road (signs for Derry), and go 0.9 mile. Turn right onto Fordway, go 0.5 mile, and then continue onto Fordway Extension for 0.9 mile. Turn left onto Bowers Road, and go 0.6 mile. Turn right onto Windham Road, and go 1.3 miles. Continue onto N. Lowell Road 0.2 mile, and then turn left onto Depot Road. Turn right into the depot parking lot after 0.2 mile. The Derry Rail Trail is located 0.2 mile northwest along the Windham Rail Trail. Again, note that parking is prohibited at Windham Depot from 30 minutes after sunset to 30 minutes before sunrise.

To reach the Hood Park trailhead from I-93, take Exit 4 for NH 102 toward Derry/Londonderry. Head northeast onto NH 102/Nashua Road (signs for Derry), and go 0.9 mile. Turn left onto Elm St., go 0.3 mile, and turn right onto Maple St. Immediately turn left onto Rollins St., and the trailhead and parking area will be on the left in about 500 feet. The northern endpoint is located about 0.4 mile north along the trail.

The Dover Community Trail snakes its way through the heart of the Garrison City—so nicknamed for the fortified log houses, or garrisons, built by 17th-century settlers—offering a variety of trail surface types and activities for visitors.

Technically starting at the southeastern endpoint on Fisher Street, the trail heads straight north and makes its way through quiet residential areas. The canopy of surrounding trees provides ample shade and a pleasant setting. After about 0.3 mile, you'll pass through a short tunnel underneath Silver Street and continue north, crossing a few roads and neighborhoods. Be sure to follow the trail signs in this area to stay on the correct course.

After passing Washington Street, the trail crosses over a beautiful trestle high above the Cocheco River and continues to the Dover train depot/station in downtown

*The canopy of surrounding trees provides ample shade and a pleasant setting for trail users.*

**County**
Stratford

**Endpoints**
Watson Road between County Farm Road and Sandpiper Dr. to Fisher St. just west of Belknap St. (Dover)

**Mileage**
3.8

**Type**
Rail-Trail

**Roughness Index**
1–3

**Surfaces**
Asphalt, Crushed Stone, Dirt

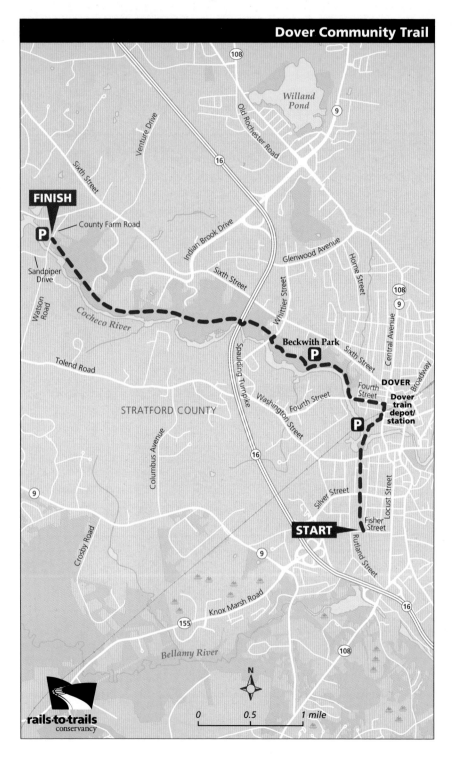

## Dover Community Trail

FINISH

P

START

P

P

Beckwith Park

DOVER

Dover train depot/station

Willand Pond

STRATFORD COUNTY

Venture Drive

Sixth Street

Old Rochester Road

County Farm Road

Sandpiper Drive

Watson Road

Cocheco River

Tolend Road

Columbus Avenue

Crosby Road

Indian Brook Drive

Sixth Street

Glenwood Avenue

Whittier Street

Home Street

Central Avenue

Broadway

Spaulding Turnpike

Washington Street

Fourth Street

Fourth Street

Sixth Street

Silver Street

Locust Street

Fisher Street

Rutland Street

Knox Marsh Road

Bellamy River

108

9

16

108
9

9

16

9

16

155

108

N

0      0.5      1 mile

rails·to·trails
conservancy

Dover (see the active railroad line that the train station services on the north side of the trestle). With a trailhead, parking, and ample restaurants and shops just one or two blocks west, this is the best place to begin your journey.

From the train station, exit the parking lot and turn left onto the sidewalk along Chestnut Street to cross the railroad tracks. Note that this section follows city sidewalks, and there are no signs to help with navigation. After two blocks, turn left onto Fourth Street and follow the sidewalk until you reach a bridge that crosses the Cocheco River.

Here, just before the bridge, turn right (heading north) to enter another off-road section of trail that skirts the north side of the river. The trail also leads you past Beckwith Park and Dover Cassily Community Garden—both great community assets. This section has a dirt and crushed-stone surface and is suitable for walking and mountain biking only; it offers a great nature escape in the center of town.

You'll cross Whittier Street and then follow the north side of Whittier Falls Way, a quiet neighborhood street, before crossing under Spaulding Turnpike and continuing off road. Here, the route continues to follow the north side of the Cocheco River and is surrounded by a nice wooded area, providing contrast to the more urban section near the center of town. The trail terminates at Watson Road, just east of the river.

There are plans to extend the trail south and ultimately connect it with other sections of trail in and around the Seacoast Region.

**CONTACT: dover.nh.gov/government/city-operations/planning/community-trail**

## DIRECTIONS

To reach the Amtrak Dover Transportation Center (Rotary Club trailhead) from the intersection of US 202 and NH 16/Spaulding Turnpike in Rochester, head south on NH 16 to Exit 8E for downtown Dover, and follow W. Knox Marsh Road 0.3 mile to a traffic circle. Enter the traffic circle, take the first exit onto Silver St./NH 9, and go 0.3 mile. Turn left onto Lexington St., and go 0.2 mile. Turn right onto Washington St., and go 0.3 mile. Turn left onto Chestnut St., go about 0.2 mile, and look for the entrance to the station on your left. The trailhead and access to the trail are located in the back of the parking area adjacent to the Cocheco River.

To reach the Watson Road trailhead from the intersection of US 202 and NH 16/Spaulding Turnpike in Rochester, head south on NH 16 to Exit 9 toward NH 9/NH 108/Dover/Somersworth. Turn left onto Indian Brook Drive (signs for Sixth St.), and go 0.5 mile. Turn right onto Sixth St., and go 0.8 mile. Turn left onto County Farm Road, go 0.2 mile, and then turn left onto Watson Road. Follow it 0.2 mile, and turn left into the trailhead parking lot.

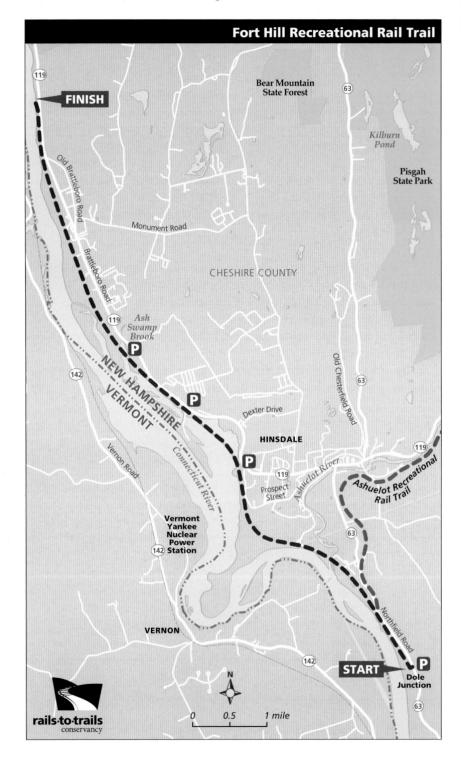

## Fort Hill Recreational Rail Trail

FINISH

119

Bear Mountain
State Forest

63

Kilburn
Pond

Pisgah
State Park

Old Brattleboro Road

Brattleboro Road

Monument Road

CHESHIRE COUNTY

Ash
Swamp
Brook

119

142

NEW HAMPSHIRE
VERMONT

Connecticut River

Vernon Road

Dexter Drive

Old Chesterfield Road

63

HINSDALE

119

Prospect
Street

Ashuelot River

Ashuelot Recreational
Rail Trail

119

Vermont
Yankee
Nuclear
Power
142 Station

63

VERNON

142

START

N

0      0.5      1 mile

Northfield Road

Dole
Junction

63

rails·to·trails
conservancy

**B**uilt in the 1910s by the Boston and Maine Railroad (B&M) as part of the Connecticut River Division Main Line, the route introduced daily service to the B&M Fort Hill Branch in the early 1920s to meet growing competition from motor trucks that had begun courting small shippers from Boston to the Canadian border. This resulted in the line being known as a peddler route (now pedaler!). The competition eventually became too much, and by 1983, the route ceased service. Thankfully, this line—like many others in the area—has been converted to trails and we can still walk, bike, and ski in the shadows of the former B&M cars.

The Fort Hill Recreational Rail Trail begins at a spacious dirt parking lot at Dole Junction in Hinsdale, which

*At the north end of the trail, you'll have a view of an old railroad bridge across the Connecticut River.*

**County**
Cheshire

**Endpoints**
Northfield Road/NH 63 across from the southern end of the Ashuelot Recreational Rail Trail at Dole Junction, 1.5 miles north of S. Parish Road and 1.5 miles south of Tower Hill Road, to an old railroad bridge over the Connecticut River at the NH–VT state line at NH 119/Brattleboro Road, 0.5 mile north of Old Brattleboro Road (Hinsdale)

**Mileage**
7.0

**Type**
Rail-Trail

**Roughness Index**
2

**Surfaces**
Ballast, Cinder, Dirt, Grass, Gravel, Sand

*Heading north from Dole Junction, travelers will be surrounded by lush vegetation on the dirt-and-grass trail.*

also serves the southern end of the 21.5-mile Ashuelot Recreational Rail Trail (see page 79). As you begin your journey north, the dirt and grass trail starts out fairly wide, though in summer, lush vegetation may creep in to grab the streams of sunlight along the rail.

In 1.3 miles, you will come to a wooden bridge over the Ashuelot River, complete with its original stone abutments. On your right, you will notice a concrete pillar marked WRJCT 69, which once notified train crews that they had 69 miles until White River Junction, Vermont.

At 2.8 miles, you will come to a second large parking area off Prospect Street in Hinsdale. From there, it's a short ride into town, with convenient off-street paths most of the way. This parking lot marks the departure from the mainland for a bit, as you head out onto a sweeping causeway into a setback of the main channel of the Connecticut River. This spot is popular for fishing and finally allows some wide-open views of New England's longest river, including the former Vermont Yankee Nuclear Power Station, which was decommissioned in 2014 and sits across the river in Vernon, Vermont. At the other end of the causeway is yet another convenient parking lot off NH 119 that is a popular access point for ice fishing, as well as north and southbound trail access.

In 0.8 mile, just before crossing a small bridge over Ash Swamp Brook, you will come to an access path on your right to the last (northernmost) parking area for the trail. The next 2.7 miles are set back from the river a bit, as the trail runs behind several businesses and residential yards. In summer, there will be enough beautiful green vegetation to give you some peace and quiet as you finish the northern end of the trail, where you will be rewarded. Built in 1912, the old truss bridge that once took B&M trains across the Connecticut River now sits silently and majestically. While the decking is decaying, preventing guaranteed passage, the crimson steel structure stands as an impressive relic of old railroad engineering and offers an opportunity to one day carry trail users into Brattleboro, Vermont, and beyond.

If you'd like to extend your journey into Vermont, the West River Trail (see page 203) is a 3.5-mile ride north from the northernmost endpoint.

**CONTACT:** nhstateparks.org/visit/recreational-rail-trails/fort-hill-recreational
-rail-trail.aspx

## DIRECTIONS

To reach the southern endpoint from I-91, take Exit 2 for VT 9/Western Ave. Turn left (east) onto Western Ave./VT 9, and follow it 1.1 miles (it becomes High St.). Turn right onto Main St., and go 0.2 mile. Turn left onto Bridge St. to enter New Hampshire. Continue onto NH 119 E/Brattleboro Road 6.7 miles. Turn right onto NH 63 S/Northfield Road, and go 2.2 miles. Parking will be on the right.

There is no parking or access at the northern endpoint. The last dedicated parking lot is at Hinsdale Town Park. To reach the park from I-91, follow the directions above to NH 119 E/Brattleboro Road, and go 4 miles. Look for a small parking area on your right. Note that this parking area is small. Another lot is available 0.8 mile farther southeast along NH 119/Brattleboro Road, directly adjacent to the trail and the Connecticut River Reservoir.

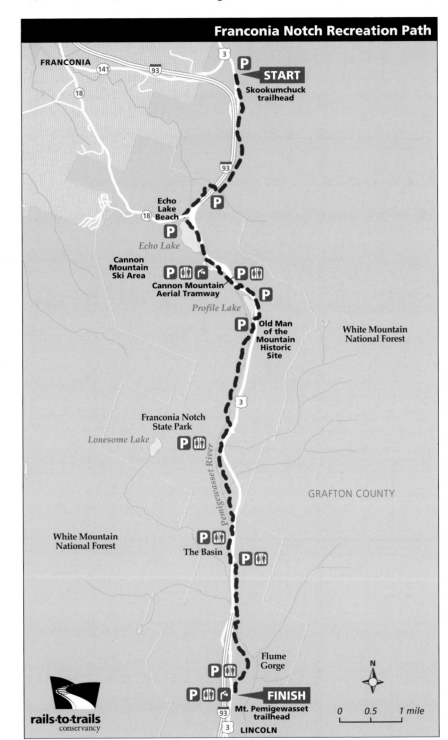

**Franconia Notch Recreation Path**

The Franconia Notch Recreation Path runs the length of the Franconia Notch State Park in the White Mountain National Forest. Commonly called the Recreation Path, the 8.7-mile trail visits most of the park's attractions, such as the Old Man of the Mountain Historic Site, Echo Lake, and Flume Gorge. The paved path roughly follows I-93 through the pass.

Heading south from the Skookumchuck trailhead, the spectacular views of peaks and forests will remind you that the Notch is indeed a mountain pass between the Kinsman and Franconia Ranges. The elevation changes are also a reminder, as the trail gains about 340 feet to the foot of Cannon Mountain, then drops 750 feet to the terminus at Mt. Pemigewasset trailhead. As satisfying as it will be to descend the hills you crest, observe the 20-mile-per-hour speed limit on the trail.

*The spectacular views of peaks and forests will remind you that the Notch is indeed a mountain pass between the Kinsman and Franconia Ranges.*

**County**
Grafton

**Endpoints**
Skookumchuck trailhead on US 3/Daniel Webster Hwy., 0.3 mile south of NH 141 (Franconia), to Mt. Pemigewasset trailhead/ Flume Gorge and Visitor Center on US 3/Daniel Webster Hwy., 0.5 mile north of Parkers Ct. (Lincoln)

**Mileage**
8.7

**Type**
Greenway/Non-Rail-Trail

**Roughness Index**
1

**Surface**
Asphalt

The main attractions are marked with walking-only signs for trail users, and they are wheelchair accessible. The route is often shaded as you reach these locations, thanks to the steep mountainsides and trees lining the path. Bring your camera because, in addition to the major sites along the route, you soon will be treated to dazzling vistas at the Sunset Bridge.

In 2.1 miles you will arrive at Echo Lake Beach, where there's a store, restrooms, and boat rentals in season. The trail follows the lake 0.5 mile before you reach the legendary Cannon Mountain Aerial Tramway. The cable car carries riders up to the 4,080-foot summit, where you can get beer and food at a café, and enjoy views of the Adirondack Mountains on clear days.

The Old Man of the Mountain Historic Site is the next stop, about 0.4 mile down the trail. The Great Stone Face, which appeared on a cliff as a person's profile, was mentioned in the 19th-century writings of Daniel Webster and Nathaniel Hawthorne and still appears in silhouette on state highway markers. Although it detached from the cliff face back in 2003, the park has provided informative signage and a viewing platform that re-creates the appearance of the stone face on the cliff for visitors.

The trail heads mostly downhill for the next 3.3 miles to The Basin, a huge granite pothole in the Pemigewasset River. The final 2 miles take you to the cascading waters and granite walls of the iconic Flume Gorge and Visitor Center before delivering you to the end of the path at the Mt. Pemigewasset trailhead and parking lot.

*Note:* Fees are charged at Flume Gorge, Cannon Mountain Aerial Tramway, and Echo Lake Beach. Bike rentals and shuttles are available at the Tramway.

**CONTACT:** cannonmt.com/recreation-path.html and nhstateparks.org/visit/state -parks/Franconia-notch-state-park.aspx

## DIRECTIONS

To reach the Skookumchuck trailhead from I-93 N, take Exit 35 onto US 3 N/Daniel Webster Hwy. toward Lancaster. Go 0.1 mile, and look for trailhead parking on the right.

To reach the Skookumchuck trailhead from I-93 S, take Exit 36 onto NH 141 toward South Franconia. Turn left onto NH 141/Butterhill Road. Go 0.8 mile, and turn right onto US 3/Daniel Webster Hwy. Go 0.3 mile, and look for parking on the left.

To reach the Mt. Pemigewasset trailhead from I-93 S, take Exit 34A and merge onto US 3 S/Daniel Webster Hwy. Go 0.4 mile, and turn left into the Flume Gorge and Visitor Center parking lot. The trail starts at the north end.

To reach the Mt. Pemigewasset trailhead from I-93 N, take Exit 34A and merge onto US 3 N/Daniel Webster Hwy. Go 0.1 mile, and turn right into the Flume Gorge and Visitor Center parking lot. The trail starts at the north end.

The year 2017 marks 20 years since a rails-to-trails project was first mentioned in the Goffstown Master Plan, and thanks to work by the Friends of the Goffstown Rail Trail and support throughout the community, this trail has become a shining example of what can become of an old rail corridor. The trail inhabits a segment of the former Boston and Maine (B&M) Railroad route that once spanned northern New England. A flood in 1936 damaged much of the line and its spurs, and in 1976, a fire consumed the covered bridge that crossed the Piscataquog River.

Beginning in Goffstown, the trail starts with little fanfare on Factory Street and sneaks behind neighborhoods with fleeting views of the glistening river to your left. Upon traveling on East Union Street about 0.3 mile, the trail picks up again past a school bus parking area and starts to take on a life of its own, with glimpses of the river far below.

You'll pass by one of many convenient access points to the trail, the Goffstown Parks and Recreation Department complex, and go another 0.5 mile to the first of two

*Throughout your journey, trees and beautiful waterways surround you.*

**County**
Hillsborough

**Endpoints**
Factory St. and VT 13 (Goffstown) to the Piscataquog Rail Trail at Agnes St., 0.3 mile northeast of Pinard St. (Manchester)

**Mileage**
5.5

**Type**
Rail-Trail

**Roughness Index**
1

**Surfaces**
Ballast, Cinder, Dirt, Gravel, Sand

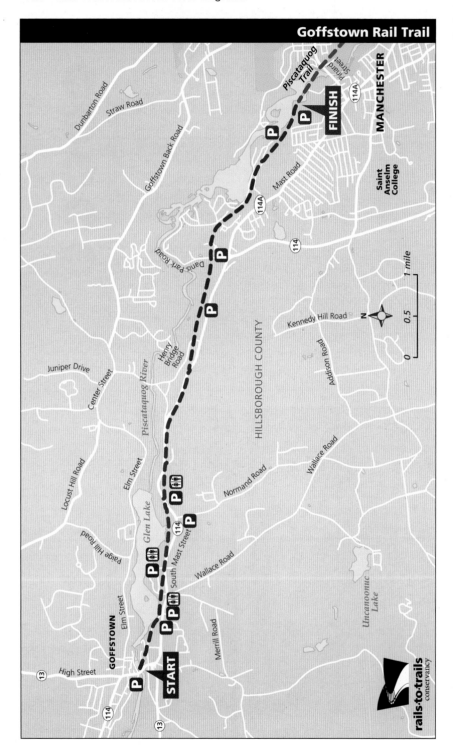

crossings over Mast Road. Though the trail is mostly hard-packed gravel, the three street crossings—two over Mast Road and one over Henry Bridge Road—are paved and have plenty of signage to help residents easily connect to the trail.

In 0.7 mile, you'll emerge from the woods and travel through the parking lot of a service station. (The trail picks up just on the other side, as signs indicate.) Here, a mile marker lets you know that you are 3.5 miles from the eastern end and the beginning of the Piscataquog Trail (see page 132).

After another mile, the trail slips behind the New Hampshire State Prison for Women and the Hillsborough County Complex and courthouse. Friendly county workers maintain this part of the trail, and trail parking is available in the municipal lot. Note the brilliant redbrick buildings to your right, which once acted as coal storage for the B&M line and are now home to administrative offices.

More of the corridor's history is apparent after you cross Danis Park Road and pass inside the deep cut where the cliffs were blasted to allow trains to travel at a proper grade. If it's a hot day, you'll also appreciate the cool breeze on your way through! Next, a secret tip: As you pass the Moose Club Park Road trailhead, keep an eye on your GPS; soon you will be at exactly 43°N latitude, the same parallel that forms most of the boundary between Nebraska and South Dakota.

Near the eastern end, about 300 feet short of mile marker 0.0, a connecting path leads to the Sarette Recreation Complex, which has ample parking. At the official eastern end of the Goffstown Rail Trail, the route seamlessly connects to the Piscataquog Trail, which heads over the Merrimack River and into Manchester.

**CONTACT: goffstownrailtrail.org**

## DIRECTIONS

To reach parking in Goffstown from I-293, take Exit 6 for Amoskeag St. toward Goffstown Road. (If coming from I-293 S, follow the right fork of the exit ramp to Amoskeag St.) Take a slight left onto Amoskeag St. (signs for Concord/Goffstown Road/I-293), go 0.1 mile, and then continue straight onto Goffstown Road 1.8 miles. Continue onto Goffstown Back Road 2.1 miles, and then continue onto Center St. 0.7 mile (taking the second exit to head straight through one traffic circle). Continue onto Elm St. 2.6 miles, turn left onto NH 114 S/NH 13 S, and go 0.1 mile. Look for parking to your right in the Goffstown Town Hall lot. To access the northern end of the trail, travel south on NH 114 S/NH 13 S 0.1 mile across the Piscataquog River bridge, and take your first left onto Factory St. Go one block, and turn right onto the trail to head southeast.

To reach the southeast endpoint in Manchester from I-293, take Exit 5 for Granite St. toward West Manchester. Head southwest onto Granite St., and go 0.1 mile. Turn left onto S. Main St., and go 0.3 mile. Turn right onto Varney St., go 0.4 mile, and continue onto Mast Road/NH 114A 1.1 miles. Turn right onto Laurier St., and go 0.2 mile. Laurier St. turns slightly left and becomes Louis St. Turn right into the Sarette Recreation Complex, and look for parking on your left.

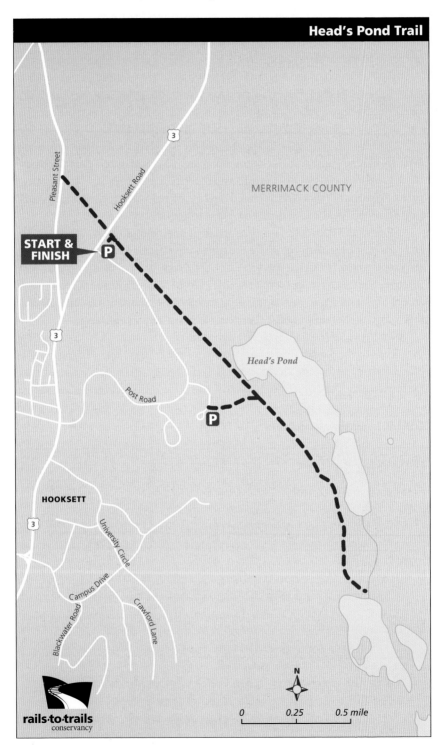

**Head's Pond Trail**

3

Pleasant Street

Hooksett Road

MERRIMACK COUNTY

START & FINISH  P

3

Post Road

P

Head's Pond

HOOKSETT

3

University Circle

Campus Drive

Blackwater Road

Crawford Lane

N

rails·to·trails
conservancy

0    0.25    0.5 mile

The Head's Pond Trail (formerly known as Hooksett Rail Trail) is a 1.9-mile rail-trail that visits two scenic ponds, including the eponymous Head's Pond, in a woodsy area of Hooksett. The trail's smooth stone dust surface is well suited to bikes, but the short length and out-and-back configuration of the path isn't. As a result, you'll mostly find local joggers and walkers (often with a four-legged friend) using the trail. Fishermen also use the trail to catch largemouth bass or chain pickerel in the ponds. History and outdoors buffs will enjoy the interpretive signs that inform about Hooksett and the local flora and fauna.

*This short but sweet trail offers lovely views of its eponymous pond in a woodsy area of Hooksett.*

**County**
Merrimack

**Endpoints**
Pleasant St., 0.5 mile south of Merrimack St. and 0.5 mile north of Daniel Webster Hwy./ NH 28/US 3, to a gate on an unnamed dirt road (Hooksett)

**Mileage**
1.9

**Type**
Rail-Trail

**Roughness Index**
2

**Surface**
Crushed Stone

A trailhead with ample parking on US 3 is the best place to begin. A steep and rocky access path leads downhill from the parking lot, but once you're on the trail, it's flat over its entire length. The trail follows a former Portsmouth & Concord Railroad alignment that linked the two cities briefly in the 1850s before operations ceased on this section and the track was removed in 1861.

From the trailhead, the Head's Pond Trail goes northwest under US 3 and ends in 0.25 mile on Pleasant Street. Most visitors continue southeast on the trail to the ponds. Pines, maples, and birches envelop the trail and provide shade in summer months. In about 0.5 mile, you can relax on a bench and enjoy a view of Head's Pond.

A nearby path connects to an adjacent neighborhood. The remainder of the trail continues as before, although the canopy opens up a bit to allow more sun as you approach the southern endpoint.

The trail ends abruptly at a gated dirt road that leads to a sand and gravel pit. You'll want to stop here anyway, as you have reached the second pond, where yet another bench welcomes you to rest and enjoy the view. (A word of caution, though: heavy rains can overflow the pond and submerge the bench legs, leading to wet feet for those who insist on sitting regardless.) Head back the way you came for a double dose of scenery.

Although there aren't any services along the trail, you can find refreshments in historic Hooksett on the Merrimack River. One option is the café at Robie's Country Store, visited every four years by candidates vying for New Hampshire's presidential primary. The store, located at 9 Riverside Street, is a historic landmark that dates to 1822.

**CONTACT:** hooksettconservationcommission.wordpress.com/2015/11/03 /heads-pond-trail

## DIRECTIONS

To reach the trailhead and parking in Hooksett from I-93, take Exit 11. From the toll plaza, turn left onto Hackett Hill Road, go 0.2 mile, and turn left onto W. River Road/NH 3A. Go 0.6 mile, and turn right onto Main St. In 0.4 mile stay straight onto College Park Dr. Go 0.5 mile, and turn left onto US 3/NH 28/Hooksett Road. Go 1.1 miles, and look for parking on the right.

Lake Winnisquam is New Hampshire's fourth largest lake, and taking the Lake Winnisquam Scenic Trail is one of the best ways to experience it. Meaning "pleasant waters," Lake Winnisquam provides beautiful vistas of the water, mountains, and wildlife. The rail-trail, also known as the Winni Trail, opened in 2016 and is very well maintained, with clear signage for sharp turns through the woods. The length and shade make the trail ideal for runners and walkers.

Starting at the eastern trailhead located near the Leslie E. Roberts Beach and Recreation Area, you will find picnic tables, a playground, a restroom, and, of course, a place to dip your toes in the water. Fishing is allowed in the lake; license-free fishing days occur in January and June. At the junction of US 3/NH 11 and Business US 3,

*Skirting the shoreline for its entire length, the path offers unparalleled vistas of Lake Winnisquam.*

**County**
Belknap

**Endpoints**
Leslie E. Roberts Beach and Recreation Area at US 3/NH 11 and Bus. US 3 to US 3/NH 11, 0.1 mile south of Union Road (Belmont)

**Mileage**
1.8

**Type**
Rail-Trail

**Roughness Index**
1

**Surface**
Asphalt

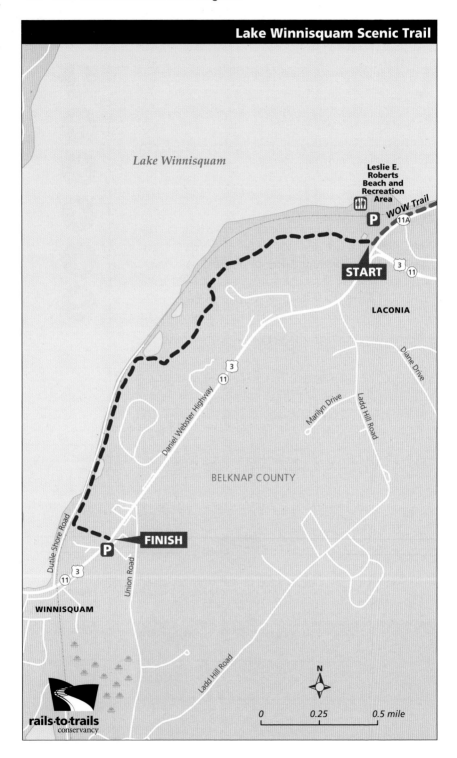

**Lake Winnisquam Scenic Trail**

Lake Winnisquam

Leslie E. Roberts Beach and Recreation Area

WOW Trail

11A

START

3

11

LACONIA

Diane Drive

3

11

Daniel Webster Highway

Marilyn Drive

Ladd Hill Road

BELKNAP COUNTY

Dutile Shore Road

FINISH

Union Road

3

11

WINNISQUAM

Ladd Hill Road

N

0    0.25    0.5 mile

rails·to·trails
conservancy

the trail connects to the southern trailhead of the 2.7-mile WOW Trail (see page 161), which travels east toward Laconia and is perfect for cyclists.

The paved 1.8-mile rail-trail winds through lush forest, where you can enjoy the shade of dense, tall trees and the chatter of wildlife. The southwestern portion provides stunning views of the water and far-reaching corners of the lake. From this trailhead, the town of Belmont plans to connect to the 5.1-mile Winnipesaukee River Trail (see page 158) to the west toward Tilton and Franklin.

**CONTACT:** belmontnh.org/projectswinnitrail.asp

## DIRECTIONS

To reach the trail from I-93, take Exit 20 for US 3/NH 11 (toward NH 140/Tilton if coming from the south, or toward NH 132/E. Main St. if coming from the north). Turn left onto US 3N/NH 11 E/Laconia Road, following signs for Belmont/Laconia. See directions below depending on the trailhead you wish to reach.

To reach the eastern trailhead at the Leslie E. Roberts Beach and Recreation Area, follow US 3 N/NH 11 E/Laconia Road about 6.5 miles. Turn left onto Leslie Roberts Dr., just before US 3 N/NH 11 E becomes Bus. US 3 N, where the parking lot can be found less than 0.5 mile to the right.

To reach the western trailhead at Osborne's Agway (a farm and garden supply store in Belmont), follow US 3N/NH 11 E/Laconia Road 5.1 miles. Turn left at Osborne's Agway. A small trail parking lot with four spots is located immediately to the left of the entrance, on the southwest side of Osborne's Agway, adjacent to the start of the trail.

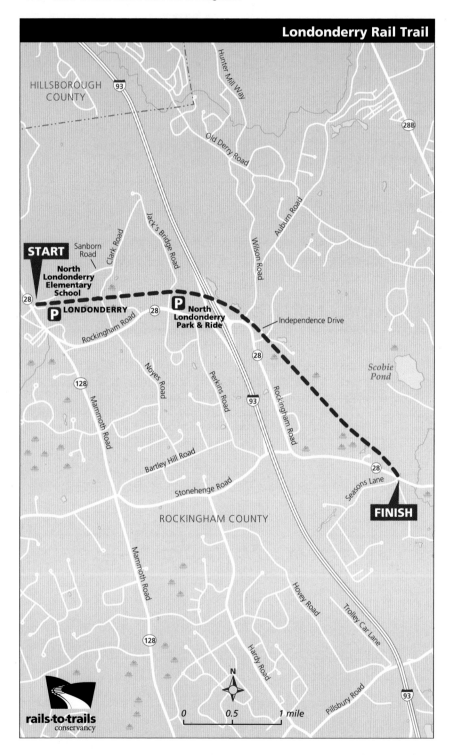

**Londonderry Rail Trail**

The smooth paved surface of the Londonderry Rail Trail offers a pleasant, tranquil 3.3-mile adventure for trail users in south-central New Hampshire. Its route follows a corridor once used by the Manchester and Lawrence Railroad, which started operations in the mid-1800s as a way to connect Manchester with Boston. The railroad ceased operations in the 1980s, and the creation of the rail-trail began in earnest in 2012.

As part of the future 125-mile Granite State Rail Trail, which one day will stretch from Massachusetts to the Vermont border, the Londonderry Rail Trail will eventually span 6 miles and serve as a connection between the developing South Manchester Rail Trail to the north and the Derry Rail Trail (see page 92) to the south.

A good place to begin your journey is at the northern trailhead on Sanborn Road. A small parking lot sits

*The trail's west end forms a straight shot through the woodlands on an elevated embankment—a remnant of the original railroad corridor infrastructure.*

**County**
Rockingham

**Endpoints**
Sanborn Road just east of Wyndmere Dr. to NH 28/Rockingham Road and Seasons Lane (Londonderry)

**Mileage**
3.3

**Type**
Rail-Trail

**Roughness Index**
1

**Surface**
Asphalt

adjacent to Sanborn Road just east of the endpoint, and additional parking is available across the street at the North Londonderry Elementary School (when school is not in session).

The trail begins by traveling east through quiet, wooded neighborhoods, with the first 1.2 miles forming a straight shot on an elevated embankment—a remnant of the original railroad corridor infrastructure—but with a few dips down across neighborhood streets. The trail's surface is well maintained, and signage is good for the entire length of the trail.

The trail opens up as it passes the North Londonderry Park & Ride, the second key parking area for the route, before passing under I-93 and veering south toward the center of town. Immediately following the underpass, you'll pass some tranquil ponds and wetlands located on the east side of the trail.

After a few street crossings, the route follows Independence Drive a short distance before entering another beautiful wooded section. The remaining 1.5 miles take you through some tranquil wetland areas—you might forget your proximity to I-93 and the town in this pristine natural sanctuary—before terminating at NH 28. Watch for turtles and other wildlife as you cross through a peat bog in this section of trail.

Please note that there is currently no parking at the southern terminus, and travel to and from this point would be challenging for nonmotorized users due to the current infrastructure. Plans are in the works to extend the trail across NH 28 and eventually create a seamless connection with the Derry Rail Trail to the south.

CONTACT: **londonderrytrails.org** and **londonderrynh.org**

## DIRECTIONS

To reach the trailhead at the northwestern end of the trail from I-93, take Exit 5 toward NH 28 N, and follow signs for North Londonderry/Manchester. Head west onto NH 28 N/Rockingham Road, and go 1.5 miles. Turn right onto Sanborn Road, go 0.1 mile, and turn right into the parking lot (located directly across the street from North Londonderry Elementary School).

To reach the parking lot at the North Londonderry Park & Ride from I-93, follow the directions above to NH 28 N/Rockingham Road, and go about 0.3 mile. Turn right onto Symmes Dr., and then turn right into the access road to the parking lot. Turn right into the parking lot and you'll see the trail toward the rear of the lot on your left. Be sure to pay attention to the signs, as some spaces have time limits or are dedicated for bus and/or commuter use only.

There is currently no dedicated parking at the trail's southeast terminus.

**M**ine Falls Park in Nashua is a 300-acre-plus urban park with a network of approximately 9.7 miles of a variety of trail types. This forested park offers an extraordinary nature experience in the heart of New Hampshire's second-most populous city along the Nashua River. The park is a beacon of recreational opportunities; in addition to the trail network, the area boasts historic exploration, wildlife viewing, ball fields, and ample fishing spots.

The Nashua River and Nashua Canal both cut right through the park, providing an interesting glimpse into the city's past. The Nashua Manufacturing Company built the canal to channel water from the river downstream to a dam, creating a crucial power source for the mills and industrial movement in the area during the 1800s.

*This forested park offers an extraordinary nature experience in the heart of Nashua.*

**County**
Hillsborough

**Endpoints**
Mine Falls Gatehouse/ Dam at Stadium Dr., 0.15 mile west of Riverside St., to the end of Pine St. Ext., near the Nashua Manufacturing Company Historic District, 0.3 mile south of Technology Way (Nashua)

**Mileage**
9.7

**Type**
Canal/Greenway

**Roughness Index**
1–3

**Surfaces**
Asphalt, Crushed Stone, Dirt, Grass

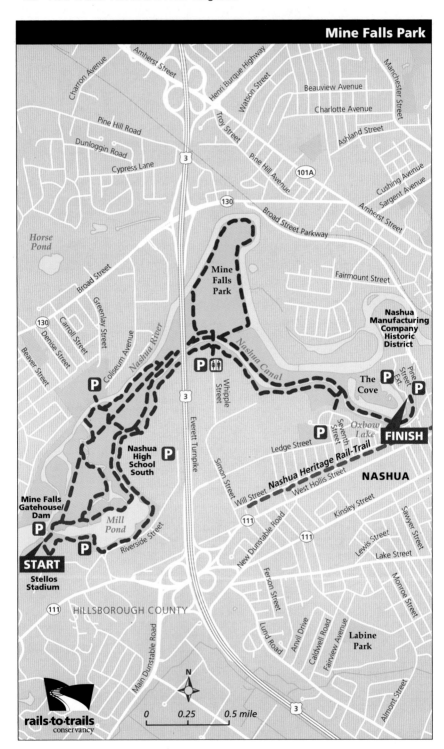

**Mine Falls Park**

Charron Avenue
Amherst Street
Henri Burque Highway
Watson Street
Beauview Avenue
Charlotte Avenue
Manchester Street

Pine Hill Road
Troy Street
Pine Hill Avenue
Ashland Street

Dunloggin Road
Cypress Lane
3
101A
Cushing Avenue
Sargent Avenue
Amherst Street

130
Broad Street Parkway

Horse Pond
Mine Falls Park
Fairmount Street

Broad Street
Greenlay Street
130
Carroll Street
Denise Street
Beaver Street
Coliseum Avenue
Nashua River
Nashua Canal
Nashua Manufacturing Company Historic District

P
Whipple Street
The Cove
P
Pine Street Ext.
P

3
Everett Turnpike
P
Seventh Street
Oxbow Lake
FINISH

Nashua High School South
P
P
Ledge Street
Nashua Heritage Rail-Trail
NASHUA

Mine Falls Gatehouse/ Dam
P
Simon Street
Will Street
West Hollis Street

Mill Pond
P
Riverside Street
111

START
Stellos Stadium
New Dunstable Road
Ferson Street
111
111
Kinsley Street
Lewis Street
Lake Street
Sawyer Street
Monroe Street

111  HILLSBOROUGH COUNTY
Main Dunstable Road
Lund Road
Anvil Drive
Caldwell Road
Fairview Avenue
Labine Park
Almont Street

N

rails·to·trails
conservancy

0    0.25    0.5 mile

3

Before you head out, it's a good idea to bring along a map of the park developed by the City of Nashua, available at **nashuanh.gov/DocumentCenter/View/2328.** The park is organized by a series of color-coded trails and corresponding numbers posted along the trails to help you navigate. The city map details all of this information. Several access points make it easy to get to the park from several places, and three primary routes traverse the park from east to west.

One great starting point for the trail is the Mine Falls Gatehouse/Dam trailhead, located on the western side of the trail system, between the Nashua River and Mill Pond, accessible from Stadium Drive. The impressive Mine Falls Dam appears right next to the parking area; here, you can also glimpse a gatehouse (currently being restored) constructed by the Nashua Manufacturing Company in 1886 as part of the canal system that is now on the National Register of Historic Places.

Mine Falls Park extends to the east, immediately presenting you with three primary pathway options. Following the northern side of the Nashua Canal, the old towpath travels east directly alongside the water. In 1.2 miles, you will cross under US 3/Everett Turnpike and come to a trail junction at the Whipple Street trailhead. There are many different trail connections throughout the park, and three bridges cross the canal.

Staying along the northern side of the canal for the remaining 1.1 miles, the trail makes its way to the eastern edge of the park. Beautiful views of the river, wetlands, and wildlife abound on the northern side of the trail overlooking Oxbow Lake and The Cove. The Nashua Manufacturing Company Historic District is located just one block east of the park at Clocktower Place and Factory Street Extension.

In addition to the canal towpath, a trail on the northern edge of the park closely follows the south bank of the Nashua River. Just after passing under US 3/Everett Turnpike, you can opt to continue straight toward the eastern side of the park or turn left to make a small loop through the wooded area that runs adjacent to the southern side of the river.

To the south, a paved trail segment begins just off of Stadium Drive near Stellos Stadium and closely follows the southern edge of the canal for the length of the park. If you choose to follow this section, you can also access the 1.3-mile Nashua Heritage Rail-Trail—which runs parallel to West Hollis Street—by turning right onto a trail junction about 2.3 miles from the stadium parking lot. To the left is a trail bridge that will take you to the northern side of the canal. From the trail junction, head straight onto North Seventh Street and go 0.3 mile, passing ball fields and a parking area. Cross over North Groton Street and enter the Nashua Heritage Rail-Trail, which heads east or west along the north side of West Hollis Street.

Throughout the park, trails suitable only for hiking offer a unique wilderness experience right in Nashua.

*The trail network offers breathtaking views of both the Nashua River and Nashua Canal.*

**CONTACT: nashuanh.gov/491/Mine-Falls-Park**

## DIRECTIONS

To reach the Mine Falls Gatehouse/Dam trailhead from US 3/Everett Turnpike, take Exit 5W, and merge onto NH 111/W. Hollis St., heading west. Go 0.5 mile. Turn right onto Riverside St., and in several hundred feet, turn left onto Stadium Dr. Go 0.2 mile, and follow signs to Mine Falls Park. You will turn right and pass Stellos Stadium on your left before entering the park. After passing the boat launch on your left, look for trail parking on your left near the gatehouse.

To reach the Whipple St. trailhead from US 3 S/Everett Turnpike, take Exit 5E if coming from the north, and merge onto NH 111/W. Hollis St. After crossing over the highway, immediately turn right to get on US 3N/Everett Turnpike. Take Exit 5A and follow signs for Simon St. Turn left onto Simon St., and go 0.2 mile. Turn left onto Whipple St., and go another 0.2 mile to the park entrance and parking.

To reach the easternmost trailhead on Pine St. Ext. from US 3/Everett Turnpike, take Exit 6 for Broad St./NH 130 toward Hollis. Head east onto NH 130/Broad St. (signs for Nashua), and go 0.4 mile. Turn right onto Broad St. Pkwy., go 1.1 miles, and turn right onto Pine St. Ext. In a few feet turn left to stay on Pine St. Ext., go 0.1 mile (the road will turn right), and then turn left again to stay on Pine St. Ext. for another 0.2 mile. Turn left into the small parking lot.

The Monadnock Recreational Rail Trail is a great example of a repurposed rail route that provides safe commuting opportunities while also allowing trail users to escape into forest environments for some peace and respite.

Beginning next to the American Legion Post ball field on Webster Street in Jaffrey, the paved trail winds its way south where crosswalks provide access to the unofficial entry point after Stratton Road, which is complete with a Rails-to-Trails sign and information kiosk. From here, your route becomes more serene as the pavement ends near another public ball field. A pleasant sitting area with a bench by the Contoocook River is located just 0.2 mile from here. *Note:* The 1½ MI marker you see denotes the distance remaining until the Jaffrey–Rindge town line.

For the next 0.75 mile, you will skirt the west boundary of Children's Woods (28 acres) and Carey Park (100 acres), both owned by the town of Jaffrey and preserved for the study and enjoyment of the region's natural history. Blazed trails lead directly from the rail-trail.

*The southern end of the trail, through Rindge, offers spectacular scenery.*

**County**
Cheshire

**Endpoints**
Webster St. between Peterborough St./US 202 and Alder Ct. (Jaffrey) to the NH–MA state line 0.9 mile east of Robbins Road, 0.5 mile west of Forristall Road, and 0.7 mile south of Woods Crossing Road (Rindge)

**Mileage**
7.5

**Type**
Rail-Trail

**Roughness Index**
2–3

**Surfaces**
Asphalt, Dirt, Grass, Gravel

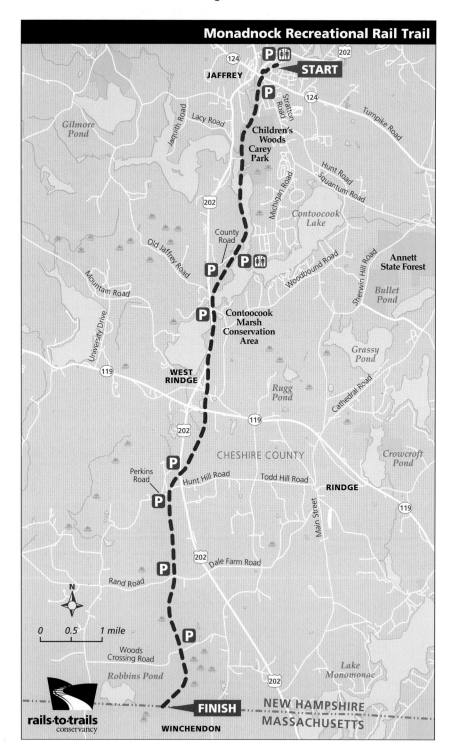

Heading farther south takes you through the wetlands on the western edge of Contoocook Lake and over a large wooden bridge that offers beautiful sweeping views of the lake and its wildlife. If you are here in summer, you'll enjoy the smell of pine trees and wildflowers. In spring be on the lookout for turtles hatching on the sandy banks; they may decide to scurry over to the other side of the marsh.

Rounding the bend to your right, you will pass from Jaffrey into Rindge, where the trail is known as the Rindge Rail Trail and the Jack Dupree Memorial Trail. Here, at County Road, you'll find a public boat launch that offers plenty of parking and access to the lake. Shortly thereafter, you'll enter the Contoocook Marsh Conservation Area, which offers a small trail loop and benches to enjoy the scenery and wildlife at the wetland's edge.

From here to the southern endpoint, the trail becomes more challenging with a dirt and grass surface, and a hybrid or mountain bike is recommended. As you pass through West Rindge, the trail becomes much narrower; if you are on a bicycle, keep to the left, as narrow wooden ties still mark the old route.

The next 3.5 miles from NH 119 offer a serene experience year-round; however, note that the 0.9-mile section between Perkins Road and Rand Road is relatively low-lying and particularly prone to flooding. A sign indicates that the trail is closed to all use in the muddy season. If flooding does occur, you may be forced to detour onto US 202, which provides wide shoulders but is very busy.

A simple granite pillar at the New Hampshire–Massachusetts border marks the trail's official end. The route continues to Winchendon, though passage is only recommended in winter when snow packs the way.

**CONTACT:** nhstateparks.org/visit/recreational-rail-trails/monadnock-recreational
-rail-trail.aspx

---

## DIRECTIONS

To reach the northern trailhead from I-293, take the NH 114 exit toward Manchester/Bedford. Merge onto NH 101 W, and go 1 mile. Turn left to remain on NH 101 W, and go 17.6 miles. Turn left again to remain on NH 101 W, and go another 14.7 miles. Turn left onto Grove St., go 0.3 mile, and continue onto US 202 W/Jaffrey Road 5.7 miles. Turn left onto Webster St., and the trail will be on your right in a few hundred feet. Look for parking just farther down on the left across from Oak St.

Technically, one car is permitted to park at the three southernmost crossroad points for the trail at Woods Crossing Road, Rand Road, and Perkins Road; however, cars must not block the access gates, and there is no guarantee that space will be available. The best place to park in the trail's southern half is just off US 202 in Rindge, about 0.2 mile north of Perkins Road. To reach the US 202 parking area from the intersection of NH 101 and US 202 in Peterborough, head south on US 202 W 6 miles, and in Jaffrey turn right onto Main St./NH 124. Immediately turn left to remain on US 202, and go another 4.6 miles. Look for parking on your left (just before the trail's access point). The trail's southern endpoint is located 2.7 miles south along the trail.

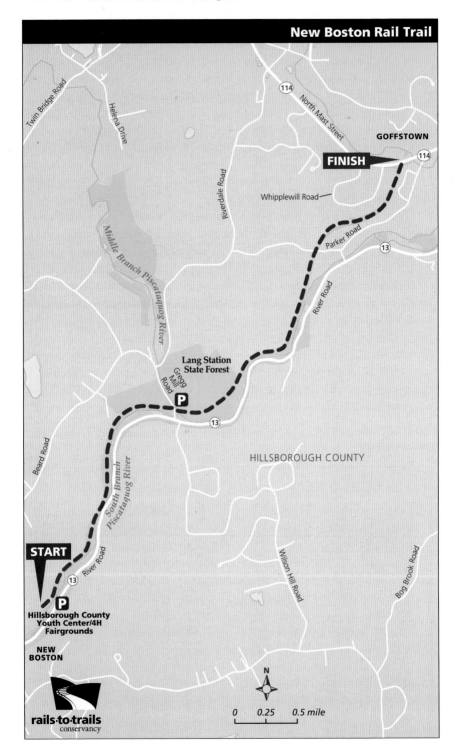

New Boston Rail Trail

The New Boston Rail Trail follows the former railroad corridor of the same name for 3.9 miles through densely wooded areas in the town of New Boston. The railroad was in operation from 1893 to 1931, and was used both for freight and passenger service. Through various efforts by the state of New Hampshire, local organizations, and the people of New Boston, the corridor and surrounding land were preserved and turned into a trail after the railroad ceased operations in the 1970s.

The trail presents two distinctly different experiences. The western section of the trail offers a traditional rail-trail experience on a wide, packed dirt surface suitable for most mountain and hybrid bicycles and pedestrian use. The eastern section is more suitable for hikers and experienced mountain bikers only. The change in these two

*The trail traverses densely wooded areas in the town of New Boston, including passage through Lang Station State Forest.*

**County**
Hillsborough

**Endpoints**
Hillsborough County Youth Center/4H Fairgrounds at Hilldale Lane and NH 13 to N. Mast St./NH 114 between Parker Road and Whipplewill Road (New Boston)

**Mileage**
3.9

**Type**
Rail-Trail

**Roughness Index**
2-3

**Surface**
Dirt

surface types is at the Lang Station trailhead, which is located close to the midway point of the trail and includes a parking area.

Starting from the western endpoint at the Hillsborough County Youth Center/ 4H Fairgrounds, the trail travels east along the peaceful South Branch Piscataquog River through a nice canopy of trees. You can easily view the river along this section of the trail, which includes several places to stop for a break and enjoy the serenity of the river. As the trail continues, it veers slightly away from the river and enters Lang Station State Forest after 1.3 miles.

As the trail approaches the Lang Station trailhead, several paths lead back to the river and feature informal camping spots. At the Lang Station trailhead, the surface changes dramatically as the eastern portion of the trail begins.

Here, the trail continues on the eastern side of Gregg Mill Road, immediately crossing the Middle Branch of the Piscataquog right before it meets the South Branch over a lovely footbridge. From this point, it immediately becomes clear that the trail is only suitable for hikers and experienced mountain bikers. As you make your way through the pristine forest, you can catch fleeting views of the river to the south. The remnants of the old New Boston Railroad are harder to distinguish but are there. The trail crosses Parker Road about 1.5 miles from Lang Station.

The route then continues through the woods until the eastern endpoint at NH 114. Please note that there is only a worn footpath to NH 114, and this is not an ideal trail access point, as it is neither visible nor easy to find from NH 114. In the future, this eastern section will be developed into a more suitable surface for all trail users, and it will eventually connect to the 5.5-mile Goffstown Rail Trail (see page 105) to the east.

If you're starting from the Hillsborough County Youth Center/4H Fairgrounds, be sure to pay attention to the signage relating to parking and access. Although this is an official trailhead accessible to the public, it's also the youth center's private property.

The official map on the trail's website shows an extra 0.75-mile section from the western endpoint to the original train depot, which is now a private residence. This section makes a nice addition to the trail, going across the youth center grounds and traveling along a private road that is open to vehicular traffic. The depot is located close to the center of New Boston, where the trail intersects with Depot Street.

**CONTACT: nbrailtrail.com** and **facebook.com/nbrailtrail**

## DIRECTIONS

To reach the trail from I-293, take the NH 114 exit toward Manchester/Bedford. Merge onto NH 101 W, and go about 1 mile. Continue straight onto NH 114 N, following signs for Goffstown/Henniker. In 3.5 miles, turn left to remain on NH 114 N, and go another 3.8 miles. Turn left onto NH 13. See directions below depending on the trailhead you wish to reach.

To reach the Lang Station trailhead, follow NH 13 S 3.9 miles, and turn right onto Gregg Mill Road. In less than 0.1 mile, the trail parking area and Lang Station will be on your left.

To reach the Hillsborough County Youth Center/4H Fairgrounds trailhead, follow NH 13 S 5.9 miles, and turn right onto Hilldale Lane. You will then cross a bridge and enter the Hillsborough County Youth Center property. Follow Hilldale Lane along the river, heading north a few hundred yards, and you'll see signs for the trail. Note that this is private property, though the youth center allows the public to park and access the trail during the day.

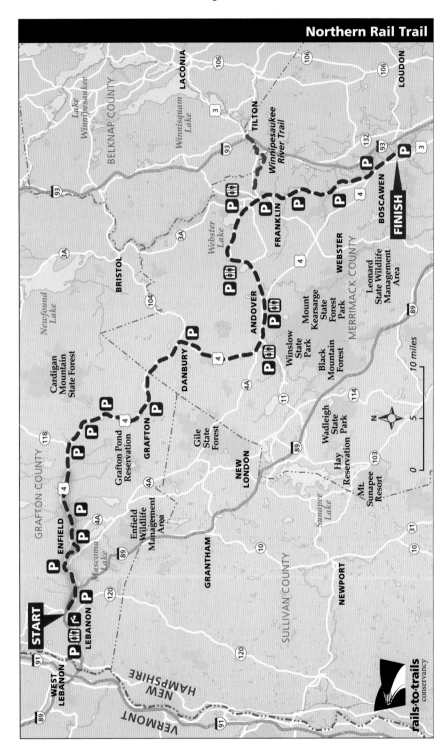

**Northern Rail Trail**

Spanning 57.6 miles from Lebanon to Boscawen, the Northern Rail Trail is New Hampshire's longest rail-trail conversion. Trail development began in 1996 after the state purchased the Boston and Maine Railroad's dormant Northern Line. Built in 1847 by the Northern Railroad, the line formed a substantial portion of a Boston-to-Quebec route that was heavily traveled during the first half of the 20th century. While the state owns the rail corridor, local groups did most of the work to open the trail for year-round use in their respective counties from 2000 to 2014.

In addition to walking and biking, permitted uses include horseback riding, cross-country skiing, snowmobiling, snowshoeing, and dogsledding.

Begin your journey in Lebanon at the trail's northern end to take advantage of the mostly downhill slope. Lebanon offers a handful of restaurants and shops, and you'll want to make sure you stock up before you set out, as there are remote sections between towns.

*Near the communities of Andover and Webster Lake, the trail intersects with Sucker Brook.*

**Counties**
Grafton, Merrimack

**Endpoints**
Spencer St. near Parkhurst St. (Lebanon) to River Road, 0.25 mile north of US 4/King St. (Boscawen)

**Mileage**
57.6

**Type**
Rail-Trail

**Roughness Index**
2

**Surfaces**
Cinder, Crushed Stone

The journey southeast from Lebanon is easy and scenic as you cross nine short bridges over the Mascoma River in the first 4 miles. The trail then skirts the northern shore of the 1,100-acre Mascoma Lake, where you may encounter bathers taking a dip on a hot day. The trail then enters the lakeside community of Enfield. Past here, the path occasionally narrows and can be overgrown with grass and other vegetation. You'll appreciate the dense tree cover in this heavily wooded country in the summer, however.

About 20 miles past Enfield you'll arrive in Danbury, a popular near-midway point for rest and replenishment. The Danbury Country Store offers snacks, restrooms, and a welcome porch. By now you have crossed into Merrimack County, where the trail is upgraded to a crushed stone surface rather than the cinders in Grafton County. Several interpretive signs scattered throughout the remainder of the trail also improve the experience and inform trail users on the rail line's history.

Seven miles past Danbury you pass Andover's Potter Place Railroad Station, restored to look as it did in 1874. The depot's museum, caboose, and nearby freight house are operated by the Andover Historical Society. In 1 mile, the trail crosses the Blackwater River next to the 1882 Keniston Covered Bridge. Andover stretches along US 4/Main Street roughly between Eagle Pond and Highland Lake; restaurants are on Main Street north of the trail.

*This beautiful bridge, which crosses the Blackwater River, is located just outside of Andover.*

East of Andover, the trail enters slightly denser environs, so expect to encounter more people using the trail. This is particularly true at the popular swimming spot Webster Lake, named for local 19th-century statesman Daniel Webster. In Franklin, 1.7 miles past the lake, a short on-road connection links to the Winnipesaukee River Trail (see page 158).

Continuing south on the Northern Rail Trail, you'll come across the stone remains of a turntable that once assisted in changing the direction of locomotives. For the remaining 11 miles south, you'll closely follow US 3 and the Merrimack River to the trail's end at a cornfield in the southern reaches of Boscawen.

Future plans call for extending the trail on both ends. In the north, the paved Mascoma River Greenway will run 4 miles from the Northern Rail Trail in Lebanon to West Lebanon. Grander plans in the south would connect the Northern Rail Trail about 7 miles to the state capital of Concord. They are all components of the Granite State Rail Trail, a 125-mile project that will eventually span southern New Hampshire from Massachusetts to Vermont.

**CONTACT: fnrt.org** and **northernrailtrail.org**

## DIRECTIONS

To reach the northern trailhead from I-89, take Exit 18 onto NH 120 toward Lebanon. Head south 0.4 mile, and turn left onto Hanover St. Go 0.4 mile, and stay straight onto US 4/S. Park St. Go 0.2 mile, and turn left onto E. Park St./Campbell St. Go 0.1 mile, turn right onto Parkhurst St., and then immediately turn left onto Spencer St. Look for parking on the left in Eldridge Park. The trail starts on the right.

The southern endpoint does not offer trailhead parking, but parking is available at Boscawen Town Park/Jamie Welch Memorial Field roughly 2 miles north. To reach this trailhead from I-93, take Exit 17 onto US 4/Hoit Road toward Boscawen. Head west 1.2 miles to a traffic circle, and take the first exit to remain on US 4/King St. Go 2.1 miles, and turn right onto Depot St. Parking is available in 0.2 mile at the park. Backtrack a short distance to access the trail.

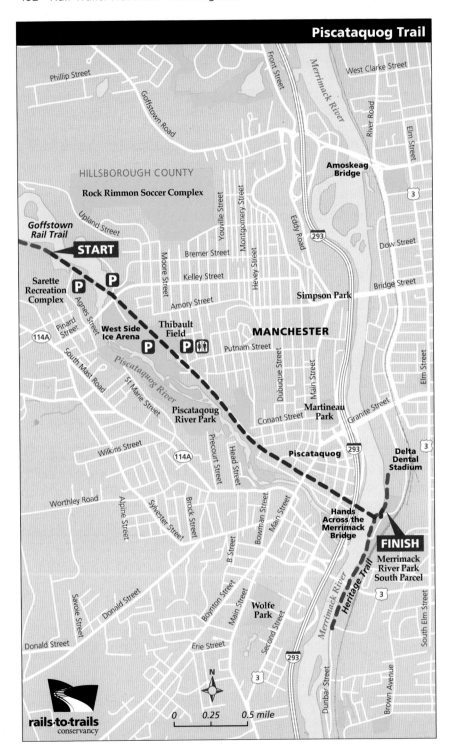

# Piscataquog Trail

Phillip Street

Goffstown Road

Front Street

Merrimack River

West Clarke Street

River Road

Elm Street

Amoskeag Bridge

3

HILLSBOROUGH COUNTY

Rock Rimmon Soccer Complex

Youville Street

Montgomery Street

Eddy Road

293

Dow Street

Goffstown Rail Trail

Upland Street

Bremer Street

Hevey Street

Bridge Street

**START**

Sarette Recreation Complex

P  P

Kelley Street

Amory Street

Simpson Park

Agnes Street

Moore Street

MANCHESTER

Pinard Street

114A

South Mast Road

**West Side Ice Arena**

P

**Thibault Field**

P 🚻

Putnam Street

Main Street

Elm Street

Piscataquog River

St Marie Street

**Piscataquog River Park**

Dubuque Street

Martineau Park

Granite Street

Wilkins Street

114A

Head Street

Conant Street

293

Piscataquog

Delta Dental Stadium

3

Worthley Road

Alpine Street

Sylvester Street

Brock Street

Precourt Street

Bowman Street

Main Street

**Hands Across the Merrimack Bridge**

**FINISH**

Donald Street

B Street

Boynton Street

Main Street

**Wolfe Park**

Second Street

Merrimack River

Heritage Trail

Merrimack River Park South Parcel

3

Savole Street

Donald Street

Erie Street

293

Dunbar Street

Brown Avenue

South Elm Street

N

0    0.25    0.5 mile

**rails·to·trails**
conservancy

The Piscataquog Trail, though only about 2 miles long, provides a vital off-road link between the communities on the western side of the Merrimack River (the West Side of Manchester) to several parks and ball fields and the downtown core.

Picking up at the eastern end of the Goffstown Rail Trail (see page 105) northwest of Agnes Street on the Manchester town line (ample parking is available at the Sarette Recreation Complex), the trail soon crosses its namesake, the Piscataquog River, over the beautifully reconstructed Irving and Bernice Singer Pedestrian Bridge, completed in 2015. Having not carried a Boston and Maine (B&M) Railroad train car since the 1980s, the trestle was removed, and

*On the east side of the Merrimack River, you'll be greeted by this bronze bull statue.*

**County**
Hillsborough

**Endpoints**
Goffstown Rail Trail at Agnes St., 0.3 mile northeast of Pinard St., to the junction with the Heritage Trail at Riverwalk Way, 0.5 mile south of Line Dr., in Merrimack River Park–South Parcel (Manchester)

**Mileage**
2.1

**Type**
Rail-Trail

**Roughness Index**
1

**Surface**
Asphalt

with a mix of funding sources, including a donation from the Singer family, the new bridge now carries happy commuters, families, and pets.

The route crosses under Pinard Street and then begins to loosely parallel the Piscataquog River, offering numerous connections to Piscataquog River Park. Preserving most of the stretch of river from the dam to the Merrimack River, the park offers its own system of hiking trails and is a popular retreat for fishing or just relaxing in nature. On the south side of the Piscataquog Trail, you'll find West Side Ice Arena—a primary trail access point with further access to the water— and baseball diamonds. On the north side, you'll find Thibault Field, which offers restrooms and convenient parking about 0.75 mile from the western endpoint.

Just after passing under Granite Street, look up and to your left for a colorful collection of birdhouses that stands guard over the trail, where you might spot a chickadee, warbler, northern cardinal, or purple finch, the latter of which is New Hampshire's state bird.

You'll sense the city nearby as you emerge from the trees and cross South Main Street in the Piscataquog neighborhood. In just 0.25 mile, you'll enter the Hands Across the Merrimack Bridge, which was completed in 2008 after a conversion from an existing B&M truss bridge. The wide, wooden plank bridge takes you up and over I-293 and then the river and offers an exciting bike-pedestrian alternative to the Granite Street bridge upstream. If you're not quite

*This pretty bridge crosses over the Piscataquog River at the west end of the trail, where it meets the Goffstown Rail Trail (see page 105).*

ready to finish the trail, you'll find numerous benches and plenty of room to stop and enjoy the river views. You may even spot a bald eagle.

Once across the river, you'll meet the bronze bull statue that was erected to "commemorate Manchester's entrepreneurial tradition as exemplified by the founders and employees of Granite State Packing Company and Jac Pac Foods." Here, you'll also find the trail's terminus in Merrimack River Park South Parcel, as well as a connection to the Heritage Trail, which you can take about 0.1 mile north to Delta Dental Stadium and the rest of New Hampshire's Queen City.

CONTACT: manchesternh.gov/Departments/Parks-and-Recreation/Parks
-Facilities/Recreational-Trails/Piscataquog-Trail

## DIRECTIONS

To reach the northwestern endpoint in Manchester from I-293, take Exit 5 for Granite St. toward West Manchester. Head southwest on Granite St., and go 0.1 mile. Use the left two lanes to turn left onto S. Main St., and go 0.3 mile. Turn right onto Varney St., go 0.4 mile, and continue onto Mast Road/NH 114A 1.1 miles. Turn right onto Laurier St., and go 0.2 mile. Laurier St. turns slightly left and becomes Louis St. Turn right into the Sarette Recreation Complex, and look for parking on your left.

To reach parking at West Side Ice Arena from I-293 S, take Exit 6 for Amoskeag St. toward Goffstown Road. Turn left onto Eddy Road, and go 0.4 mile. Turn right onto Bremer St. and go 1.1 miles. Turn left onto Electric St. and cross over the trail, going 0.2 mile to the arena straight ahead. From I-293 N, take Exit 6, and turn left onto Amoskeag St. Immediately after crossing under I-293, turn left onto Eddy Road, and follow the directions above.

To reach parking at Thibault Field from I-293, follow the directions above, but take Bremer St. for only 0.6 mile. Turn left onto Boutwell St. and go 0.2 mile. Turn right onto Amory St., and then immediately turn left onto Cumberland St. Go 0.2 mile, and turn right onto Putnam St. Immediately turn right onto Douglas St., and head straight into the parking lot.

To reach parking along South Commercial St. (street has a 10-hour limit) from I-293, take Exit 5. Head east on Granite St., and turn right onto S. Commercial St. in 0.2 mile. No designated trail parking is available at Delta Dental Stadium.

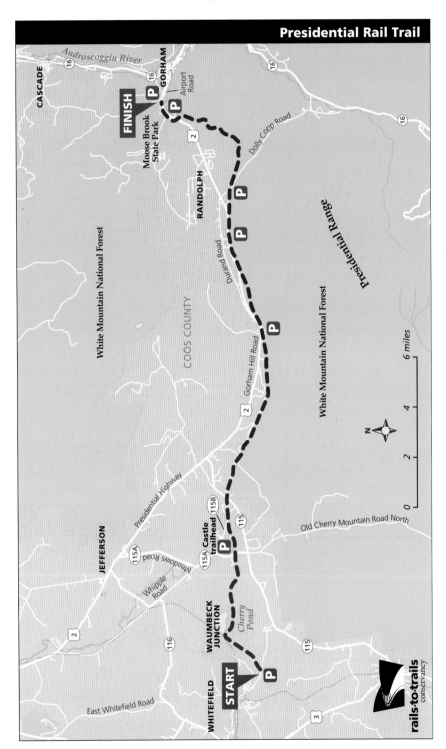

L ocated in the scenic Presidential Range in the White Mountains, the Presidential Rail Trail is a scenic and pleasant route, providing an alternative view of Mount Washington and the surrounding area. The mountain peaks provide the area with both its name—each peak is named after a different president—and its reputation for having some of the worst weather in the United States. The areas surrounding the peaks are a different story; weather off the peaks is pleasant in summer, and the trail provides stellar views of the range. The area is also home to a wide range of wildlife, including moose, black bears, wild turkeys, and other birds, as well as beavers and otters.

Starting at the western trailhead on Airport Road, the terrain is gentle, sloping slightly upward. Nearby is a hiking trail that leads 1.6 miles to Cherry Pond. Around Waumbeck Junction, about 1.5 miles into the trail, you'll

**County**
Coös

**Endpoints**
Airport Road at Cherry Pond Trail, 1.4 miles west of NH 115 (Whitefield), to US 2/Lancaster Road between High St. and Lilac Lane (Gorham)

**Mileage**
19.2

**Type**
Rail-Trail

**Roughness Index**
2

**Surfaces**
Crushed Stone, Grass, Gravel

*The Presidential Range provides a postcard-perfect backdrop for a trail ride.*

pass near the pond on your left. The trail then crosses several small brooks, starting with Stanley Slide Brook in 1.8 miles. The trail crosses NH 115A in 0.6 mile, then 0.1 mile after that is Mill Brook, and 0.2 mile after that is Red Brook.

The trail then passes through a sprawling residential area, where the terrain is slightly rough and grassy in places. The western half of the trail is less traveled and a bit rougher in spots.

In 6.6 miles you'll come to the Castle trailhead, after crossing NH 115A. Continuing east the trail crosses a historic pony truss bridge over Snyder Brook, 3 miles after the Castle trailhead. The route passes by a parking lot in Randolph near the Appalachia trailhead (not to be confused with the Appalachian Trail), just a few feet from US 2, and then begins the downhill slope toward Gorham. This portion makes for an especially fun ride, as the trail smooths out and slopes gently downward, with more stunning views of the mountain range. Several bridges here cross over the Moose River, the first one 2.3 miles after Snyder Brook.

After the last Moose River crossing, the trail approaches Gorham for the remaining 1.7 miles, intersecting other trails that are mostly for snowmobile use. The eastern endpoint of the trail is located in Gorham, home of the Gorham Historical Society and Railroad Museum and Moose Brook State Park, a great place for camping, picnicking, and fishing. The Appalachian Trail is located just a few miles farther east, cutting a north-south path beside the Rattle River and over US 2 (go to **appalachiantrail.org** for more info).

**CONTACT: friendsofthepresidentialrailtrail.org**

## DIRECTIONS

To reach the western trailhead in Whitefield from I-93, take Exit 40, and turn right (east) on US 302. In 11.1 miles turn left onto US 3. In 2 miles turn right onto NH 115 N. Go 4.4 miles, and turn left onto Hazen Road. In 0.5 mile, continue onto Airport Road. In 0.9 mile, an industrial road will appear on the left, with the western trailhead and parking lot on the right.

To reach the eastern endpoint in Gorham from I-93, take Exit 40, and turn right (east) on US 302. In 11.1 miles turn left onto US 3. In 2 miles turn right onto NH 115, and go 9.7 miles. Turn right onto US 2, go 11.6 miles, and a parking lot will appear to the left with signs for the Presidential Rail Trail. The trail begins on the north side of the lot.

Crossing through wooded areas and featuring magnificent wetland vistas, the Rockingham Recreational Rail Trail (Fremont Branch) offers an 18.3-mile trail adventure from Epping to Windham. The northern section of this route has a dirt surface, but it is generally usable and enjoyable for mountain biking and hiking. In winter snowmobiling is permitted on this stretch. The longer southern section, from NH 107 in Fremont to Windham, has a loose sand surface difficult for any type of bike and is only suited for hiking. ATVs and motorbikes also use this section in spring, summer, and fall.

*Crossing through wooded areas and wetlands, the trail offers a challenging but rewarding adventure from Epping to Derry.*

**County**
Rockingham

**Endpoints**
Main St. south of Railroad Ave. at the intersection with Rockingham Recreational Trail (Portsmouth Branch) (Epping) to just east of Depot Road at Frost Road at the intersection with Windham Rail Trail (Windham)

**Mileage**
18.3

**Type**
Rail-Trail

**Roughness Index**
2–3

**Surfaces**
Dirt, Sand

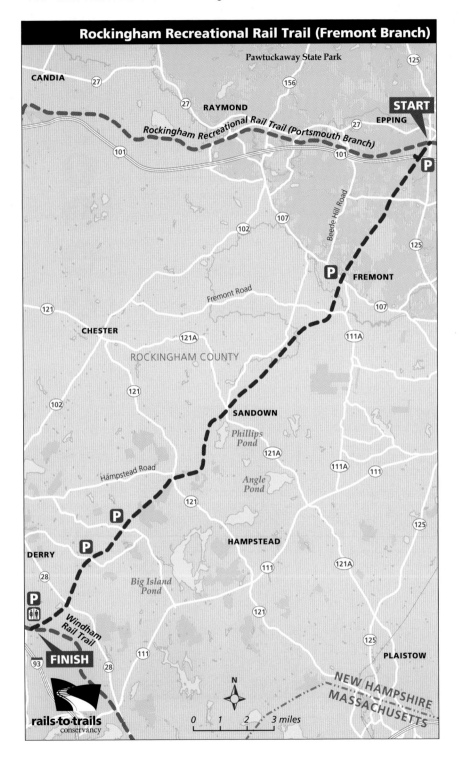

**Rockingham Recreational Rail Trail (Fremont Branch)**

Pawtuckaway State Park

CANDIA

RAYMOND

Rockingham Recreational Rail Trail (Portsmouth Branch)

START

EPPING

Beede Hill Road

FREMONT

CHESTER

ROCKINGHAM COUNTY

SANDOWN

Phillips Pond

Fremont Road

Hampstead Road

Angle Pond

HAMPSTEAD

DERRY

Big Island Pond

Windham Rail Trail

FINISH

PLAISTOW

NEW HAMPSHIRE
MASSACHUSETTS

N

0   1   2   3 miles

rails-to-trails
conservancy

Starting in Epping, the trail's endpoint intersects the Rockingham Recreational Rail Trail (Portsmouth Branch), see page 143, at Main Street; here, you can take the 28-mile trail east to Newfields or west to Manchester. Traveling south on the Fremont Branch from the Epping trailhead, you'll immediately cross underneath NH 101 via a narrow but passable tunnel. The trail then continues through a delightful wooded section and passes by some farms.

The route alternates between wooded areas and large wetland clearings, with ample opportunities for viewing wildlife and colorful summer wildflower displays. Continuing south, you'll enter the town of Fremont in about 4.5 miles.

A clearly marked trailhead in Fremont includes a parking area right after you cross NH 107. Bicycle use is not recommended after this point. The remaining 12 miles between Fremont and Windham are open to and actively used by ATVs and motorbikes. Use caution while walking along this section of trail.

This segment offers a delightful setting for hikers as it makes its way south below high tree canopies and bisects wetlands and ponds. In Sandown, you will pass an old railroad car and a former railroad station that offer a glimpse into the corridor's past. The trail then enters Derry through forested areas and ends in Windham about 1.3 miles after you pass NH 28.

The Rockingham Recreational Rail Trail (Fremont Branch) makes a seamless junction with the Windham Rail Trail (see page 155) near the latter trail's northern terminus by the Windham Depot, where parking is available. The Windham Depot also connects to the Derry Rail Trail (see page 92) about 0.2 mile farther northwest. Note that both of these trails are paved, and while they do accommodate snowmobiling in winter, ATV use is not permitted on either trail.

**CONTACT: nhstateparks.org/visit/recreational-rail-trails/rockingham-recreational -trail-fremont.aspx**

**SEE NEXT PAGE FOR DIRECTIONS**

# DIRECTIONS

To reach the Epping trailhead from I-93, take Exit 7 onto NH 101 toward Portsmouth. Head east 19 miles, and take Exit 7 for NH 125 toward Epping/Kingston. Turn left (north) onto NH 125, and go 0.4 mile. Turn left onto Main St., and then turn left into the parking lot; look for spaces immediately to your right.

To reach the Fremont trailhead from I-93, take Exit 7 onto NH 101 toward Portsmouth. Head east 14.6 miles, and take Exit 5 for NH 107. Turn left (south) onto NH 107/Freetown Road, go 0.8 mile, and then turn left to continue on NH 107 S/Main St. for 3.5 miles. Turn right into the trailhead parking lot, which is across from Jackie Bernier Dr.

To reach parking near the southern endpoint on Island Pond Road from I-93, take Exit 4 for NH 102 toward Derry/Londonderry. Head northeast onto NH 102/Nashua Road (signs for Derry), and go 0.9 mile. Turn right onto Fordway, go 0.1 mile, and turn left onto South Ave. After 0.5 mile, turn right onto Birch St., and go 0.6 mile. Turn left onto Rockingham Road, and go 0.7 mile. Continue straight onto Island Pond Road for 2.3 miles. Look for a small parking area on your right.

To reach the trailhead at Windham Depot from I-93 N, take Exit 3 onto NH 111 W toward Windham. Head west 1.6 miles, and turn right onto N. Lowell Road. Go 2.6 miles, and turn right onto Depot Road. Go 0.1 mile, and turn right into the depot parking lot. Parking is prohibited at Windham Depot from 30 minutes after sunset to 30 minutes before sunrise.

To reach the trailhead at Windham Depot from I-93 S, take Exit 4 onto NH 102 toward Derry/Londonderry. Turn left (east) onto NH 102/Nashua Road (signs for Derry), and go 0.9 mile. Turn right onto Fordway, go 0.5 mile, and then continue onto Fordway Extension for 0.9 mile. Turn left onto Bowers Road, and go 0.6 mile. Turn right onto Windham Road, and go 1.3 miles. Continue onto N. Lowell Road 0.2 mile, and then turn left onto Depot Road. Turn right into the depot parking lot after 0.2 mile. Again, note that parking is prohibited at Windham Depot from 30 minutes after sunset to 30 minutes before sunrise.

The Rockingham Recreational Rail Trail brings at least two superlatives to mind: it's one of New Hampshire's longest rail-trails at just more than 28 miles, and it begins in Manchester, the state's largest city. Travelers will find lakes and forests here, as well as former mill towns where they can stock up, relax, or visit historic buildings and relics left over from the railroad days.

The Boston and Maine Railroad was the last to run trains on the Portsmouth Branch between Newfields and Manchester, selling the corridor to the state in 1988. The oldest railway section dates to about 1850 and was built by the Portsmouth and Concord Railroad. Succeeding railroads finished other sections of the Portsmouth Branch to Manchester in the early 1860s. The eastern section of the branch from Newfields to Portsmouth is still in service, while service to Epping, Raymond, Candia, Auburn, and Manchester ended in 1982.

The first 2 miles of trail in Manchester are scheduled for paving by the end of 2018, while gravel or crushed rock covers the rest. There are few at-grade road intersections east of

*In Raymond you'll find a restored train station, which displays a locomotive, a caboose, and a push car.*

**Counties**
Hillsborough, Rockingham

**Endpoints**
Mammoth Road/NH 28A between Nelson St. and Porter St. (Manchester) to Ash Swamp Road near Exeter Road/NH 108 (Newfields)

**Mileage**
28.1

**Type**
Rail-Trail

**Roughness Index**
2

**Surfaces**
Asphalt, Crushed Stone, Dirt, Grass, Gravel, Sand

# Rockingham Recreational Rail Trail (Portsmouth Branch)

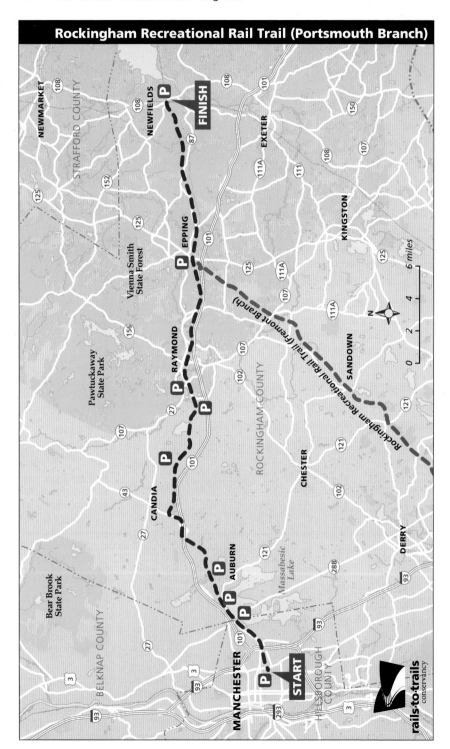

town, as the old railbed passes beneath the roads. Some of these underpasses have low ceilings, however, as the bottom of the culverts are planked with wood, so cyclists and equestrians should be prepared to dismount. In winter cross-country skiing, snowshoeing, snowmobiling, and dogsledding are permitted.

Beginning on the paved trail at Mammoth Road/NH 28A, you head east for 0.9 mile to a tunnel under I-93/NH 101. The packed gravel starts at Lake Shore Road (mile 2). In another 0.5 mile you arrive at the trailhead for 2,500-acre Massabesic Lake, the source of water for Manchester. It's also home to deer, fox, loons, and other wildlife. This is a popular trailhead for the rail-trail because of adequate parking and the scenic location. Motorized use is prohibited west of here in Manchester.

About 8.5 miles from that trailhead, you'll cross paths with railroad history at a marker for the demolished site of an 1889 railroad station on Depot Road in East Candia. The railbed rises above the forest floor in places here, while other stretches thread through high-walled cuts blasted through New Hampshire's famous granite.

From East Candia, you'll travel 4 miles to a surviving railroad station in Raymond. Originally built in 1893 and restored by the Raymond Historical Society, the station features local museum collections inside and railroad relics, such as a locomotive, a caboose, and a push car, outside. You'll find plenty of places for food and refreshment near the depot and on the outskirts of town in 1 mile.

In 4.7 miles the trail passes through Epping, where you'll find more services and a junction with the Fremont Branch of the Rockingham Recreational Rail Trail (see page 139), which heads south a little over 18 miles to Windham.

The last 7.3 miles passes through more forestland and ends at the still-standing circa 1891 Rockingham Junction railroad station, which served the Boston and Maine Railroad's Main Line and Portsmouth Branch. Trains operated by Pan Am Railways still pass this station.

CONTACT: nhstateparks.org/visit/recreational-rail-trails/rockingham-recreational -trail-portsmouth.aspx

## DIRECTIONS

While a small parking lot is located at the western end of the trail, the best place to park is at Massabesic Lake, which has ample parking. To reach the Massabesic Lake trailhead from I-93, take Exit 7 onto NH 101 toward Portsmouth. Head east 1.5 miles, and take Exit 1 onto NH Bypass 28B/Londonderry Turnpike toward Auburn. Turn right, go 0.3 mile, and turn right into the parking lot, just after the traffic circle. The trail begins 2.6 miles west in Manchester.

To reach the Newfields trailhead from I-93, take Exit 7 onto NH 101 toward Portsmouth. Head east 25.8 miles, and take Exit 10 onto NH 85 N toward Newfields. Turn left, go 3.3 miles, and turn left onto NH 108/College Road/Exeter Road. Go 0.8 mile, and turn left onto Ash Swamp Road. Go 0.2 mile, and the trailhead and parking are on the right (just before Ash Swamp Road makes a sharp turn right).

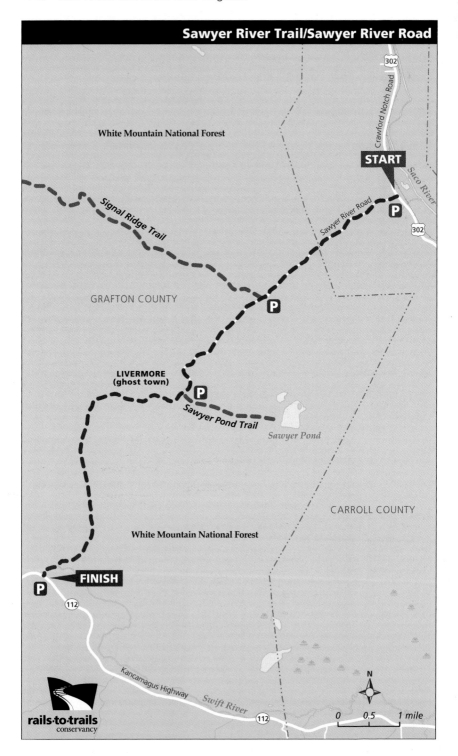

# Sawyer River Trail/Sawyer River Road

302

Crawford Notch Road

White Mountain National Forest

START

Signal Ridge Trail

Sawyer River Road

Saco River

P

302

GRAFTON COUNTY

P

LIVERMORE
(ghost town)

P

Sawyer Pond Trail

Sawyer Pond

CARROLL COUNTY

White Mountain National Forest

FINISH

P

112

rails·to·trails
conservancy

Kancamagus Highway   Swift River

112

N

0        0.5        1 mile

The Sawyer River Trail/Sawyer River Road lies deep in the forested heart of the 1,200-square-mile White Mountain National Forest. The 7.5-mile route traces an old logging railroad that's now part forest road and part singletrack. Alert visitors might even stumble across the foundations of a ghost town in the undergrowth.

The corridor follows the old Sawyer River Railroad, which served the logging operations of the Grafton County Lumber Co. between 1876 and 1927. The Saunders family owned the lumber company, the mill, the railroad, and the town of Livermore located in the center of logging operations. The rough terrain and frequent use of aging equipment contributed to more than 30 derailments over the life of the railroad, which was finally done in by a devastating flood in 1927. Most Livermore residents left soon thereafter.

*Deep in the heart of White Mountain National Forest, the Sawyer River Trail provides a scenic trek along an old logging railroad.*

**Counties**
Carroll, Grafton

**Endpoints**
US 302/Crawford Notch Road 1.5 miles south of Lucy Road (Hart's Location) to NH 112/Kancamagus Hwy. between Livermore North trailhead (near Lily Pond) and Sugar Hill Overlook (Lincoln)

**Mileage**
7.5

**Type**
Rail-Trail

**Roughness Index**
3

**Surfaces**
Ballast, Dirt, Grass, Sand

The lightly traveled Sawyer River Road starts at US 302 and follows the forested river valley 4 miles to a U.S. Forest Service gate, where it meets the 3.5-mile Sawyer River Trail. The road is closed in winter when snowmobilers, cross-country skiers, snowshoers, and dogsledders take to the corridor. In summer visitors hike or ride mountain bikes down the road or drive to trailheads deeper in the forest.

Starting at the trailhead at Sawyer River Road on US 302/Crawford Notch Road (technically located in Carroll County), you'll begin a trek that gains almost 900 feet through the forest to Kancamagus Highway, although most elevation gain is in the first 4 miles. In 2 miles, keep your eyes open for crumbled walls and building foundations among the trees. This is the abandoned town of Livermore, once home to nearly 200 people. As you poke through the woods and down the hillside toward the Sawyer River, you might identify the remains of the brick power plant, the store, and houses, including the Saunders's mansion that stood here until it burned down in the 1960s.

The junction with the Signal Ridge Trail is also in this vicinity, climbing 5 miles to the Mount Carrigain Fire Tower. You'll arrive at parking and a major trail junction in another 1.9 miles at a U.S. Forest Service gate at the end of Sawyer River Road. Past the gate, the Sawyer Pond Trail heads left over a footbridge, while the Sawyer River Trail stays straight. You'll pass a snowmobile trail on the right. Continue over a logging bridge and Sawyer River Trail turns off to the right and becomes a singletrack trail.

Flooding caused by beaver dams creates some detours on the Sawyer River Trail. The grade flattens out, but the trail still provides mountain bikers with technical challenges. You might see old railroad ties, bridge supports, and other hints to the trail's past.

Approaching the trail's end, you'll reach the Swift River, where boulders facilitate crossing. *Note:* High water can make the crossing difficult and dangerous in spring. This is a great spot for lunch, however, and one of the best swimming holes around. Just beyond the river is the Kancamagus Highway trailhead.

CONTACT: 603-447-5448; **www.fs.usda.gov/recarea/whitemountain /recarea/?recid=74933**

## DIRECTIONS

To reach the northern trailhead from I-93, take Exit 40 onto US 302/NH 10 toward Bethlehem and Twin Mountain. Turn right (east), go 29.9 miles, and look for Sawyer River Road on the right. Parking is available next to the road, as well as at trailheads 2 miles and 3.9 miles down Sawyer River Road.

To reach the southern trailhead from I-93, take Exit 32 onto NH 112 E/Kancamagus Hwy. Turn left (northeast), go 16.6 miles, and look for trailhead parking on the left.

**V**isitors to the Sugar River Trail (also known as the Sugar River Recreational Rail Trail) can be forgiven if they lose track of which side of the river they're traveling. The 9.5-mile trail crosses its namesake river seven times—twice on covered bridges—between Newport and the outskirts of Claremont. The trail meets the Bobby Woodman Trail, which completes the run into Claremont.

The route follows a railroad corridor built in the 1870s by the Sugar River Railroad for the Concord and Claremont Railway. The Boston and Maine Railroad acquired this electric railway in 1887 and renamed it the Claremont Branch. In the first decade of the 1900s, the railroad rebuilt many of the river crossings as covered bridges; two remained after the railroad stopped using the railbed between Newport and Claremont in 1977.

*The Sugar River Trail offers not just one but two covered bridges.*

**County**
Sullivan

**Endpoints**
Belknap Ave. near N. Meadow Road (Newport) to Washington St./NH 11/NH 103 at Roberts Hill Road and Bobby Woodman Trail (Claremont)

**Mileage**
9.5

**Type**
Rail-Trail

**Roughness Index**
2

**Surfaces**
Gravel, Ballast

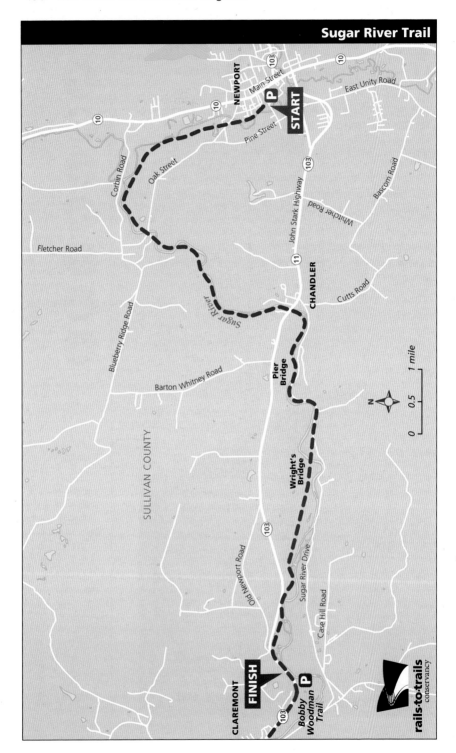

**Sugar River Trail**

NEWPORT

START
P
103
10
Main Street
East Unity Road
10
Pine Street
Corbin Road
Oak Street
John Stark Highway
103
Whitcher Road
Bascom Road
Fletcher Road
11
CHANDLER
Cutts Road
Sugar River
Blueberry Ridge Road
Barton Whitney Road
Pier Bridge
N
1 mile
0.5
0
SULLIVAN COUNTY
Wright's Bridge
103
Old Newport Road
Sugar River Drive
Case Hill Road
CLAREMONT
FINISH
P
Bobby Woodman Trail
103

rails·to·trails
conservancy

The Sugar River Trail is one of only a few state trails that allow ATV use, as well as trail bikes (a type of off-highway recreational vehicle), after the snows melt; mountain bikers, hikers, equestrians, snowmobilers, and cross-country skiers also use the trail year-round (snowshoeing and dogsledding are also permitted). Wildlife is abundant in the secluded woodlands; watch for deer, rabbits, beavers, raccoons, wild turkeys, and even the occasional moose around the next bend.

The trail takes a circuitous route between the historic mill towns of Newport and Claremont as it follows the Sugar River valley. Beginning in Newport, you'll find the town has several historical buildings and a Main Street that looks like a movie set for the 1800s, with brick storefronts, clock towers on public buildings, and church steeples. The trailhead on Belknap Avenue is only a few blocks from downtown.

Passing through forest for 2.5 miles, the trail crosses three trestles in quick succession. In another 3 miles, you'll arrive at the first covered bridge, known as Pier Bridge for its central pier. The second covered bridge, Wright's Bridge, appears 1.2 miles after you pass through Chandler.

The Boston and Maine Railroad built these in 1907 and 1906, respectively, as replacement spans. These are two of eight surviving railroad covered bridges in the United States. Unlike covered bridges on New England roadways, these are much narrower and taller, with 21 feet of vertical clearance. While covered bridges sheltered pedestrians and horse-drawn wagons in historic times, the railroads covered their wooden bridges to protect the trusses from the ravages of weather.

The trail passes through woods and then meets up with NH 11/NH 103 before reaching a junction with the Bobby Woodman Trail on the outskirts of Claremont. The Bobby Woodman Trail heads 2.3 miles into downtown Claremont. You'll find many opportunities for food and services along the way.

**CONTACT:** nhstateparks.org/visit/state-parks/sugar-river.aspx

## DIRECTIONS

To reach the Newport trailhead from I-89, take Exit 9 onto NH 103 W toward Newport. Turn right (west), go 19.1 miles, and make a slight left to join NH 11 W. Go 3.2 miles into Newport, and take the second right off the traffic circle onto N. Main St./NH 10. Go 0.2 mile, and turn left onto Belknap Ave.; then go 0.2 mile, and look for the trailhead parking on the right at Newport Recreation Department.

To reach the trailhead on the outskirts of Claremont from I-89, take Exit 12 onto NH 11 W toward Sunapee. Head west 7.6 miles, and bear right to join NH 103. Go 3.2 miles into Newport, and take the fourth right off the traffic circle onto N. Main St./NH 11/NH 103. Go 0.2 mile, and turn right onto NH 11/NH 103/Elm St.; then go 0.2 mile, and veer left to stay on NH 11/NH 103. Go 6.9 miles, and look for trailhead parking on the left.

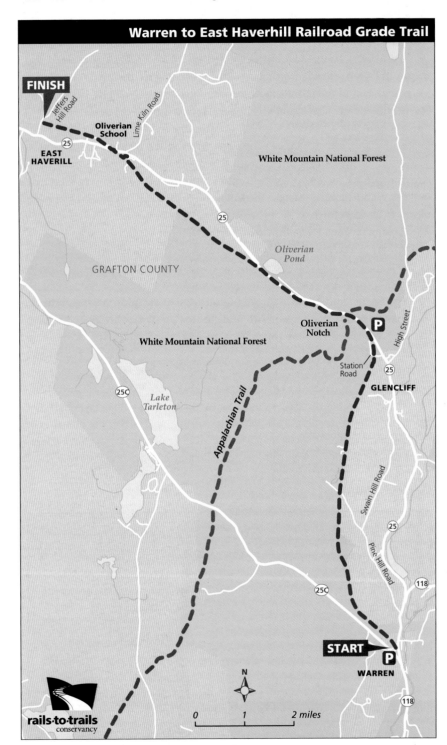

## Warren to East Haverhill Railroad Grade Trail

**FINISH**

Jeffers Hill Road

**Oliverian School**

Lime Kiln Road

(25)

**EAST HAVERILL**

White Mountain National Forest

(25)

*Oliverian Pond*

**GRAFTON COUNTY**

Oliverian Notch

**P**

High Street

White Mountain National Forest

Station Road

(25)

**GLENCLIFF**

(25C)

*Lake Tarleton*

Appalachian Trail

Swain Hill Road

(25)

Pine Hill Road

(118)

(25C)

**START**

**P**

**WARREN**

N

(118)

**rails·to·trails**
conservancy

0     1     2 miles

Many rail-trails start at a vintage depot, an old caboose, or a rusty locomotive acquired by the local historical society. The Warren to East Haverhill Railroad Grade Trail, however, starts at the base of a surplus 70-foot Redstone missile delivered in 1971 to inspire local youth about the space program. It's the same type of missile that launched Derry native Alan Shepard into space in 1961. It's a good place to blast off down a 10.8-mile dirt trail into the White Mountains.

Warren and Haverhill were two stops on the Boston and Maine Railroad's White Mountains Division that ran between Concord and Woodsville on the Vermont border. The original charter in 1844 went to the Boston, Concord and Montreal Railroad, which finished the line through New Hampshire by 1853. Mergers eventually put it under the control of the Boston and Maine Railroad in 1895. The line supported the timber and tourism industries until it ceased operations in 1954 as cars and trucks took over.

*The trail's hard-packed dirt surface is popular for all types of trail uses, including horseback riding.*

**County**
Grafton

**Endpoints**
Water St. and School St. (Warren) to Jeffers Hill Road between Dickinson Road and Mt. Moosilauke Hwy./NH 25 (Haverhill)

**Mileage**
10.8

**Type**
Rail-Trail

**Roughness Index**
3

**Surface**
Dirt

Formerly the Warren Recreational Trail and also known as the Jesse E. Bushaw Memorial Trail or New Hampshire Snowmobile Corridor No. 5, the rail-trail takes an easy grade uphill from Warren to the westernmost pass through the White Mountains at Glencliff, and then descends to East Haverhill. Off-highway recreational vehicles, including trail bikes, are allowed only as far as Glencliff, but snowmobiles can continue beyond. In addition to snowmobiling and cross-country skiing, snowshoeing and dogsledding are permitted in winter.

The Redstone rocket trailhead is set amid the village school, town hall, a church, and a restaurant (an ice cream parlor is a block away). The trail starts uphill on the railroad grade and soon enters a forest.

About 4.6 miles up the trail, you'll cross Station Road in Glencliff. Originally called Warren Summit, the town was renamed Glencliff after confusion over its name—being similar to that of nearby Warren—resulted in a train collision. Beginning in 1909, the railroad depot here served passengers heading to the Glencliff Sanatorium, a treatment center for tuberculosis patients seeking fresh mountain air. The complex on Mount Moosilauke is still open today as a home for the elderly.

If you see haggard backpackers here, they're probably headed to the community's post office. The Appalachian Trail passes over Oliverian Notch here, and hikers use this as a mail drop. A hostel and grocer in the village also cater to hikers. You'll cross the Appalachian Trail 0.4 mile ahead as it runs close to NH 25/Mt. Moosilauke Highway.

The rail-trail runs alongside the road, passing the Oliverian Pond, and then veers back into the forest. Concrete blocks restrict motorized use on the rail-trail through a wildlife preserve. You'll arrive at athletic fields for the Oliverian School 2.5 miles past the pond, cross NH 25, and then take the trail across the boarding school campus (motorized vehicles are prohibited on the trail here). The route continues another mile to Jeffers Hill Road.

**CONTACT:** nhstateparks.org/visit/recreational-rail-trails/warren-recreational-trail.aspx

## DIRECTIONS

To reach the Warren trailhead from I-93, take Exit 26 onto NH 3A/NH 25 toward Rumney. Head southwest 4 miles, and take the first exit off the traffic circle to stay on NH 25 W. Go 7.4 miles, and stay straight where NH 118 joins NH 25. Go another 8.1 miles, and bear left onto NH 25C/Lake Tarleton Road; then turn right onto School St. The trailhead is about 0.2 mile ahead where Water St. and School St. intersect. Street parking is available along School St.

There is no official trail parking at the northern end.

The Windham Rail Trail passes through the woodsy periphery of Windham in southern New Hampshire, but it sits in the heart of the future cross-state Granite State Rail Trail. Its connections to the Derry Rail Trail (see page 92) in the north and the Salem Bike-Ped Corridor in the south make up the longest paved section—10 miles— of a future 125-mile route between Massachusetts and Vermont that will combine several trails.

The trail follows a railbed taken out of service by the Boston and Maine Railroad in 1980. Rail service first came to Windham in the 1840s with the Manchester and Lawrence Railroad, which carried freight and passengers to the growing industrial belt. A 3-mile section through Windham cost the most to build because of extensive rock cutting and the filling of lowlands. The Boston and Maine gained control in 1887. After the line fell into disuse, it became a gravel multiuse trail; Windham finished paving the path in 2016.

At the northern trailhead near the Derry town line, explore the Boston and Maine Railroad C-16 caboose and the restored 1849 Windham Depot and freight terminal. The station served the busy junction between the Manchester and Lawrence Division and the Worcester, Nashua & Portland Division of the Boston and Maine Railroad. Today the trailhead serves as a rail-trail crossroads with

**County**
Rockingham

**Endpoints**
Derry Rail Trail at N. Lowell Road/Windham Road at Brown Road to Salem Bike-Ped Corridor at Range Road at NH 28/N. Broadway (Windham)

**Mileage**
4.3

**Type**
Rail-Trail

**Roughness Index**
1

**Surface**
Asphalt

*At the northern trailhead near the Derry town line, explore the Boston and Maine Railroad C-16 caboose and the restored 1849 Windham Depot and freight terminal.*

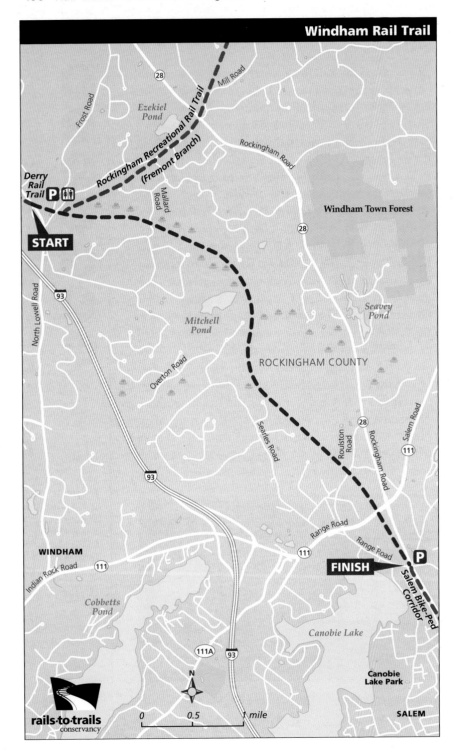

# Windham Rail Trail

28

Mill Road

Frost Road

*Ezekiel Pond*

Rockingham Recreational Rail Trail

(Fremont Branch)

Rockingham Road

**Windham Town Forest**

Derry Rail Trail P 🚻

**START**

Mallard Road

28

93

North Lowell Road

*Mitchell Pond*

*Seavey Pond*

ROCKINGHAM COUNTY

Overton Road

93

Searles Road

Roulston Road

28

Rockingham Road

Salem Road

111

**WINDHAM**

111

Indian Rock Road

Range Road

111

Range Road

P

**FINISH**

Salem Bike-Ped Corridor

*Cobbetts Pond*

*Canobie Lake*

111A   93

N

**Canobie Lake Park**

**rails-to-trails**
conservancy

0      0.5      1 mile

**SALEM**

the Rockingham Recreational Rail Trail (Fremont Branch), see page 139, heading northeast and the future Windham Greenway heading west.

You'll meet the Derry Rail Trail 0.2 mile northwest of the trailhead. That paved trail continues north 4 miles into downtown Derry. In the other direction, the trail passes between the old station and freight house and enters a wooded area that borders most of the path.

You'll pass two marshy areas as you follow Flatrock Brook and cross over Mallard Road in the first mile. Mitchell Pond comes into view on the right in 0.8 mile. This area presented problems for the railroad builders as the railbed kept sinking into a meadow. Not far past the pond, you'll fall into the shade of the first pass through rock, which also slowed railroad construction.

Scottish immigrants began settling in the Windham area in 1719 and turned to farming. You'll see the low stone walls that separated their fields as you head south along the path. Old stone cellars dug below the settlers' houses can also still be found in the woods. An old stone arch bridge, made of local granite, carries the trail across a stream at about mile 3. Not far past the bridge, you'll enter a rocky, 0.25-mile-long railroad cut through a nearly 30-foot hill. The effects of the shade, water seepage, and the cool breeze funneled through the cut—called the Rainforest Ledge—create a natural air-conditioning system in summer.

The only road crossing on the trail is at Roulston Road (no parking here), then you'll cross NH 111 on a modern pedestrian bridge at mile 3.6. The trail ends in 0.4 mile on Range Road, where you'll find a bicycle shop. Cross Range Road to pick up the Salem Bike-Ped Corridor.

**CONTACT: windhamrailtrail.org**

## DIRECTIONS

To reach the Windham Depot trailhead from I-93 N, take Exit 3 onto NH 111 W toward Windham. Head west 1.6 miles, and turn right onto N. Lowell Road. Go 2.6 miles, and turn right onto Depot Road. Go 0.1 mile, and turn right into the depot parking lot. Parking is prohibited at Windham Depot from 30 minutes after sunset to 30 minutes before sunrise.

To reach the Windham Depot trailhead from I-93 S, take Exit 4 onto NH 102 toward Derry/Londonderry. Turn left (east) onto NH 102/Nashua Road, and go 0.9 mile. Turn right onto Fordway, go 0.5 mile, and continue onto Fordway Extension 0.9 mile. Turn left onto Bowers Road, and go 0.6 mile. Turn right onto Windham Road, and go 1.3 miles. Continue on N. Lowell Road 0.2 mile, and turn left onto Depot Road. Turn right into the depot parking lot in 0.2 mile. Parking is prohibited at Windham Depot from 30 minutes after sunset to 30 minutes before sunrise.

To reach the southern trailhead for the Windham Rail Trail from I-93, take Exit 3 onto NH 111 E toward North Salem. Head east 0.9 mile, and turn right onto Range Road. Go 0.6 mile, and look for parking on the left at the corner of NH 28/N. Broadway.

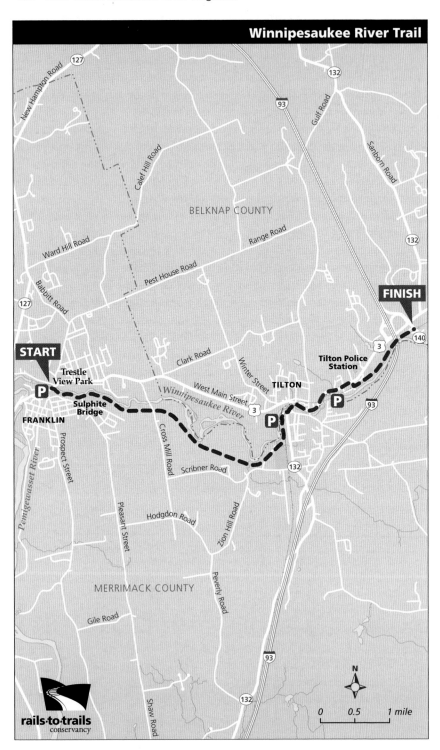

The Winnipesaukee River Trail runs along a rail line that previously connected the paper industry between Franklin and Tilton. Nicknamed the Paper City, Franklin saw the industry boom from the 1900s until the Great Depression. Historical remnants can still be found along the 5-mile trail. The flat path consists of a mixture of asphalt and crushed stone that hikers, bikers, and even four-legged friends can appreciate.

Before hitting the trail at Trestle View Park in Franklin, located on Central Street, enjoy some local restaurants and shops. The park also provides access to the Winnipesaukee River if you want to bring your kayak. From here, the 58-mile Northern Rail Trail (see page 128) is just a 1.4-mile bike ride away, heading west on Central and South Main Streets.

The western trailhead at Trestle View Park is hard to miss, as it's marked by a 15-foot-tall, black steel mill wheel. The Winnipesaukee River provides a welcoming call to trail users with the soothing sound of flowing water along the route. About 0.5 mile in, you will pass the Sulphite Bridge, also called the Upside Down Covered Bridge, to

*The Upside Down Covered Bridge—which allowed trains to cross the river on top of its structure, instead of through the center—is the last remaining bridge of its kind in the country.*

**Counties**
Belknap, Merrimack

**Endpoints**
Trestle View Park at US 3/NH 11/Central St. between E. Bow St. and Prospect St. (Franklin) to NH 140/Tilton Road, 400 feet east of US 3/NH 140 intersection (Tilton)

**Mileage**
5.1

**Type**
Rail-Trail/Rail-with-Trail

**Roughness Index**
2

**Surfaces**
Asphalt, Dirt, Crushed Stone, Gravel

your left. The bridge—which previously allowed trains to cross the river on top of its structure, instead of through the center—is listed on the National Register of Historic Places and is the last remaining bridge of its kind in the country. A fire in 1980 burned the interior of the bridge, which closed to traffic in 1973.

About 0.25 mile farther down the trail, you can see remnants of the paper mill on the far side of the river. Some sections of the path veer away from the river, but trail users can still experience the sights and sounds of birds, wildflowers, peaceful ponds, and perhaps even a beaver or two.

You approach the town of Tilton about 3 miles into the trail. Be cautious when entering this more urban area, as crosswalks are not clearly defined. Downtown Tilton offers local shops and restaurants, great places for a short break.

A wide sidewalk on the north side of East Main Street connects this newer trail section. Continue onto East Main Street 0.5 mile until you reach the Tilton Police Station trailhead to your right. Again, caution should be used when crossing the road here, as there is no designated crosswalk. This trailhead welcomes you with a beautiful wildflower garden and trestle bridge.

The remaining 0.9 mile runs along the rail line away from the road. Crossing under the I-93 overpass signifies that you are nearing the trail's end at Tilton Road. Even though this endpoint does not have any signage, it would be an ideal pickup or drop-off location. Alternatively, you can turn around to begin the return journey and enjoy a well-deserved treat back in Franklin.

**CONTACT: winnirivertrail.org**

## DIRECTIONS

To reach the western trailhead at Trestle View Park in Franklin from I-93, take Exit 20 for US 3/NH 11/NH 132 (toward NH 140/Tilton/Laconia if coming from the south, or toward E. Main St. if coming from the north). Turn right onto US 3 S/NH 11 W/Laconia Road, and go 4.2 miles, following signs for Tilton/Franklin. Keep an eye out for the 15-foot black steel mill wheel to your right, which signals your arrival at the park. The parking entrance will be to your right after passing the mill wheel and a small park sign.

To reach the eastern endpoint in Tilton from I-93 N, take Exit 20 and head straight onto NH 140/Tilton Road. From I-93 S, take Exit 20, and turn left onto US 3 N/NH 11 E. In 0.25 mile turn left onto NH 140/Tilton Road. In 400 feet, after passing an industrial road to your right, the eastern endpoint appears, emerging from its path through several parking lots.

To reach the Tilton Police Station trailhead from I-93, take Exit 20 for US 3/NH 11/NH 132 (toward NH 140/Tilton/Laconia if coming from the south, or toward E. Main St. if coming from the north). Turn right onto US 3 S/NH 11 W/NH 132 S/E. Main St. for about 1 mile. The police station will be on your right, with a dirt parking lot located across the street. Look for the wildflowers and boulders in the parking lot.

The WOW Trail is named after the three bodies of water that can be seen from this rail-trail: Lake Winnipesaukee, Opechee Bay, and Lake Winnisquam. This picturesque 2.7-mile trail shares a corridor with the Winnipesaukee Scenic Railroad between Meredith and Lakeport. The trail will eventually stretch 9 miles between Laconia and Belmont. This urban path provides diverse experiences for users, offering the serenity of nature as well as the comforts of local restaurants and shops. The route runs through the heart of downtown Laconia and connects to the Lake Winnisquam Scenic Trail (see page 111), also known as the Winni Trail, to the west.

Start your journey at the eastern trailhead in Laconia's Lakeport neighborhood, where the first mile of trail runs along the banks of Opechee Bay to the right. Beautiful murals and public art brighten this section of the trail, and

*The WOW Trail is named after the three bodies of water that can be seen from the route: Lake Winnipesaukee, Opechee Bay, and Lake Winnisquam.*

**County**
Belknap

**Endpoints**
Elm St. between Railroad Ave. and Union Ave. (Laconia) to Leslie E. Roberts Beach and Recreation Area at US 3/ NH 11 and Bus. US 3 (Belmont)

**Mileage**
2.7

**Type**
Rail-with-Trail

**Roughness Index**
1

**Surface**
Asphalt

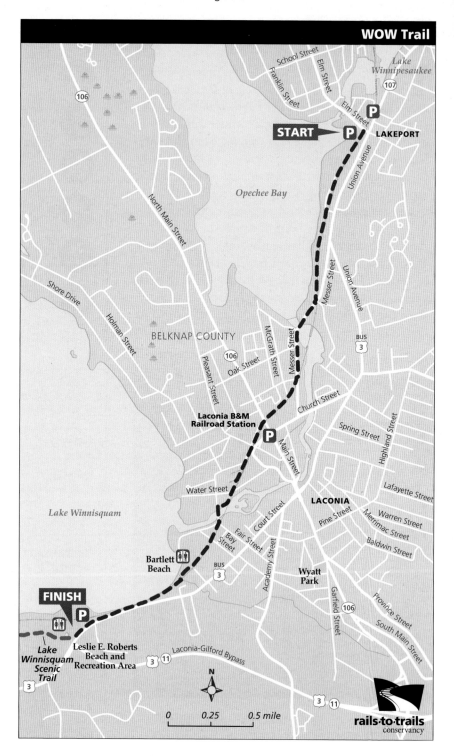

picnic tables are available if you want to stop and enjoy the view. After crossing over the bay, the next section runs through the heart of Laconia. In 0.5 mile from the bridge, you can't miss the former Laconia B&M Railroad Station, on the left just after you cross Main Street. Although passenger service ended in 1965, you can find shops and restaurants inside, as well as parking.

The remaining 1.2 miles of trail follow Lake Winnisquam, delivering picturesque vistas of the water, mountains, and wildlife. About 0.75 mile from the railroad station, Bartlett Beach is another site worth seeing. Here, there are seasonal restrooms, a playground, a volleyball court, picnic facilities, and water access. Look for signs for local restaurants if you need a bite to eat. The remaining portion of the trail continues along the water, ending at the Leslie E. Roberts Beach and Recreation Area, which has water access, restrooms, and parking. Fishing is allowed at the lake, with license-free fishing days occurring in January and June.

Here, the WOW Trail connects to the northern endpoint of the Lake Winnisquam Scenic Trail, a 1.8-mile path that winds through additional lakefront and wooded areas. The town of Belmont plans to connect the Lake Winnisquam Scenic Trail to the 5.1-mile Winnipesaukee River Trail to the west, toward Tilton and Franklin.

**CONTACT: wowtrail.org**

## DIRECTIONS

To reach the trail from I-93, take Exit 20 for US 3/NH 11 (toward NH 140/Tilton if coming from the south, or toward NH 132/E. Main St. if coming from the north). Turn left onto US 3 N/NH 11 E/Laconia Road, and go 6.5 miles, following signs for Belmont/Laconia. See directions below depending on the trailhead you wish to reach.

To reach the northeastern trailhead in Laconia, continue onto Bus. US 3 N 2.8 miles, then turn left onto Elm St. Take the first left onto Park St. to enter the parking lot. The trailhead is located near the Lake Opechee Inn and Spa.

To reach parking and a drop-off area for the trail at the former Laconia B&M Railroad Station, continue onto Bus. US 3 N 0.9 mile. Turn left onto Fair St., and go 0.4 mile. Make a slight right to continue onto New Salem St. for about 0.2 mile. The train station will appear to your right. Parking is available on either side of the station.

To reach the southwestern trailhead at the Leslie E. Roberts Beach and Recreation Area, turn left onto Leslie Roberts Dr. just before US 3 N/NH 11 E becomes Bus. US 3 N. The parking lot can be found less than 0.5 mile to the right.

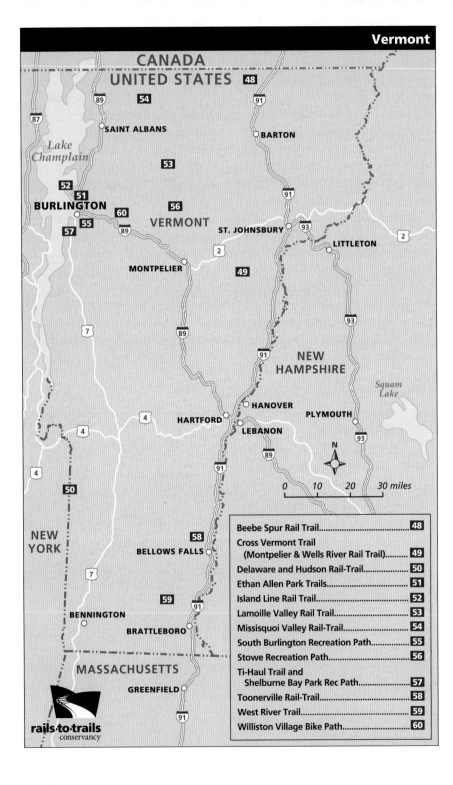

CANADA
UNITED STATES

Lake Champlain

SAINT ALBANS

BURLINGTON

VERMONT

MONTPELIER

BARTON

ST. JOHNSBURY

LITTLETON

NEW YORK

NEW HAMPSHIRE

Squam Lake

HANOVER

HARTFORD

LEBANON

PLYMOUTH

0    10    20    30 miles

BELLOWS FALLS

BENNINGTON

BRATTLEBORO

MASSACHUSETTS

GREENFIELD

rails·to·trails
conservancy

# Vermont

*The Montpelier & Wells River Rail Trail, a component of the Cross Vermont Trail (see page 169), traverses Groton State Forest and three state parks.*

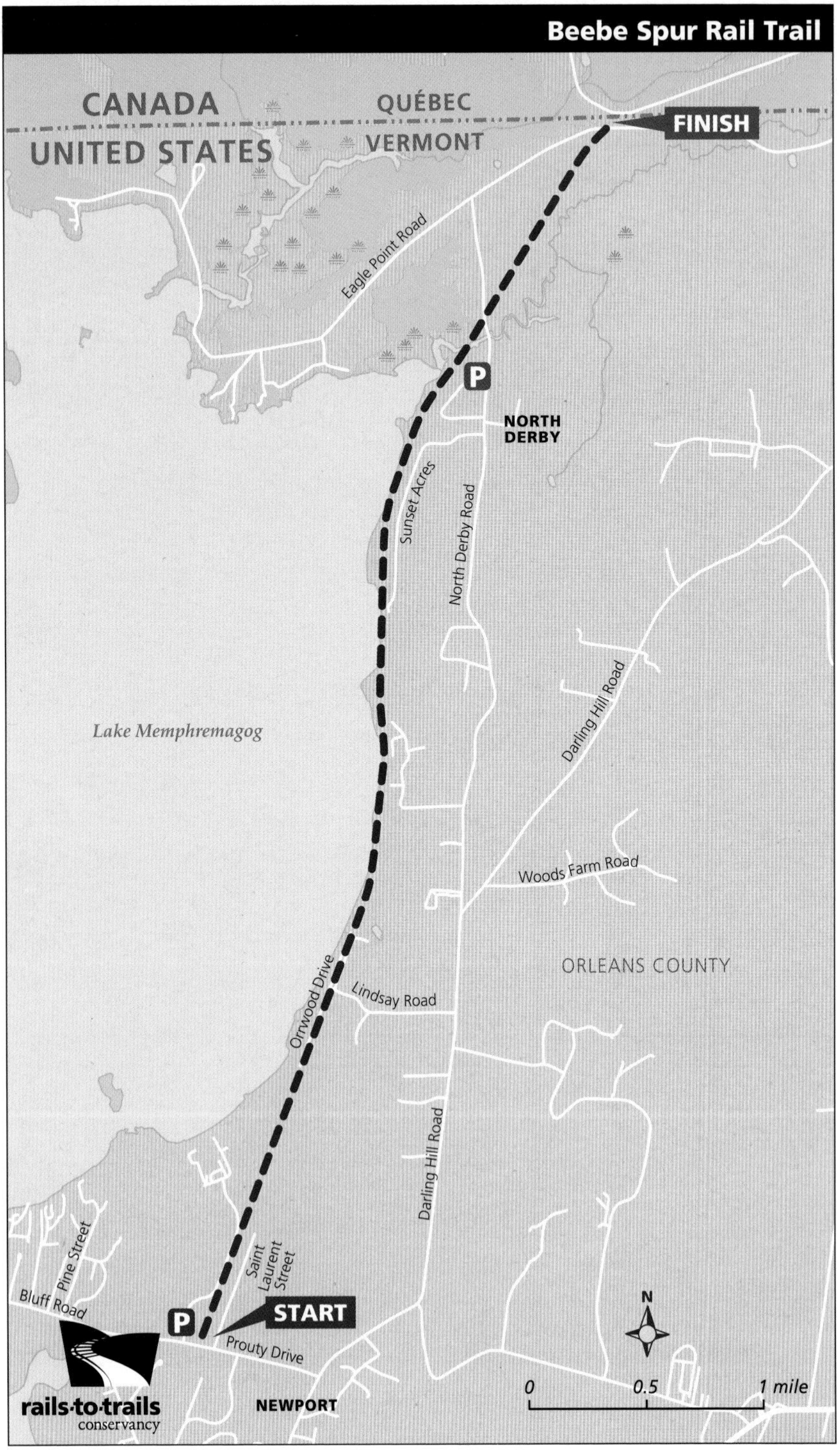

# Beebe Spur Rail Trail

CANADA

UNITED STATES

QUÉBEC

VERMONT

FINISH

Eagle Point Road

P

NORTH
DERBY

Sunset Acres

North Derby Road

Darling Hill Road

Lake Memphremagog

Woods Farm Road

ORLEANS COUNTY

Ortwood Drive

Lindsay Road

Darling Hill Road

Pine Street

Bluff Road

Saint Laurent Street

P

START

Prouty Drive

NEWPORT

N

0        0.5        1 mile

rails·to·trails
conservancy

The Beebe Spur Rail Trail (also known as the Newport-Beebe Bike Path) makes a level run along the eastern shore of Lake Memphremagog to Vermont's border with Canada. At less than 4 miles, the distance isn't taxing, although the gravel surface can make for a challenging bicycle ride without wide tires. At the north end, travelers who want to cross into Canada need to take a 1.5-mile detour and carry a passport.

The trail's name is derived from the historic community of Beebe Plain, which straddles the US–Canada border; a mid-19th-century post office served both countries from opposite ends of the building. The town served as a railroad connection between a branch of the Connecticut and Passumpsic Rivers Railroad completed in 1867 and Canada's Massawippi Valley Railway built in 1870. The Quebec Central Railway took control of the line in 1926.

*You'll enjoy views of Lake Memphremagog as the pathway traces its eastern shore.*

**County**
Orleans

**Endpoints**
Prouty Dr. between Lakemont Road and St. Laurent St. (Newport) to N. Derby Road, 0.5 mile east of its intersection with Eagle Point Road near the Canadian border (North Derby)

**Mileage**
3.8

**Type**
Rail-Trail

**Roughness Index**
2

**Surface**
Gravel

A subsequent owner, Canadian Pacific Railway, discontinued use on the line in 1990 and removed the tracks in 1992.

The Beebe Spur Rail Trail follows that old Connecticut and Passumpsic Rivers Railroad line from Newport to the border, while the 19-kilometer (11.8-mile) Sentier Nature Tomifobia uses the Massawippi Valley Railway corridor in Canada.

Starting at the south end in Newport, the trail reveals spectacular views of Lake Memphremagog in less than a mile. This glacial lake's name means "where there is a big expanse of water." It spans Vermont and Quebec over its 32-mile length and allows unobstructed views of the Green Mountains to the west. A small trailside pond surrounded by ferns and wildflowers contrasts with the wide-open lake behind it, providing a perfect spot for a snapshot or selfie.

As you gaze across the water, be aware of the legendary lake monster Memphre. With a horse-shaped head at the end of his long neck and a body the size of a house, the creature has elicited sightings for more than 100 years. It hasn't been seen since 2005, despite the whimsically named In Search of Memphre ultramarathon swim across 25 miles of Lake Memphremagog every July and September.

Heading north, you'll pass by many lakefront homes—some with tidy boathouses—with screened-in porches for enjoying views of this shoreline setting. You'll likely feel a friendly vibe, as trail users who bicycle, walk their dogs, or simply gaze at the water offer cheerful greetings.

After 3 miles, the trail veers away from the lake, passes parking for the trail, and enters residential North Derby. This is no longer a border crossing, but signs direct you 1.5 miles east to Beebe Road, which enters Canada.

CONTACT: discovernewportvt.com/newport-beebe-bike-path.html

## DIRECTIONS

To reach the southern trailhead from I-91, take Exit 28, and head west on US 5 S/VT 105 W. Go 0.7 mile, then turn right onto Shattuck Hill Road. Go 1.2 miles, and turn left onto Darling Hill Road. Go 0.4 mile, and turn right onto Prouty Dr. In 0.5 mile turn right into the parking lot for North Country Hospital. After parking, retrace your route about 0.1 mile along Prouty Dr. to the trail and turn left.

To reach the northern trailhead from I-91, take Exit 28, and head west on US 5 S/VT 105 W. Go 0.7 mile, then turn right onto Shattuck Hill Road. Go 1.2 miles, and turn right onto Darling Hill Road. Go 1.1 miles, and bear left onto N. Derby Road. Go 1.8 miles, and turn left at a sign for Department of Fish and Wildlife. You'll find parking here; the trail ends 0.8 mile to the north.

Locals lovingly describe the Cross Vermont Trail as a patchwork quilt that will ultimately form a 90-mile trail from Lake Champlain in the west to the Connecticut River in the east. A component of the Cross Vermont Trail, the Montpelier & Wells River Rail Trail is named for a former railroad that followed the same route, but most residents know the pathway by the name Cross Vermont Trail.

Part of a larger system that includes segments in East Montpelier, Plainfield, and Wells River, among others, this 22.9-mile portion is the most scenic of the off-road paths, stretching past three state parks and through Groton State Forest.

Starting in Marshfield at US 2 and School Street (parking is available 0.1 mile south along School Street at the Marshfield Town Office), you'll technically begin your journey on a 1-mile on-road portion (School Street becomes

*The rustic trail weaves in and out of tunnels of trees, the canopy offering a visual cue for where the railroad once carved its path.*

**Counties**
Caledonia, Washington, Orange

**Endpoints**
US 2 at School St. (Marshfield) to US 302/ Scott Hwy. between Wallace Hill Road and Butson Trail (Wells River)

**Mileage**
22.9

**Type**
Rail-Trail

**Roughness Index**
3

**Surfaces**
Ballast, Dirt, Gravel, Sand

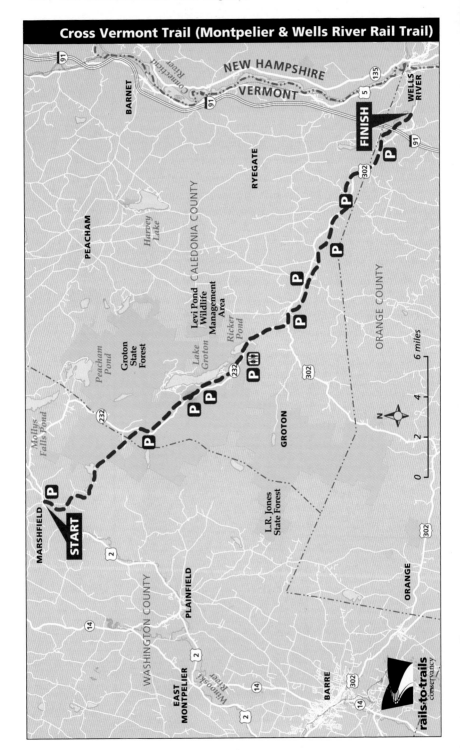

## Cross Vermont Trail (Montpelier & Wells River Rail Trail)

Lower Depot Road) that heads southeast and then curves southwest to Railroad Bed East, just past the intersection of Bemis Farm Road (right) and Upper Depot Road (left). Follow signs for the Cross Vermont Trail to find your way. Note that this portion is difficult to navigate because the beginning of the off-road portion is not marked. After passing Bemis Farm Road and Upper Depot Road, immediately look for Railroad Bed East, a short road that veers right (Bailey Pond Road will continue to stretch southeast). After veering right, the route takes you almost immediately onto the off-road portion of trail.

Heading southeast, the trail follows the Wells River, which flows east from the river's source in Groton State Forest, where three state parks provide numerous opportunities to camp and fish alongside impeccable views of the forest and mountains. In 4.4 miles, you'll reach Kettle Pond State Park, followed by Stillwater State Park by Lake Groton in another 2.4 miles, and then Ricker Pond State Park in 2.8 more miles; parking and trail access are available in each location, close to or adjacent to the trail.

As you journey out of Marshfield toward Groton State Forest, the trail is best described as rustic; it is well suited for hikes, mountain bikes, and snowmobiles but not road or hybrid bikes. Prepare for some steep climbs and majestic views as you pass lakes and ponds, with mountains as your backdrop. You'll even find a few picnic spots nestled among the trees. The trip is nothing short of gorgeous as you weave in and out of tunnels of trees, the canopy offering a visual cue for where the railroad once carved its path.

Along the way, you'll see relics from Vermont's logging history. Note specifically the remnants of Ricker Mills dam at the outlet of Ricker Pond along the southern edge of Groton State Forest. From the late 1700s through the 1960s, many mills could be seen along Lake Groton.

The southern portion of the trail between Groton and Boltonville—also primarily used for hiking, mountain biking, and snowmobiling—is more rustic. Assuming you have the right gear, the end of the trip can be a tranquil experience, taking you through the quiet village of South Ryegate and delivering views of pastures and forested hills along a long stretch of old railbed. At US 302/Scott Highway, you'll meet an on-road section of the Cross Vermont Trail that extends about 3.3 miles into Boltonville. Turn right onto US 302, and follow it to Church Street. Turn left onto Church Street, and then turn right onto Creamery Road. Follow Creamery Road until it meets up again with US 302/Scott Highway. Turn left onto US 302, and follow the road until you pass Boltonville Road on your left. Immediately to your left is another 1.8-mile off-road section of trail that leads you through woods and underneath I-91 to US 302 in Wells River.

**CONTACT: crossvermont.org**

# DIRECTIONS

To reach the northern endpoint and parking at the Marshfield Town Office from I-91, take Exit 21 to merge onto US 2 W (toward VT 15). Head west on US 2 for 19 miles, and turn left onto School St. Go 0.1 mile, and turn right into the parking lot at Marshfield Town Office. The on-road portion of trail begins approximately 0.1 mile north at US 2, and the off-road trail begins about 0.9 mile south along the trail at Railroad Bed E.

At the southern edge of Groton State Park, parking is available at the Ricker Mills trailhead located at 58 State Forest Road in Groton. From I-91, take Exit 17 toward US 302 W/Scott Hwy. Head west on US 302/Scott Hwy. (from I-91 N, you'll turn left; from I-91 S, you'll turn right), and go 8.7 miles. Turn right onto VT 232, and go 1.6 miles. Turn right into the parking lot adjacent to the south end of Ricker Pond.

To reach parking at Mills Memorial Field in Groton from I-91, take Exit 17 toward US 302 W/Scott Hwy. Head west on US 302/Scott Hwy. (from I-91 N, you'll turn left; from I-91 S, you'll turn right), and go 3.7 miles. Turn left into the Mills Memorial Field parking lot. The southern endpoint for the off-road section of trail is just 0.2 mile north along US 302/Scott Hwy., to your left at Brown Dr.

The Delaware and Hudson Rail-Trail follows the flowing contours of the western Vermont countryside, rambling in and out of New York state, where you'll find a 4-mile gap. This border area is known as the Slate Valley for the quarrying industry that has been active here since the 1830s. The nearly 26-mile trail connects with Amtrak's Ethan Allen Express in Castleton.

The trail traces the railbed laid by the Rutland and Washington Railroad in the 1850s to serve the slate quarries that mined the sheets of rock used primarily as roofing material. By 1871 foreclosures and mergers led to the

*Sweeping views of the hills surrounding Slate Valley will delight trail users.*

**Counties**
Bennington and Rutland, VT; Washington, NY

**Endpoints**
Main St./VT 4A between Mill St. and Ellis Orchard Road (Castleton) to NY 22A near Prouty Road (Hampton, NY); Depot St. just east of LaFountain Lane (Middle Granville, NY) to 4WD Road and Rupert Road/CR 153 (Salem, NY)

**Mileage**
25.8

**Type**
Rail-Trail

**Roughness Index**
2

**Surfaces**
Asphalt, Cinder, Dirt, Grass, Gravel

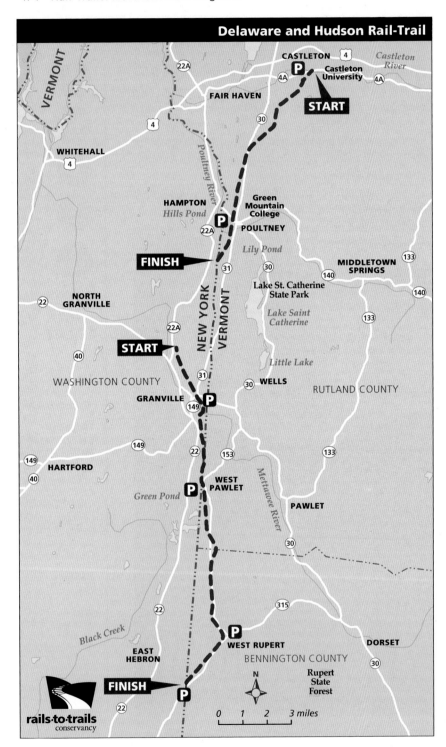

**Delaware and Hudson Rail-Trail**

CASTLETON

Castleton River

VERMONT

22A

4A

Castleton University

**START**

FAIR HAVEN

30

WHITEHALL

4

Poultney River

HAMPTON
Hills Pond

Green Mountain College

POULTNEY

22A

**FINISH**

Lily Pond

31

30

MIDDLETOWN SPRINGS

133

140

Lake St. Catherine State Park

NORTH GRANVILLE

22

Lake Saint Catherine

133

140

NEW YORK

VERMONT

22A

Little Lake

**START**

31

30   WELLS

RUTLAND COUNTY

WASHINGTON COUNTY

40

GRANVILLE

149

149

22

153

149

HARTFORD

40

133

Green Pond

WEST PAWLET

Mettawee River

PAWLET

30

22

315

EAST HEBRON

WEST RUPERT

DORSET

BENNINGTON COUNTY

Rupert State Forest

30

Black Creek

**FINISH**

22

N

0   1   2   3 miles

**rails·to·trails**
conservancy

Delaware & Hudson Railroad (D&H) leasing the line, which by now was known as the Slate Picker. Improvements in highways and truck transportation led to the eventual demise of the line in 1983.

The Vermont portion was developed into a rail-trail in the late 1980s, leaving a 4-mile gap between East Granville, New York, and a farm field near the state line. Long-range plans requiring acquisitions of private land are under way to finish the route in New York.

The trail welcomes walkers, mountain bikers, and horseback riders in warmer weather and snowshoers, cross-country skiers, and snowmobilers in the winter.

To explore the northern section, start at the trailhead across the street from the Amtrak Castleton Station, which dates to 1850. Castleton was first settled in the 1770s and saw action during the Revolutionary War. You'll pass through the Castleton University campus before entering farmland and pockets of hardwood trees. In about 8 miles, you'll arrive on the sleepy downtown streets of Poultney, home to Green Mountain College. Leaving town, the trail ends just over the state line in a farm field.

The southern section of trail begins on Depot Street in Middle Granville, New York, and heads southeast past a dairy farm and airport to Granville, New York, in 2.5 miles. The D&H railroad depot at the trailhead serves as a bed-and-breakfast today.

As the hub of slate quarrying in this area, the town hosts the Slate Valley Museum at 17 Water Street, just a block from the trailhead. You'll learn about the history of slate quarrying here, as well as the cultural changes foisted on the town by the arrival of Welsh miners in the 19th century. Although slate usually comes in basic gray, the local slate is desirable for its array of hues, such as green, purple, and red.

Crossing a bridge over the Mettawee River and skirting a furniture factory, the trail crosses back into Vermont about 2.5 miles past the Granville trailhead and arrives in West Pawlet 1.5 miles later. A quarry looms over the east side of town.

The forest opens up a bit south of town and offers sweeping views of the surrounding hills and countryside. Don't be surprised to see deer all along this trail. After passing a parking area outside the small village of West Rupert, the trail continues only 0.5 mile farther before reaching its southern terminus at the state border.

CONTACT: fpr.vermont.gov/state_lands/management_planning/documents /district_pages/district_2/dh_rail_trail

# DIRECTIONS

To reach the northern trailhead in Castleton, Vermont, from I-89, take Exit 1 toward Rutland on US 4. Turn left (southwest) on US 4, and go 9.8 miles. Turn left to stay on US 4, and go another 30.9 miles. In Rutland, turn left again to remain on US 4, and go 2.2 miles. Turn right onto US 4, and continue another 10.7 miles. Take Exit 5 toward Castleton. Turn left (heading south) onto E. Hubbardton Road, go 0.4 mile, then turn right onto VT 4A/Main St. Go 0.7 mile, and turn left onto Seminary St. Go 0.2 mile, and turn right into the visitor parking area. At the end of the lot, you'll find a row of spaces for trail users; the trail passes the lot. The endpoint is located 0.6 mile north along the trail.

To reach the trailhead in Granville, New York, from I-87, take Exit 17N to US 9 N toward South Glens Falls. Merge onto US 9 N, go 1.7 miles, and turn right onto NY 197/Reynolds Road. Go 4.7 miles, and turn right onto NY 197 E/US 4 S. Go 0.4 mile, then turn left to stay on NY 197 E/Argyle St. Go 2.1 miles (remain on NY 197 by turning right where Argyle St. becomes Baldwin Ave.), and turn left onto County Road 42. Then go 2.8 miles, and turn right onto NY 196. Go 7.7 miles, and turn left onto NY 40. In 1.6 miles, turn right onto NY 149. Go 7.6 miles, and turn left to stay on NY 149/Quaker St. Go 0.8 mile and bear right to stay on NY 149/Main St. The trailhead and parking are 0.3 mile ahead on the right.

To reach the trailhead in West Rupert, Vermont, from I-91, take Exit 2, and turn left onto VT 9 heading east toward Brattleboro. Go 1.1 miles, and turn left onto VT 30/US 5/Main St. Go 0.3 mile, and turn left to stay on VT 30/Park Pl. Go 0.1 mile, and turn right to stay on VT 30/ Linden St. In 38.5 miles in Peru, Vermont, turn left to remain on VT 30/VT 11. Go 6.4 miles, turn right onto Main St./VT 7A, and then immediately turn left onto VT 30/Bonnet St. Go 8.1 miles, then turn left onto VT 315. Go 8.7 miles (VT 315 becomes VT 153). Go 2.3 miles, then turn right onto Hebron Cross Road. Look for a small parking lot on the right in 0.2 mile. The endpoint is located 0.5 mile south along the trail.

L ocated in Burlington's North End, 67-acre Ethan Allen Park has approximately 4 miles of woodland trails and smaller spurs, which create nested loops around the scenic park and offer views of the surrounding Green Mountains. Local civic leader and landowner William Van Patten opened the park in 1905. Van Patten let his horse, Mattie, find the easiest trails to get to the top of the park's rocky hill, where he then built a gazebo overlooking Burlington and Lake Champlain. The gazebo remains today and adds to the park's charm while also providing respite on rainy days.

The park became an entertainment spot in the early decades of the 20th century for picnics, dancing, concerts, and bootleg liquor. Centuries earlier, native Abenaki used this spot to watch for approaching friends and foes.

Although pedestrian access points are situated along the west side of the park along Ethan Allen Parkway, the

*The trails within Ethan Allen Park offer breathtaking vistas of the surrounding Green Mountains.*

**County**
Chittenden

**Endpoints**
Just east of Ethan Allen Pkwy. and North Ave. to Ethan Allen Pkwy. and Sandy Lane, to Ethan Allen Pkwy. and Farrington Pkwy., or to 127 Bike Path at VT 127, 2 miles north of Manhattan Dr. and 1.1 miles south of Plattsburg Ave. (Burlington)

**Mileage**
2.3 (major spines), 4.0 (total with connecting spurs)

**Type**
Greenway/Non-Rail-Trail

**Roughness Index**
1

**Surfaces**
Asphalt, Dirt

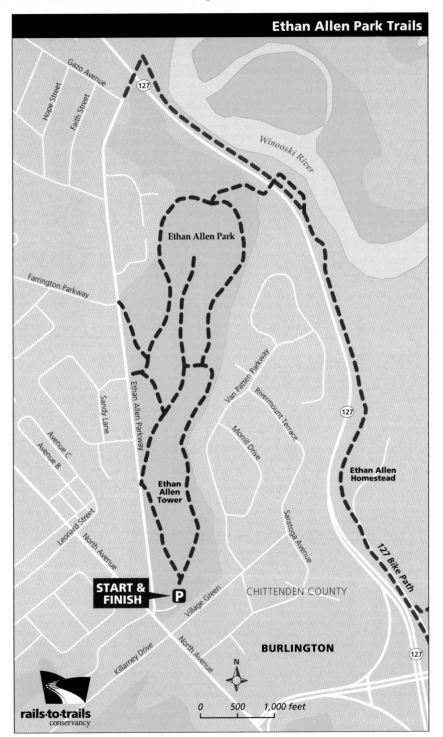

# Ethan Allen Park Trails

Gazo Avenue

Hope Street

Faith Street

127

Winooski River

Ethan Allen Park

Farrington Parkway

Van Patten Parkway

Rivermount Terrace

127

Ethan Allen Homestead

Sandy Lane

Ethan Allen Parkway

Avenue C

Avenue B

Morrill Drive

Ethan Allen Tower

Leonard Street

North Avenue

Saratoga Avenue

127 Bike Path

START & FINISH

P

Village Green

CHITTENDEN COUNTY

Killarney Drive

North Avenue

BURLINGTON

N

127

0   500   1,000 feet

**rails·to·trails**
conservancy

park's only dedicated parking area is located at the trail system's southernmost tip at Ethan Allen Parkway and North Avenue. A short pathway heads northwest from the parking lot to a small playground. To reach the gazebo and corresponding picnic area, head north at the V along the left trail for about 0.6 mile (you'll be under trees for the duration of your journey). Note the steady climb to the top of the hill.

In about 0.2 mile, you'll pass another landmark, Ethan Allen Tower, honoring Vermont's Revolutionary War hero. The Adirondack Mountains and Lake Champlain are visible from a lookout tower at the top of this monument (opening times vary throughout the year).

Other trails loop around the perimeter of the park and take trail users up and down and around numerous hills. The park has scattered picnic sites and a bike rack in the southeast section. (Note that currently there are no dedicated restrooms in the park.) All trails are located beneath dense tree canopy, which provides shade in the summer months, as well as beautiful forest to ponder and enjoy in every season.

At the park's northeastern end, a wooden-deck trestle bridge for pedestrians and cyclists crosses over VT 127 and seamlessly connects trail users to the 127 Bike Path, a critical link to other nearby trails and sites, including the Ethan Allen Homestead located just 0.8 mile south along the 127 Bike Path.

**CONTACT:** enjoyburlington.com/venue/ethan-allen-park

---

## DIRECTIONS

To reach the southern trailhead from I-89, take Exit 14W, merge onto US 2 W/Williston Road toward Burlington, and continue to follow US 2 W 1.5 miles. Turn right onto S. Willard St., go 0.8 mile, and then turn left onto Archibald St. In 0.4 mile turn right onto Spring St., and immediately turn left onto Manhattan Dr. Go 0.2 mile, and turn right onto VT 127 N. In 0.9 mile take the exit toward North Ave./Beaches, and go 0.7 mile. Turn right onto North Ave., go 0.3 mile, and turn right onto Ethan Allen Pkwy. Turn right into the trailhead.

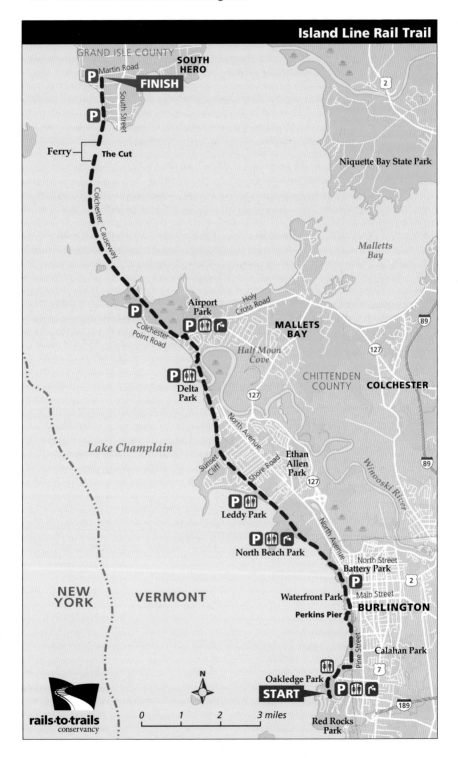

# Island Line Rail Trail

GRAND ISLE COUNTY

**SOUTH HERO**

Martin Road

**FINISH**

South Street

Ferry — **The Cut**

Colchester Causeway

2

Niquette Bay State Park

*Malletts Bay*

Holy Cross Road

Airport Park

Colchester Point Road

**MALLETS BAY**

*Half Moon Cove*

89

127

**CHITTENDEN COUNTY**

**COLCHESTER**

Delta Park

127

*Lake Champlain*

North Avenue

Sunset Cliff

Shore Road

Ethan Allen Park

127

*Winooski River*

89

Leddy Park

North Beach Park

North Avenue

North Street

**Battery Park**

2

**NEW YORK**

**VERMONT**

Waterfront Park

Main Street

**BURLINGTON**

**Perkins Pier**

Pine Street

Calahan Park

7

N

Oakledge Park

**START**

**rails·to·trails** conservancy

0    1    2    3 miles

**Red Rocks Park**

189

**rail-trail**
**Hall of Fame**

Lake Champlain virtually laps at your feet for long sections of the 13.4-mile Island Line Rail Trail. Rolling through waterfront parks in Burlington and Colchester, the trail crosses the lake on a spectacular 3-mile causeway that requires a ferry ride to cross a 200-foot gap to destinations on South Hero Island.

The Rutland-Canadian Railroad built the Island Line in 1899 to connect coastal markets in New England with the Great Lakes, eventually reaching Lake Ontario. As rail transportation fell into decline, the railroad scratched its passenger service in 1955 and freight service in 1961. It wasn't until the 1980s that the idea of a pedestrian trail took hold; now more than 150,000 visitors use the trail each year.

The southern 8 miles of trail are paved, and the remainder is hard-packed crushed limestone. Since 2015, Burlington's section of the rail-trail (known as Burlington Greenway) has been undergoing a face-lift with new paving and landscaping. You'll notice improvements between Perkins Pier downtown and North Beach Park. If you encounter work on the trail, look for signs to the detour around the project.

**Counties**
Chittenden, Grand Isle

**Endpoints**
Austin Dr. in Oakledge Park between Dunder Road and Ambrose Pl. (Burlington) to Martin Road between Railroad St. and South St. (South Hero)

**Mileage**
13.4

**Type**
Rail-Trail

**Roughness Index**
1

**Surfaces**
Asphalt, Gravel

*The Lake Champlain causeway offers a unique trail experience.*

The southern terminus at Oakledge Park in Burlington—a good place to begin your journey—has plentiful parking and restrooms. Heading north along a sandy beach, you'll get your first view of New York's Adirondack Mountains across the lake. At the park's north end, 14 granite boulders in Burlington's Earth Clock create a calendar, clock, and compass—an example of this town's artistic reputation.

You'll pass some industrial sites and a rail yard for the Vermont Railway, a short line railroad. Just after passing the ferry docks on King Street, you'll see Union Station, built from brick, limestone, and granite in 1916. Used as an office building now, it's also the base for a tourist train, as well as local bike advocacy group Local Motion. A block past the station is Waterfront Park, which can get congested if a concert or festival is scheduled.

In 4.5 miles, you come to a boardwalk through Delta Park and a 600-foot pedestrian bridge over the mouth of the Winooski River. Here the trail becomes the Colchester Bike Path and Causeway.

In 2.4 miles, after passing Airport Park, you come to the marble causeway that many consider the highlight of the route. American elms rise from the shoreline but don't interrupt the view east to the Green Mountains or west to the Adirondacks. At 2.7 miles, the causeway ends at The Cut, but you can ride a ferry on weekends and holidays in the spring and fall and all week in the summer. (Find rates and hours at **localmotion.org**.) The trail continues for another mile once you get to South Hero Island.

After getting off the ferry across The Cut, it's another 0.4 mile to the shoreline. Here the trail becomes Allen Point Fishing Access and proceeds as a road for state fish and wildlife vehicles until it ends at Martin Road in 0.8 mile.

**CONTACT: localmotion.org**

## DIRECTIONS

To reach Oakledge Park in Burlington from I-89, take Exit 13 onto I-189 toward Shelburne/Burlington. Follow I-189 W 1.4 miles, then turn right onto US 7. In 0.5 mile turn left onto Flynn Ave., and follow Flynn Ave. into Oakledge Park. Parking is at the end of the road in 1 mile.

To reach the Airport Park trailhead in Colchester from I-89, take Exit 16 onto US 7 N/US 2 W toward Colchester. Head north on US 7/US 2, go 1.7 miles, and turn left onto VT 127. Go 3.7 miles, and continue straight on W. Lakeshore Dr. 1.8 miles (it becomes Holy Cross Road after 0.8 mile). Bear left slightly onto Colchester Point Road, go 0.6 mile, and then turn right into the parking lot (just before Buckingham Dr.).

To reach the northernmost parking in South Hero from I-89, take Exit 17 and head west on US 2. Go 8.5 miles, crossing over Lake Champlain, and turn left onto South St. In 2.5 miles turn right onto Martin Road. Go 0.3 mile, and turn left into the trail access road. Look for parking to your left.

The Lamoille Valley Rail Trail (LVRT) is a growing, year-round trail across northern Vermont that will one day stretch 93 miles between St. Johnsbury and Swanton. The trail passes through the spine of Vermont's Green Mountain Range, from the Connecticut River to Lake Champlain. When finished, the LVRT, covering four counties and 18 towns, will be one of the longest rail-trails in New England. The LVRT's grade never exceeds 3 percent, making it accessible to a variety of trail users and abilities.

The developing trail is being built along the former route of the Lamoille Valley Railroad, which once served as a vital east–west transportation corridor from 1877 until its closing in 1994. The railroad was known as the covered bridge line and was a leaf peeper train for scenic

*The Cambridge Junction Bridge, one of Vermont's iconic covered bridges, is a highlight of the route.*

**Counties**
Caledonia, Franklin, Lamoille

**Endpoints**
Channel Dr. 0.5 mile west of VT 15 (West Danville) to Main St. just south of Bay St. (St. Johnsbury); Park St./VT 15A and Darling Road (Morrisville) to Cambridge Junction Road and Cambridge Junction Road Extension by the Lamoille River (Cambridge); Robin Hood Dr. between First St. and Bushey St. (Swanton)

**Mileage**
34.2

**Type**
Rail-Trail

**Roughness Index**
2

**Surfaces**
Crushed Stone, Gravel

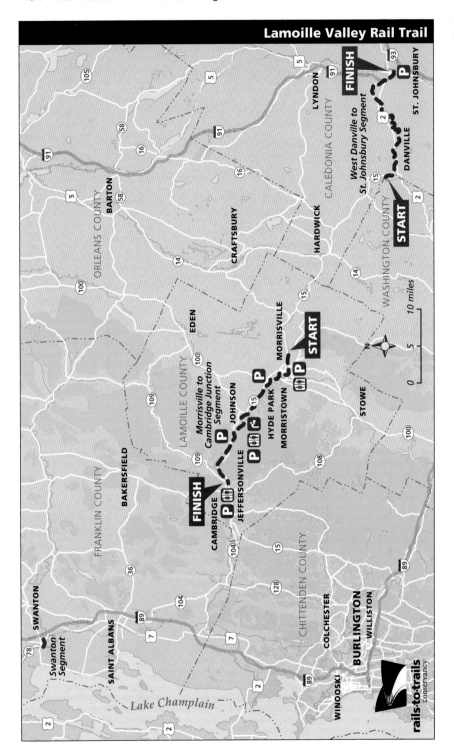

**Lamoille Valley Rail Trail**

tourism. The Vermont Association of Snow Travelers has supported the project for many years and helps to maintain the trail.

### West Danville to St. Johnsbury Segment: 16.3 miles

This section of the LVRT is loaded with a variety of scenic landscapes, including gorgeous wetlands and Joe's Pond, a locally popular fishing, boating, and residential area. Trail users looking for an easier grade should plan to start in West Danville and head east toward St. Johnsbury. Beginning at Chanel Drive, you'll head south along Joe's Pond and then east, paralleling VT 15. Most of this section is flanked by trees, with a small residential area near the intersection of VT 15 and US 2.

As you continue east and pass Danville, the trail snakes in and out of wooded areas and farm fields and crosses over a few local roads. You'll encounter dramatic outcrops of bedrock—ledge cuts left over from the time of the railroad—as well as dense shaded forest and ferns in the warmer months.

Closer to St. Johnsbury, tunnels help trail users avoid road crossings at US 5 and I-91 and also provide a cool spot in the warmer months. After heading under I-91 and reaching Mt. Vernon Street, you'll enter the last 1.5-mile section of trail, also known as the Three Rivers Bike Path, which heads to the southern edge of St. Johnsbury, where you'll find a small parking lot.

### Morrisville to Cambridge Junction Segment: 16.9 miles

This segment travels from Morrisville to Cambridge as it follows both VT 15 and the Lamoille River. The quiet route passes through a wide range of landscapes—from small towns to agricultural areas, meadows, and forests.

Although the route technically begins at Park Street and Darling Road on the outskirts of Morrisville, the best place to begin your journey is the Portland Street trailhead, which has ample parking and restrooms. Heading northwest, you'll skirt around the western side of Morrisville and through trees and farmland to Hyde Park. Passing a mostly residential area, you'll continue through vast farmland and riverside areas and through Johnson. Here, The Old Mill Park is home to a trailhead with parking, restrooms, and water.

Continuing northwest past Ithiel Falls, you'll eventually reach Cambridge Junction and Cambridge, where a seamless connection to the Cambridge Greenway takes you toward Jeffersonville. As you enter Cambridge, you'll pass a restored train station that has been converted into a community playground with a train theme. This junction (Cambridge Junction) is marked by one of Vermont's iconic covered bridges, the Cambridge Junction Bridge (also known as the Poland Covered Bridge), built in 1887. Several small businesses, including cafés, ice cream shops, and breweries, have popped up throughout this section and cater to trail users.

## Swanton Segment: 1.0 mile

A small segment in Swanton stretches from Robin Hood Drive across the Missisquoi River to South River Street, offering neighborhood connections for locals.

**CONTACT:** lvrt.org

---

# DIRECTIONS

To reach the endpoint in West Danville from I-89, take Exit 8 toward US 2/VT 12/Montpelier/St. Johnsbury. Merge onto Memorial Dr., and go 1.7 miles. Take a slight left onto River St., and go 1.2 miles. At the traffic circle, take the second exit onto US 2 E/E. Montpelier Road/River St., and go 24.4 miles. Turn left onto VT 15 W, and go 2.2 miles. Turn left onto Channel Dr. Look for the small parking area to your right in 0.5 mile.

To reach the St. Johnsbury trailhead from I-91, take Exit 20 for US 5 toward St. Johnsbury. If you're coming from I-91 N, turn right from the exit onto US 5 N. If you're coming from I-91 S, turn left off the exit onto US 5 N. Go 0.4 mile, and turn right onto Main St. Make an immediate right into the small parking lot and trailhead.

To reach the Morrisville trailhead from I-89, take Exit 10 for VT 100 N toward Stowe. Head northeast on VT 100 N, and go 18.2 miles. Turn right onto Bridge St., and go 0.3 mile. Turn left onto Portland St., and go 0.1 mile into the parking lot.

To reach the Cambridge trailhead from I-89, take Exit 10 for VT 100 N toward Stowe, and head northeast on VT 100 N. Go 7.1 miles, and turn left onto Moscow Road. Go 1.5 miles, turn right onto Barrows Road, and go 1.8 miles. Turn right onto Luce Hill Road, and go 0.5 mile. Turn left onto VT 108 N (parts of this road may be closed in winter due to weather). Go 15.3 miles, and then take a slight right onto VT 108. Go 0.3 mile, and at the traffic circle, take the first exit onto VT 15 E. Go 0.7 mile, and turn left onto Cambridge Junction Road. Go 0.1 mile, and turn left toward Cambridge Junction Road, and turn right (just before crossing the Lamoille River) into the parking lot. (Cambridge Junction Road Extension may be closed at certain times or days.)

The Swanton Segment of the trail has no dedicated parking lots.

Saint Albans used to be called Rail City for all the train traffic it saw, but it could be known as Rail-Trail City now. The town sits at the front door of the Missisquoi Valley Rail-Trail, among the longest and most scenic in the state. The 26.3-mile trail rolls past the dairy farms and cornfields of northwestern Vermont to within a couple of miles of the state's border with Québec.

The crushed-stone trail follows the railbed of Central Vermont Railroad's Richford Branch. The line between Saint Albans and Richford was chartered as the Missisquoi Railroad in the late 1860s, and the much larger Central Vermont leased it in 1872. Eventually, the Central Vermont came under control of the Canadian National

*The Missisquoi River Valley offers a scenic backdrop for the pathway.*

**County**
Franklin

**Endpoints**
US 7/N. Main St. between VT 105/Seymour Road and Rewes Dr. (Saint Albans) to VT 105/Troy St. between Liberty St. and S. Richford Road (Richford)

**Mileage**
26.3

**Type**
Rail-Trail

**Roughness Index**
2

**Surface**
Crushed Stone

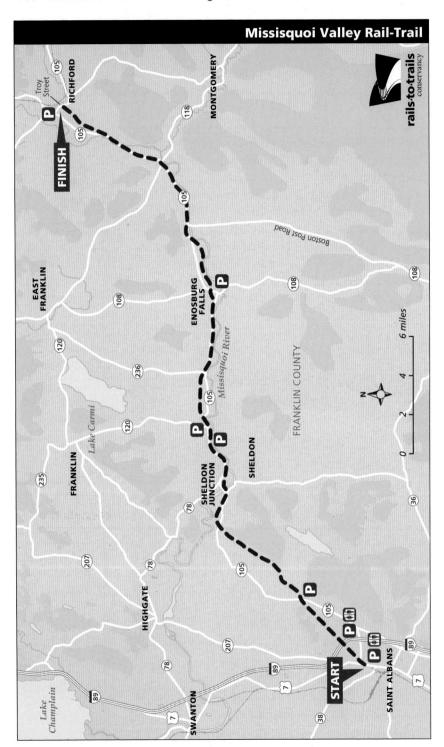

**Missisquoi Valley Rail-Trail**

*In Sheldon, you'll relish the views of the Missisquoi River and surrounding mountain peaks.*

Railway. A train derailment on a trestle near Sheldon in June 1984 spelled the end of the line but raised an opportunity to build a rail-trail. One span was so badly damaged that the railroad decided it wasn't cost effective to repair due to dwindling traffic. Local traffic on either side of the bridge continued sporadically for a few years, but the railroad discontinued use on it in the early 1990s.

The trail starts on the north side of Saint Albans, in the midst of chain restaurants and mini-marts, although parts of town reflect its former life as a flourishing railroad junction. Heading northeast, within 2 miles you're riding past cornfields, dairy farms, and red barns. About 9 miles down the trail, you'll cross a bridge over the Missisquoi River at Sheldon Junction; this is where the previously mentioned trail derailment occurred. The replacement span doesn't match the other two here. At 523 feet, it's the longest bridge on the trail.

The next few miles are known as Corn Alley, as the corn grows right next to the trail. In 7.6 miles, you'll arrive at Enosburg Falls, historically the center of the dairy industry in the area. The June Dairy Days festival relives those days the first weekend of the month. You'll see a red caboose and freight depot; both house museum artifacts and local railroad memorabilia. They're open June–October, Saturday, 10 a.m.–2 p.m. There's shade at Lincoln Park a couple of blocks south on VT 108, and you'll also find cafés, coffee shops, and an ice cream parlor in the vicinity.

It's mostly cornfields and pastureland for roughly the last 10 miles to Richford. The last bridge on the trail is about 3 miles before Richford. The Historic District of Richford is less than a mile away from the trailhead; to get there turn left onto Troy Street and right onto Main Street. Most of the historical buildings are concentrated near or at the junction with River Street just across the Missisquoi River. The river powered the mills here in boom times more than a century ago, but prosperity has abandoned the commercial district. Two blocks left on River Street you'll see an example of a prominent businessman's mansion built in 1890, now a bed-and-breakfast. Plans are in the works to extend the trail to the Canadian border.

**CONTACT:** champlainbikeways.org/documents/Missisquoi%20VRT%20FINAL.pdf

## DIRECTIONS

To reach the trailhead in Saint Albans from I-89, take Exit 20 onto VT 207/Highgate Road toward Saint Albans. Head southwest on VT 207, go 0.4 mile, and turn left onto US 7/Swanton Road. Go 1 mile, and turn left onto VT 105/Seymour Road. Go about 500 feet, and turn right into the parking area. The trail endpoint is 0.2 mile south.

To reach the trailhead in Richford from I-89, take Exit 21 onto VT 78. Head east on VT 78, go 7.2 miles, and turn left to remain on VT 78. Go another 2.8 miles, and turn left onto VT 105. In 7.3 miles, turn left onto VT 108, and go 0.5 mile. Veer right to continue on VT 105, go 9.5 miles, and turn right onto VT 105/Troy St. In 0.4 mile look for parking at the trailhead on the right.

Residents in South Burlington formed a grassroots coalition in the late 1980s to create a safer way to travel within Burlington's extensive system of parks, schools, and neighborhoods. In the early 1990s, the city government devoted funds to complete the project, creating the South Burlington Recreation Path, a 26-mile network of paved, off-street trails. The multiuse trail network provides major pathways for commuting to segments that travel through parks and forested landscapes.

Those who prefer nature and the great outdoors might begin their journey at Overlook Park on Deerfield Road, where you'll find spectacular views of Lake Champlain and the mountains across the lake in New York. Overlook Park provides westward views and is a good spot to watch the sun set. Heading northwest, you'll travel along a segment that twists its way through Farrell Park, a heavily forested oasis of green, and toward Red Rocks Park along the water. You'll eventually cross US 7 and then

**County**
Chittenden

**Endpoints**
Overlook Park at Spear St. and Deerfield Road to Davis Road just west of Spear St. at the University of Vermont Archie Post Athletic Complex or to Central Ave. near Lyons Ave. in Red Rocks Park or to just west of Home Ave. and Batchelder St.; Catkin Dr. west of Bower St. to Main St./US 2 just east of East Terrace or to Airport Dr. and Airport Cir. (South Burlington)

**Mileage**
26.0

**Type**
Greenway/Non-Rail-Trail

**Roughness Index**
1

**Surface**
Asphalt

*On the west side of the path, explore the beautiful forested settings of Farrell and Dorset Parks.*

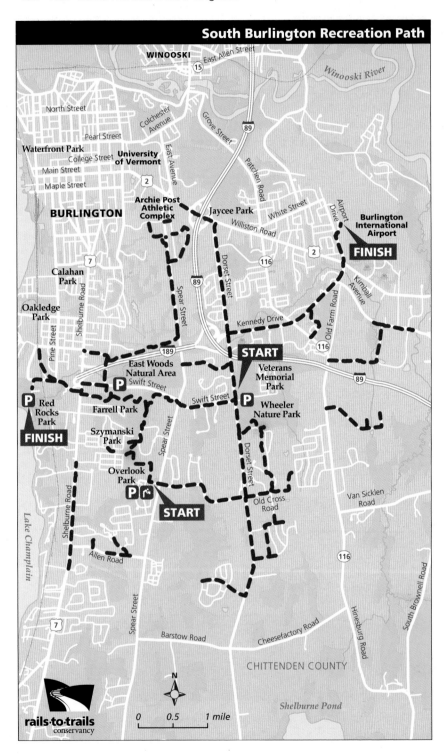

## South Burlington Recreation Path

cut an immediate left and right to join the section paralleling Queen City Park Road before reaching Red Rocks Park at Central Avenue, where you'll turn left.

Trail users will be rewarded with great views of Lake Champlain and a popular swimming hole on warm summer days. A trail parking area is located where Central Avenue meets Shelburne Bay.

You can head east from Farrell Park along Swift Street for approximately 0.8 mile to Dorset Park, which provides access to walking paths in a similarly beautiful forested setting. At Farrell Park, recreationists can also head south through Szymanski Park, with its popular tennis courts and playgrounds for children.

For a scenic route, you may wish to start at Overlook Park and head north on Spear Street on an on-road section for 1.5 miles. You can access off-road trail again to your left just after passing under I-189. On your left side, a golf course dominates, but you'll also enjoy bucolic views of the University of Vermont's farm. This segment then terminates at the Archie Post Athletic Complex on the University of Vermont campus, where there is no dedicated parking for trail users.

Accessing the trail on Dorset Street from Veterans Memorial Park, you travel north past C. Douglas Cairns Arena, where the trail then turns right along the north side of Kennedy Drive and then heads northeast toward US 2/Williston Road. Here, just before you reach the airport, you'll find a variety of shops and restaurants accessible from the trail.

Segments of the South Burlington Recreation Path also extend south beyond Overlook Park and east beyond Dorset Park. These segments are not connected to main stems of the recreation path, but they do offer safe, off-street access to adjacent neighborhoods.

**CONTACT:** 802-846-4108; **southburlingtonvt.gov/parks_and_facilities/recreation _path_and_trails**

## DIRECTIONS

The northern access point is only accessible to pedestrians and bicyclists from the University of Vermont campus. To reach the trail access point at Overlook Park from I-89, take Exit 13 for I-189 toward US 7/Shelburne/Burlington. Continue onto I-189 W 1.4 miles. Turn left onto Shelburne Road/US 7, go 0.2 mile, and turn left onto Swift St. In 1 mile, turn right onto Spear St. Go 0.8 mile, and turn right into Overlook Park, just before Deerfield Road.

To reach the western trail access point, follow the directions above to Shelburne Road/US 7, and turn left. Go 0.2 mile, then turn right onto Queen City Park Road. In 0.1 mile, turn right to stay on Queen City Park Road. Go 0.4 mile, and turn left onto Central Ave. Look for the parking lot to your left in 0.3 mile.

To reach parking on Dorset St. from I-89, take Exit 14E to merge onto US 2 E/Williston Road toward South Burlington. In 0.2 mile turn right onto Dorset St., go 1.8 miles, and turn left onto Swift St. Look for parking on your right.

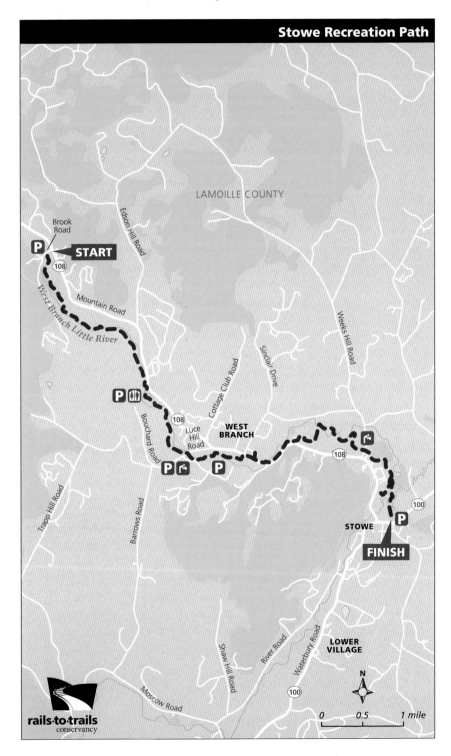

# Stowe Recreation Path

LAMOILLE COUNTY

Brook Road

P

START

108

West Branch Little River

Mountain Road

Edson Hill Road

P

P

108

Luce Hill Road

Bouchard Road

Cottage Club Road

Sinclair Drive

WEST BRANCH

P

108

Weeks Hill Road

P

STOWE

P 100

FINISH

Trapp Hill Road

Barrows Road

Shaw Hill Road

River Road

Waterbury Road

LOWER VILLAGE

100

Moscow Road

N

0    0.5    1 mile

rails·to·trails
conservancy

The Stowe Recreation Path encapsulates the best parts of Vermont mountain life. During summer the vegetation is lush and green, and the nearby West Branch Little River keeps the trail cool and provides excellent fishing and swimming opportunities. In the winter, the trail gives visitors a reason to go outside and explore the elements, and the views of snowcapped peaks are more than photo-worthy.

Trail users can enjoy this out-and-back path in either direction, but most people start at the northern segment because it's all downhill from there! The northern trailhead also lies approximately 3 miles south of the base of the world-class Stowe Mountain Resort.

The first several miles of gently sloping trail travel through the forested banks of the West Branch Little River and provide opportunities for quiet enjoyment in a rural atmosphere. Be on the lookout for wildlife along the trail;

*The path offers a delightful mix of forested landscapes and open pastoral countryside.*

**County**
Lamoille

**Endpoints**
Brook Road between W. Branch Lane and Mountain Road/VT 108 to Main St./Maple St./VT 100 at Sunset St. in Lintilhac Park (Stowe)

**Mileage**
5.5

**Type**
Greenway/Non-Rail-Trail

**Roughness Index**
1

**Surface**
Asphalt

as you travel south, you'll quickly pass a horse farm where horses often graze by the side of the trail, and lucky recreationists may even get to see a moose feeding in the distance. Portable restrooms, benches, and picnic tables are provided at a series of smaller parking lots along the trail.

After 2.5 miles, the trail crosses under Luce Hill Road, where development becomes denser and the trail more popular. A variety of restaurants, breweries, and lodging line the trail from here until the trail's end in Stowe Village. Several of these establishments have created doors with direct access points from the trail to welcome in trail users.

Given the popularity of this trail, Stowe prioritizes clearing snow and ice from the Stowe Recreation Path in the winter for year-round use. You can still enjoy snowshoeing and cross-country skiing in the snow along the sides of the trail. A free shuttle during the winter months transports trail users up the mountain for a one-way trip back down.

**CONTACT:** stowerec.org/parks-facilities/rec-paths/stowe-recreation-path

## DIRECTIONS

To reach the northern trailhead from I-89, take Exit 10 for VT 100 and head north on VT 100 toward Stowe. Go 9.8 miles, and turn left onto VT 108 N. Go 4.3 miles, and turn left onto Brook Road. The parking lot is on the left in 400 feet.

To get to the southern trailhead in Stowe from I-89, take Exit 10 onto VT 100. Follow VT 100 N toward Stowe 10 miles, where the entrance to the Stowe Recreation Path parking lot will be in Lintilhac Park on the left next to Stowe Community Church.

**N**ature and history enthusiasts will delight in the Ti-Haul Trail and Shelburne Bay Park Rec Path, two short but scenic trails linked by a pleasant 104-acre park in Shelburne, Vermont. Forming an almost seamless connection near the southern tip of Shelburne Bay, the trails create a meandering and historic journey through woodsy terrain, offering glimpses of the wildlife and water for which Vermont is well known. Both trails are recommended for bird-watching, and locals say to specifically look for black-crowned herons, great blue herons, and several species of ducks.

The best place to begin your journey is at the Bay Road trailhead, located in Shelburne Bay Park on the north side of Bay Road between Harbor Road and US 7. Heading north, the 1-mile Shelburne Bay Park Rec Path travels through a wooded oasis for just over 0.75 mile

*On this journey through woodsy terrain, you'll have a good chance of spotting wildlife.*

**County**
Chittenden

**Endpoints**
Shelburne Dog Park at
Harbor Road between
Depot Road and Turtle
Lane to Harbor Road just
south of Pheasant Hill
Road (Shelburne)

**Mileage**
2.5

**Type**
Rail-Trail/Greenway

**Roughness Index**
1–2

**Surface**
Gravel

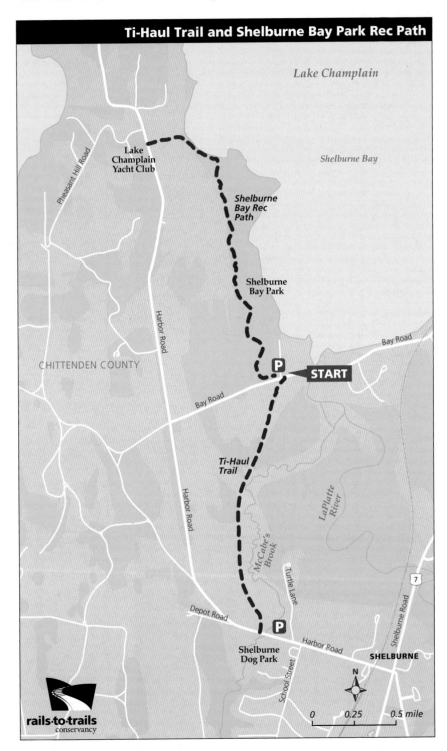

**Ti-Haul Trail and Shelburne Bay Park Rec Path**

Lake Champlain

Pheasant Hill Road

Lake Champlain Yacht Club

Shelburne Bay

*Shelburne Bay Rec Path*

Shelburne Bay Park

Harbor Road

CHITTENDEN COUNTY

Bay Road

Bay Road

P

**START**

*Ti-Haul Trail*

Harbor Road

LaPlatte River

McCabe's Brook

Turtle Lane

7

Depot Road

P

Shelburne Dog Park

Harbor Road

School Street

Shelburne Road

**SHELBURNE**

N

0    0.25    0.5 mile

**rails·to·trails**
conservancy

before skirting the Lake Champlain shoreline and offering an amazing view of Shelburne Bay.

Walking, biking, and cross-country skiing are permitted on this gravel route. Note that numerous small hills make for a pleasant and fun bicycle ride; however, cyclists should be prepared for sand and a few intense uphill climbs toward the northern end.

At Shelburne Bay, trail users can pause and take in the beauty of the shallow water, which is perfect for skipping rocks. Woodsy canopies provide shade, making for a cool respite from the sun in the summer. Boat access points and picnic tables are available in the northern section of the trail, near the trail's endpoint at the Lake Champlain Yacht Club.

The Ti-Haul Trail, located just across Bay Road from Shelburne Park, is a quintessential rail-trail—a flat, easy bike ride or a perfect stroll with glimpses of farms peeking between the trees. Though this trail also has a gravel surface, it has few hills and is wheelchair accessible.

Heading south, you'll journey through mostly woodsy landscapes with a few marshy areas before ending in about a mile at Shelburne Dog Park on Harbor Road. The Ti-Haul Trail has an interesting history, having begun as a road specifically built to move the old steamboat *Ticonderoga* from Lake Champlain to its present home at the Shelburne Museum. The 2-mile trek took 65 days to complete at an average pace of 150 feet per day as the boat was carted along railroad tracks that were built literally as the journey progressed; workers pulled up the railroad tracks behind the boat and placed them ahead. You can learn more about the steamboat and her journey at the museum, located on Shelburne Road, about 1.4 miles from the trail's southern trailhead.

Also nearby, at the intersection of Bay Road and Harbor Road, is Shelburne Farms, a working farm and education center dedicated to conservation and sustainability, built on an estate designed by Frederick Law Olmsted Sr. in the late 19th century.

**CONTACT: shelburnevt.org**

## DIRECTIONS

From I-89, take Exit 13 for I-189 toward US 7/Shelburne/Burlington, and continue on I-189 W. In 1.4 miles, turn left onto US 7 S/Shelburne Road, and go 2.9 miles. Turn right onto Bay Road, and go 1.2 miles. Turn right into the trailhead, just after crossing the LaPlatte River. Access the Shelburne Bay Park Rec Path on the west side of the parking lot. The Ti-Haul Trail is accessible to the south, just across Bay Road.

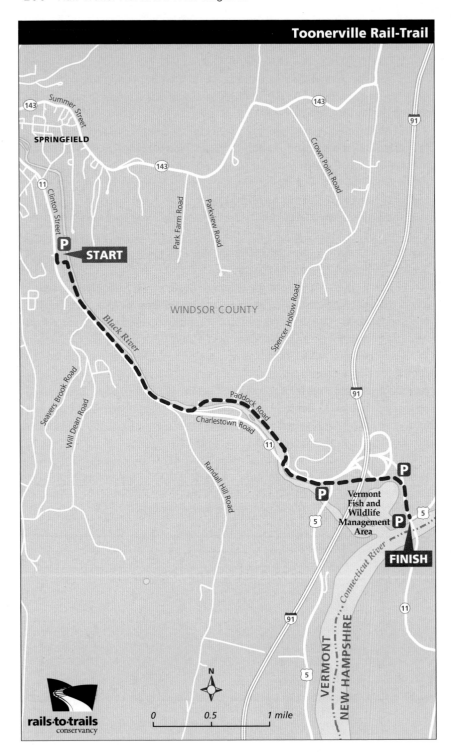

Toonerville Rail-Trail

The Toonerville Rail-Trail shadows the Black River for most of its 3.2-mile length in eastern Springfield to the border with New Hampshire across the Connecticut River. The route originally carried an electric trolley that locals nicknamed the Toonerville Trolley, referencing a nationally syndicated newspaper comic that ran 1908–1955 and was adapted to early comedy film shorts. That name has survived on this paved trail long after most have forgotten the comic strip or the trolley.

The trolley's actual name was the Springfield Electric Railway, which later became the Springfield Terminal Railway. The city of Springfield funded the 4-mile interurban railway in 1896 to make connections to the railroads that passed through Charlestown, New Hampshire, across the Connecticut River. It later fell under control of the Boston and Maine Railroad. Although the trolley stopped running in 1947 (it was the state's longest running at the time) and freight stopped using the tracks in 1984, the Springfield Terminal name still survives as a subsidiary of Pan Am Railways.

*Stop along the benches lining the trail to take in the views of the verdant Black River valley.*

**County**
Windsor

**Endpoints**
Clinton St./VT 11 and Sioux Dr. to Charlestown Road/US 5/VT 11 and Connecticut River Road/US 5 (Springfield)

**Mileage**
3.2

**Type**
Rail-Trail

**Roughness Index**
1

**Surface**
Asphalt

The paved multipurpose trail (also known as the Springfield Greenway) opened in 1999. It begins about a mile east of downtown on VT 11/Clinton Street in a field shared by the Springfield Farmers Market on Saturdays, June–early October. There's plenty of parking here.

The trail heads away from the highway briefly into the woods and along the banks of the Black River—a gradual downhill experience. There are plenty of opportunities to stop and gaze at the river and watch for waterfowl, including kingfishers, blue herons, and copious duck species, fishing for their food. The river's falls in downtown Springfield fed the mill boom in the 1800s and enticed companies to relocate here. One of those, Jones & Lamson Machine Co., became a world-renowned toolmaker. Its inventions were spun off into new companies, and the area became an early-20th-century tech boom center known as Precision Valley.

A cascading waterfall is visible about 1.2 miles after the trailhead, where a small tributary joins the main channel; at certain times, the falls project rainbows of light, providing copious photo opportunities. About 0.2 mile later, the trail crosses the river on Gould's Mill Bridge. A 0.4-mile side trip down Perley Gordon Road right before the bridge visits the Eureka Schoolhouse; completed in 1790, it's the state's oldest surviving one-room schoolhouse. Crews moved it here in 1968 from its original location.

Crossing the bridge, the trail route detours onto lightly trafficked Paddock Road for 0.7 mile. The path returns on the right side of the road and then goes beneath VT 11. In the final mile, the trail runs alongside VT 11, crosses US 5, passes a truck stop, goes beneath I-91, and then stops at a Vermont Fish and Wildlife Management Area on the shores of the Connecticut River.

While the original trolley provided a connection to downtown Springfield, the city has plans to extend the trail about 0.7 mile northward to Bridge Street, allowing easier access to downtown.

**CONTACT: springfieldvt.com/attractions**

## DIRECTIONS

To reach the Springfield trailhead from I-91, take Exit 7 onto VT 11/Charlestown Road toward Springfield. Go 2.5 miles on VT 11 W/Charlestown Road (Charlestown Road becomes Clinton St.), and turn right into a parking lot at Robert S. Jones Industrial Center.

To reach the Hoyts Landing trailhead from I-91, take Exit 7 onto US 5 toward Charlestown. Go about 0.3 mile on US 5 N/VT 11 E, and turn right onto Youngs Road; immediately look for parking on the right.

The West River Railroad, which once followed its namesake river for 36 miles, began passenger service in the late 1800s as a way to trim the two-day voyage between Brattleboro and South Londonderry to a brisk 2 hours. Plagued with difficulties from the start, the narrow line often succumbed to downed trees, falling rocks, and flooding. The line steadily lost passengers, and the railroad officially discontinued use on it in 1936, after years of attempts to keep it active.

The same challenges that inevitably doomed the West River Railroad make it an exciting location for a trail. Hikers will be rewarded with spectacular views and challenging but manageable hills. Cyclists will enjoy several miles of open dirt trail; however, note that the two northern open sections of trail contain challenging terrain and are not entirely passable to even the most seasoned of mountain bikers.

**County**
Windham

**Endpoints**
W. River St. and VT 100 (South Londonderry) to Depot St. east of Salmon Hole Lane at Jamaica State Park (Jamaica); VT 30 at Ritchie's Road to VT 30 just north of Dam Road (Townshend); Rice Farm Road 1 mile south of Quarry Road and 1.25 miles north of Howland Road (Dummerston) to Spring Tree Road just west of US 5/ VT 9 (Brattleboro)

**Mileage**
16.1

**Type**
Rail-Trail

**Roughness Index**
3

**Surfaces**
Dirt, Sand, Gravel, Asphalt

*The West River will be a near constant companion on this challenging trail adventure.*

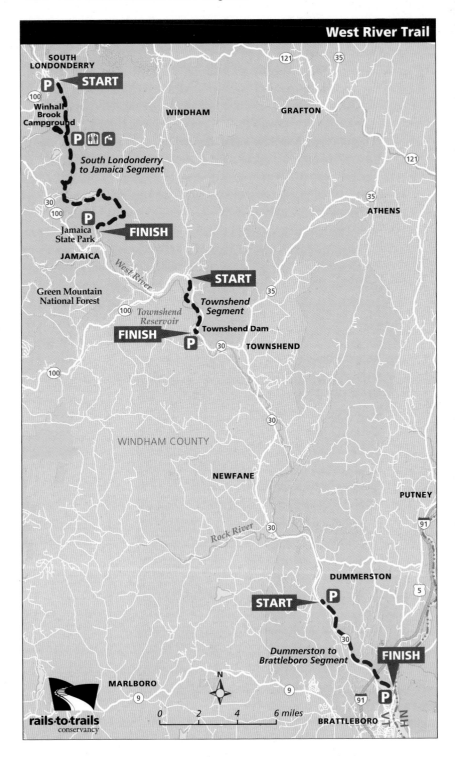

# West River Trail

SOUTH LONDONDERRY

**START**

100

Winhall Brook Campground

WINDHAM

GRAFTON

121

121

*South Londonderry to Jamaica Segment*

30
100

35

ATHENS

**FINISH**

Jamaica State Park

JAMAICA

*West River*

Green Mountain National Forest

100

*Townshend Reservoir*

**START**

35

*Townshend Segment*

**FINISH**

Townshend Dam

30

TOWNSHEND

100

30

WINDHAM COUNTY

NEWFANE

PUTNEY

91

*Rock River*

30

DUMMERSTON

5

**START**

91

*Dummerston to Brattleboro Segment*

**FINISH**

MARLBORO

9

N

9

91

0   2   4   6 miles

BRATTLEBORO

**rails·to·trails**
conservancy

The trail is currently divided into three sections; however, the Friends of the West River Trail intend to eventually complete the missing 18 miles to fully complete the 36-mile trail.

## South Londonderry to Jamaica Segment: 10.5 miles

Starting from the north at the South Londonderry trailhead on West River Street, you may wish to journey 0.5 mile north to an old train depot that now serves as a historical museum and rentable office space. Inside, you'll find exhibits and old photographs memorializing the area's railroad past.

Heading south, the wide rail-trail follows the West River through dense forest. Keep in mind that while the trail is well maintained, you may come across an odd root or puddle, so take care. After about 2 miles, the trail winds through the Winhall Brook Campground on lightly used paved streets. Restrooms and water fountains, as well as the welcoming smell of nearby campfires, are available throughout the campground.

After passing Winhall Brook Campground, the trail continues for approximately 2.5 miles until the rail-trail dead-ends. The West River Trail continues south into the mountainside, but it is only passable on foot for the next 3 miles; cyclists should not attempt to walk their bikes through this section, as the trail gets very narrow and crosses waterfalls and rocky sections on its way to the Ball Mountain Dam. The bicycle-friendly portion of rail-trail re-emerges approximately 0.5 mile past the Ball Mountain Dam and continues another 3 miles to the Jamaica State Park trailhead.

## Townshend Segment: 2.3 miles

A completed section of trail in Townshend, which begins at VT 30 and Ritchie's Road and ends 3 miles later at the Townshend Dam, is advisable only for experienced hikers. This section is incomplete, may be flooded during spring, and is not entirely passable by bicycle.

## Dummerston to Brattleboro Segment: 3.3 miles

The southern section in Dummerston, which begins at the Black Mountain trailhead, located on Rice Farm Road about 0.6 mile south of where it turns into Quarry Road, travels 3.5 miles along a picturesque portion of the West River to the Marina trailhead just north of Brattleboro, crossing underneath I-91 about 2.5 miles along the route. Note that after leaving the Black Mountain trailhead and heading south, the trail is on-road for about 0.4 mile.

Plans exist to complete the remaining 1.5 miles of trail to the Brattleboro Train Station, the original starting point for the West River Railroad.

**CONTACT:** **westrivertrail.org**

# DIRECTIONS

To reach the northern trailhead in South Londonderry from the intersection of VT 30 and US 7 in Manchester, take Exit 4 off US 7 to VT 11 E/Depot St. Head east for 13.2 miles, and turn right onto VT 100 at Londonderry. Go 2.8 miles and turn left onto W. River St. (before you turn left, VT 100 will turn right where it becomes Main St.). Go 0.5 mile, and look for parking where the street ends. Parking is also available at the old train depot in South Londonderry, located about 0.5 mile north of the trailhead on W. River St.

To get to the southern trailhead in Jamaica from the intersection of VT 30 and US 7 in Manchester, take Exit 4 off US 7 to VT 11 E/Depot St. Head east 4.8 miles, and turn right onto VT 30 S. Go 14 miles, and turn left onto Depot St. in Jamaica. Parking is available at the end of the road, about 0.6 mile ahead.

To get to the Black Mountain trailhead in Dummerston from I-91, take Exit 3 toward Brattleboro onto Chesterfield Road. In 0.1 mile at the traffic circle, take the first exit onto Putney Road. Go 0.3 mile, and turn right onto Black Mountain Road. Go 0.6 mile, and turn left to remain on Black Mountain Road. Go another 0.4 mile and turn left again to remain on Black Mountain Road. In 0.7 mile turn left onto Rice Farm Road. Go 0.4 mile, and turn left to stay on Rice Farm Road. In another 1.2 miles, look for parking on your right. From the trailhead on Rice Farm Road, a 0.5-mile on-road section heads south to the current access point.

To get to the southern trailhead in Brattleboro from I-91, take Exit 3 toward Brattleboro onto Chesterfield Road. In 0.1 mile at the traffic circle, take the first exit onto Putney Road. After 1.3 miles, take a sharp right onto Spring Tree Road. Go 0.4 mile, and turn right into the parking lot.

The Williston Village Bike Path links neighborhoods, schools, parks, shopping areas, and restaurants in the suburban town of Williston via a collection of connector trails. The eastern 1.2-mile segment of trail begins at North Williston Road—just 0.3 mile southeast of Williston Community Park and its athletic fields, where there is also a parking area—and heads northwest, completely looping around the soccer field, baseball diamond, and a disc golf course. On the eastern side, you can also pick up the Allen Brook Nature Trail, a walking trail that passes through a wooded area adjacent to Allen Brook.

The Williston Village Bike Path continues northwest and crosses over Allen Brook, reaching Old Stage Road soon after. Portions of the trail are included in the Cross Vermont Trail—a project to connect 90 miles of multiuse trail from Lake Champlain to the Connecticut River.

At Old Stage Road, you will come to a 0.7-mile on-road section through a suburban neighborhood, which is marked with small bicycle route signs. To return to

*This easy, family-friendly path connects neighborhoods, schools, and parks across Williston.*

**County**
Chittenden

**Endpoints**
N. Williston Road between US 2/Williston Road and Lefebvre Lane to Marshall Ave. at Trader Lane; Williston Road/ US 2 at S. Brownell Road to Dunmore Lane just east of Chelsea Pl.; and VT 2A/Essex Road between Cascade St. and Eastview Cir. to Beaudry Lane just east of VT 2A/ Essex Road (Williston)

**Mileage**
7.9

**Type**
Greenway/Non-Rail-Trail

**Roughness Index**
1

**Surfaces**
Asphalt, Concrete

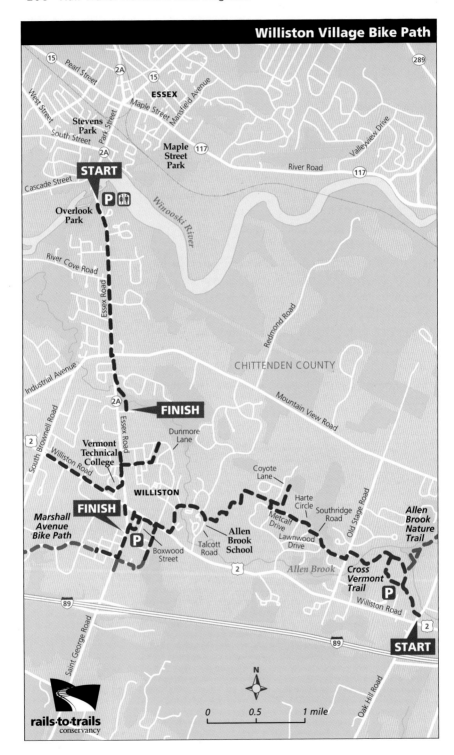

# Williston Village Bike Path

off-road trail, turn left onto Old Stage Road and then take an immediate right onto Lawnwood Drive. Go 0.2 mile, turn right onto Southridge Road, and go 0.2 mile. Turn right onto Harte Circle, go 0.1 mile, and turn right onto Metcalf Drive. Go 0.2 mile to Coyote Lane; here, you can pick up the spur access point to return to off-road trail immediately to your right. Optionally, you can turn right onto Coyote Lane, go a couple hundred feet, and turn left onto the trail.

Totaling 3.1 miles, including spurs and loops, this section of trail will take you past Allen Brook School and on to Taft Corners, a popular shopping district. Trail parking is available just off Boxwood Street. Note that after a brief winding section of trail before and after the school, you'll reach Talcott Road, a quiet neighborhood street with another 0.2-mile on-road segment. Bicycle symbols will then direct you to cross to the south side of Talcott Road, where you'll meet up with off-road trail for another 0.2 mile to US 2/Williston Road.

Turn right at US 2 to stay on the trail, which, after 0.1 mile, crosses Zephyr Road. Immediately afterward, the route turns left and crosses over US 2. Be cautious when crossing; though a crosswalk signal is located here, this section of the highway can experience high levels of traffic.

At Taft Corners the path continues through the complex, providing access to multiple shopping centers and restaurants. Here, the trail connects to the Marshall Avenue Bike Path, which follows the southern side of Marshall Avenue.

A separate 1.4-mile section of trail connects South Brownell Road to Vermont Technical College and businesses and ends at Dunmore Lane. An additional northern segment begins at Overlook Park and heads south 1.5 miles on VT 2A/Essex Road, passing shops, businesses, and a few residential areas before ending at Beaudry Lane.

**CONTACT:** **town.williston.vt.us** and **trailfinder.info/trails/trail/williston-village -bike-path**

---

## DIRECTIONS

To reach the eastern endpoint and parking at the Williston Community Park (100 Library Lane) from I-89, take Exit 12 for VT 2A toward US 2/Williston/Essex Jct. Head north on VT 2A (from I-89 N, turn right; from I-89 S, turn left), and go 0.7 mile. Turn right onto US 2 E, and go about 2 miles. Turn left onto Central School Dr., and follow the drive to the right and then to the left, ending at the parking lot adjacent to the soccer field complex.

To reach the western endpoint and parking at Taft Corners from I-89, take Exit 12 for VT 2A toward US 2/Williston/Essex Jct. Head north on VT 2A, and go 0.7 mile. Turn right onto US 2, and head east 0.2 mile. Turn right onto Boxwood St. and the parking lot is immediately to your left.

To reach the northern endpoint at Overlook Park from I-89, take Exit 12 for VT 2A toward US 2/Williston/Essex Jct., and head north. Go 2.9 miles on VT 2A N, and turn left into the parking lot at Overlook Park, just before crossing the Winooski River.

# Index

*New Hampshire's Ammonoosuc Rail Trail (see page 76)*

# Photo Credits

*Page iii:* Andrew Dupuy; *page vi:* Neil A. Gerdes; *page ix:* Jim Kosinski; *page x:* Anthony Le; *page 7:* TrailLink user mcwpage8; *page 9:* Maine Bureau of Parks and Lands; *page 13:* Katie Guerin; *pages 15 and 17:* Maine Bureau of Parks and Lands; *page 19:* Jim Kosinski; *page 23:* Washington County Council of Governments; *page 25:* Patrick Wojahn; *page 29:* Corey Templeton; *pages 31 and 33:* Katie Guerin; *page 35:* TrailLink user brockharmon; *page 39:* TrailLink user mcwpage8; *page 41:* The Forks Area Chamber of Commerce; *page 45:* Maine Bureau of Parks and Lands; *page 47:* Katie Guerin; *page 51:* Michael Corr; *page 55:* Andrew Dupuy; *page 57:* Maine Bureau of Parks and Lands; *page 61:* Patrick Wojahn; *page 63:* Dale Calder; *page 67:* Katie Guerin; *page 68:* Patrick Wojahn; *page 71:* Andrew Dupuy; *page 73:* Katie Guerin; *page 75:* Eli Griffen; *page 77:* Joe LaCroix; *page 79:* Pete Banach/SpokenShutter.com; *pages 83, 84, and 87:* Kevin Mills; *page 89:* Joe LaCroix; *pages 93 and 95:* Ben Carter; *pages 99 and 100:* Charles F. Martin; *page 103:* Eli Griffen; *page 105:* TrailLink user letswalk4949; *page 109:* Eli Griffen; *page 111:* Anthony Le; *pages 115, 117, and 120:* Ben Carter; *page 121:* TrailLink user tmaguire; *page 125:* Ben Carter; *pages 129 and 130:* Suzanne Matyas; *pages 133 and 134:* Derek Strout; *page 137:* Meredith Suniewick (courtesy of Jim Brown); *page 139:* Ben Carter; *page 143:* Jack Shine; *page 147:* Joshua R. Powe; *page 149:* Bob Gladue; *pages 153 and 155:* Andrew Riedl; *pages 159 and 161:* Anthony Le; *pages 165, 167, and 169:* Kevin Belanger; *page 173:* Scott Pastorell; *page 177:* Kevin Belanger; *page 181:* David Alexander; *page 183:* Kevin Belanger; *page 187:* Dennis Coello; *page 189:* Neil A. Gerdes; *pages 191 and 195:* Kevin Belanger; *page 197:* Brandi Horton; *pages 201 and 203:* Kevin Belanger; *page 207:* Shawn and Meg Freebern; *page 215:* Joe LaCroix.

# Support Rails-to-Trails Conservancy

The nation's leader in helping communities transform unused rail lines and connecting corridors into multiuse trails, Rails-to-Trails Conservancy (RTC) depends on the support of its members and donors to create access to healthy outdoor experiences.

Your donation will help support programs and services that have helped put more than 23,000 rail-trail miles on the ground. Every day, RTC provides vital assistance to communities to develop and maintain trails throughout the country. In addition, RTC advocates for trail-friendly policies, promotes the benefits of rail-trails, and defends rail-trail laws in the courts.

Join online at railstotrails.org, or mail your donation to Rails-to-Trails Conservancy, 2121 Ward Court NW, Fifth Floor, Washington, D.C. 20037.

Rails-to-Trails Conservancy is a 501(c)(3) nonprofit organization, and contributions are tax deductible.

# Find your next trail adventure on TrailLink

Visit TrailLink.com today.

**TrailLink**
by Rails-to-Trails Conservancy

# Love Reading About Trails?

In each issue of *Rails to Trails* magazine, you'll find:

- Features on transformational trails around the country
- Travel recommendations for hot trail destinations
- Insider info on developing trail projects
- Gorgeous photos, trail maps and more!

# Subscribe at railstotrails.org/magazine.